Blake's Humanism

Blake's Humanism

John Beer

Manchester University Press
Barnes & Noble Inc, New York

Published by the
University of Manchester at
The University Press
316–324 Oxford Road
Manchester 13

USA
Barnes & Noble, Inc.
105 Fifth Avenue
New York, N.Y. 10003

GB SBN 7190 0300 8

Made and Printed in Great Britain by
Butler & Tanner Ltd, Frome and London

Contents   page

List of Illustrations

The author and publishers gratefully acknowledge permission to reproduce the illustrations from the individuals and institutions whose names are listed below

1 (Frontispiece) Blake: human and visionary (the double portrait of William Blake by Frederick Tatham) *Collection of Mr and Mrs Paul Mellon*

The Fall

2 'The Fall' (woodcut by Lucas Cranach) *Fitzwilliam Museum, Cambridge*

3 Adam and Eve in organized innocence (water-colour drawing 'The Archangel Raphael with Adam and Eve' from Blake's illustrations to *Paradise Lost*) *Museum of Fine Arts, Boston*

4–6 Visionary or vegetative? The contradictions of human nature (title page, 'What is Man!', and 'I found him beneath a Tree' from *The Gates of Paradise*) *British Museum, London*

7–10 The Sons of Reason ('Water', 'Earth', 'Air' and 'Fire' *ibid.*)

11 The Sons of Urizen (Utha, Grodna, Thiriel and Fuzon from *The Book of Urizen* pl. 24) *Alverthorpe Gallery, Jenkintown, Pennsylvania*

12–15 Images of disorganized desire ('At length for hatching ripe he breaks the shell', 'Alas!', 'My Son! My Son!' and 'I want! I want!' from *The Gates of Paradise*) *British Museum*

16–19 Images of imprisoned desire and of the keys to the prison ('Help! Help!', 'Aged Ignorance', 'Does thy God O Priest take such vengeance as this?' and 'Fear & Hope are—Vision' *ibid.*)

20–23 Images of hope ('The Traveller hasteth in the evening', 'Death's Door', 'I have said to the Worm: Thou art my Mother & Sister' and 'Conclusion' *ibid.*)

24 Urizen and the Sun of Reason ('The Ancient of Days' frontispiece to *Europe*) *Fitzwilliam Museum*

The fourfold vision

Preface

Anyone who now studies the work of William Blake finds his path eased by the wealth of scholarship which has preceded him. In the last few years, particularly, the devoted work of scholars such as Sir Geoffrey Keynes, G. E. Bentley, Junior, and David Erdman has made Blake's text universally accessible —down to the last thumb-nail scoring by a passage in Swedenborg which impressed him. The visual art is still not as generally available as one could wish, but here the Trianon Press editions mark a great step forward; through the labours of Geoffrey Keynes and others, moreover, most of the paintings and drawings are now published somewhere.

In detailed interpretations of the work of Blake I have been particularly helped by the studies of S. F. Damon, Northrop Frye and David Erdman. There are few books which do not add to the corpus of knowledge about his work, however, and to acknowledge specific debts is not always easy. Interpretations which seemed unlikely when first read may become, in a fuller context, thoroughly acceptable, by which time one may have forgotten where one first came across them. If due acknowledgment has been omitted anywhere, I ask to be pardoned.

Among writers on Blake Kathleen Raine should be particularly mentioned. Her work has not at the time of writing been published in its final form, but I have been able to follow its progress in published articles and also to watch it unfolding in various lectures which I was privileged to attend. Although my own view of Blake differs from hers in certain important respects her work has been a constant stimulus, without which my own would have suffered. The studies by Harold Bloom and Desirée Hirst were published when my work was largely completed, but enabled me to mention some points which I found particularly valuable.

It is one of the delights of studying Blake that those who have

gained most from him are often to be found a long way from
the universities. Some of the most enlightening commentary,
for example, is to be found indirectly in the creative work of
writers who have learned from him—writers as diverse as W. B.
Yeats, E. M. Forster, D. H. Lawrence, Saul Bellow and Kathleen Raine herself. I remember with pleasure conversations
with enthusiasts such as Frank Freeman, Judith Law, William
Hughes and the late Alfred Winter.

I am particularly grateful for the help and encouragement
of my wife, who was reproved by her grandfather for reading
Blake at the age of seven and has been enjoying him ever since.

The study on which this book is based was first begun
towards the end of my tenure of a Research Fellowship at
St John's College, Cambridge. My thanks are due to the
College not only for that Fellowship but for providing me with
rooms and dinners for a few months after its expiry in May
1958, thus enabling me to survive as a scholar at a crucial time.
The University of Manchester, under the auspices of which the
major part of the work was done, has always been extremely
generous in allowing time for research and grants for travel,
besides providing the opportunity for discussions with col-
leagues such as Professor Frank Kermode, Professor John
Jump and Dr Arnold Goldman, and for seminars which enabled
various theories to be given an airing. A room for research
was provided by the munificence of Manchester Central
Library, where the use of a study carrel for several years enabled
work on this and other projects to go forward. My particular
thanks are due to the Librarians and staff of that library for
their unfailing courtesy and efficiency, and to the staffs of the
John Rylands Library; the Manchester University Library;
the Pierpont Morgan Library; the Harvard University Library;
the Fogg Museum; The Cambridge University Library; the
Fitzwilliam Museum; the Victoria and Albert Museum; and
the Reading Room, Students' Room and Print Room of the
British Museum. Nor should I forget the efficiency of the Lost
Property Department of British Railways, which rescued an
early draft of the manuscript after it had been thrown off a
train in which I was travelling by an over-zealous porter at
Stafford. Sir Geoffrey Keynes, Mr Martin Butlin of the Tate

Gallery, Mr Malcolm Cormack and Mr E. C. Chamberlain
of the Fitzwilliam Museum and Mr David Erdman of the
New York Public Library have all responded with kindness and
alacrity to my requests for help on particular points. My
final debt of gratitude is to the Master and Fellows of Peter-
house, where this book has been finally prepared for publication and where I have been enabled, after several years, to
bring together my teaching and research into one place again.

J. B. B.
Cambridge 1967

A Note on Texts and Blake's Punctuation

The text of this book has been corrected generally to
accord with that of *The Poetry and Prose of William Blake*, edited
by David V. Erdman, commentary by Harold Bloom, New
York, 1965 (E). Blake's own punctuation, used here, is eccen-
tric—it often indicates emphasis rather than connection, for
example—but it is not perverse and the real obscurities in the
text are not elucidated by making it orthodox. Since English
readers are more likely to have access to the Nonesuch editions
of Blake, edited by Geoffrey Keynes, nevertheless, references
are also given in the notes to the Nonesuch edition of 1939
(NB) and to the Nonesuch Variorum edition of 1958 (NC).
The original Nonesuch edition of 1927 (NA) has a different
pagination from either of these editions; a conversion table
from NB to NA is furnished by A. S. Roe in *Blake's Illustrations
to the Divine Comedy*, Princeton, 1953.

The reader who wishes to consult a text with Blake's own
'illuminations' should, ideally, have access to the facsimile
editions published by the Trianon Press. Failing this, the most
compendious edition of the illuminated books is still (surprisingly) the third volume of Blake's *Works*, edited by E. J. Ellis
and W. B. Yeats, London, 1893.

1 Blake and his Readers

When generalizations are made about art or poetry William Blake is one of the first exceptions who has to be accounted for: the necessary adjustment is usually made either by calling him a 'genius' (with the suggestion that this compensates for certain disadvantages) or by referring to him as 'mad' (with an indulgent inflection of the voice to allow for admiration of his achievements). He has always been an odd man out, the joker in our neatly sorted eighteenth-century pack.

To write connectedly and at length about such a figure might seem to be attempting the impossible. It is not just that he refuses to reduce to our categories, escaping like quicksilver from our carefully wrought patterns of organization. With Blake, there is a further disturbing fact. His words sometimes improve when taken out of context.

I behold London; a Human awful wonder of God!

Such a line takes on new virtue when read in isolation from the page on which it occurs[1]—it is as though the very space around the line gives the words greater resonance.

The final truth about Blake does not rest there, however. He had no desire to go down to history as a writer of inspired fragments—on the contrary, he wanted to produce work on the grand scale, to write an epic poem: and the effects of his desire are inevitably a part of his presented work. We must study the total context of that work if we want to see it as anything more than an obscure landscape lighted by periodic flashes; and we must sometimes do this in order to get the full effect of the 'flashes' themselves. The sort of positive qualities which Blake possessed automatically involved a certain relationship with the art, the literature and the society of his time: even his antagonisms and defensive gestures give his art some of its essential character.

Once we look into that relationship, moreover, we find ourselves involved with the widest issues. Blake was one of those men who, by standing at an angle to his age, causes us to look at it, as a whole, with new eyes. Its artistic, social and religious presuppositions are both challenged and thrown into relief. We may begin with the question of genius and madness. The idea that there is a link between the two is one of those persistent commonplaces which remain alive because their suggestion is more potent than their statement. In the eighteenth century it had a particularly strong appeal. Reason and social conformity were the current values. It was only natural that any phenomena which did not fall in with them should be classified in the same category and assumed to be of the same order.

Nowadays the word 'genius' is a term of overwhelming approval; in the eighteenth century it was not so absolute. A poet could refer to his Genius in the same way that he might refer to his Muse. It was a convenient way of referring to forces beyond his rational control; it involved humility as well as presumption. In 1776 Elizabeth Gilding could publish her poems under the title of *The Breathings of Genius* without appearing presumptuous: and James Beattie could, without offence, subtitle *The Minstrel* 'The Progress of Genius'. Genius was not then absolute and self-justifying, but a mysterious, somewhat attractive power which might excuse artistic divagations from the strict path of reason.

With the growth of romanticism, however, genius became the subject, first of Gothic approval, then of critical discussion. It began to be referred to, coolly, as a necessary element in all true art.

Coleridge took the discussion a stage further in *Biographia Literaria* by examining more closely the relationship between genius and power.[2] He discriminated between two forms of genius, 'absolute' and 'commanding'. Men of commanding genius might be found in any field: but their genius demanded to be made actual in some outstanding way, so that they were likely to exercise themselves in vast works of physical creation or destruction. Men of absolute genius, on the other hand, who were more likely to be artists, demanded no such violent expression: such men, he wrote, 'rest content between thought and reality, as it were in an intermundium of which their own living spirit supplies the *substance*, and their imagination the ever-varying *form*'. His prime examples of the two types of genius were Napoleon and Shakespeare.

Coleridge's distinction is particularly relevant to Blake. He, of all men, lived content between thought and reality: in one sense the substance and form of his work were provided, respectively, by his own spirit and imagination.

Here we have a link between the phenomena of genius and madness. The madman, too, lives between thought and reality. And although Blake's sanity has been frequently and successfully defended by his biographers,[3] one has to acknowledge a perceptible affinity between the spirit of some of his designs, particularly those which show a spiky flaminess, and those executed by patients suffering from paranoia.

This need not astonish us. The distinction between sanity and madness, popularly regarded as a defined frontier, is, we know, nothing of the sort. There is always, for one thing, a social element involved. Insanity is often measured in the public mind by the degree of anti-social behaviour involved, while anti-social behaviour is always liable to be treated as madness. Two results follow. The madman, by being automatically released from social constraints, may reveal to society facets of the human personality normally suppressed by social man: equally, anyone who wishes to express those facets may, by the very fact of his rejection of society, induce some of the secondary phenomena of madness.

This was especially true in the latter part of the eighteenth century. A prophet who cried out against the dominance of Reason was bound to be regarded by many as insane—even to be pushed towards the borders of sanity by their treatment of him. Blake is the culminating figure in a line which includes men such as Collins, Smart and Cowper.

The complicated issues of cause and effect which are raised by such a situation must be ignored here. A more important question is that of control. All men, whether they know it or not, exist between thought and reality. We judge them according to their success in reconciling the two—and even then we allow a degree of freedom. If we sense danger when thought begins to exist in a self-sufficient circle away from the world of sense-data, we also recognize that the mind has its own dynamisms, and should be allowed the graces and gestures that express them. We allow the mythologist a good deal of play in embellishing his narrative so long as we think that he knows what he is doing.

These criteria, so easy to apply to *The Pilgrim's Progress* or *Prometheus Bound*, lose their clarity when one opens the writings of Blake. Reasoning mingles with fantasy, social realism with visionary assertion. The reader, confused by the contradiction between lucidity of style and apparent incoherence of events, might easily give up in despair.

Blake was sometimes carried too far by his own creative excitement. There are in the Prophetic Books bursts of rhetoric or narrative which can be justified neither as interpretative mythologizing nor as poetic utterance. To read Blake is to witness an extraordinary contest between enthusiasm and control—the greatest, perhaps, that has ever taken place in an artist. There is hardly a single piece of Blake's poetry where his devotion to mythology does not compromise the singleness of the work of art. Yet he never finally relinquishes his grasp of reality. A link always exists, however tenuous: indeed it is precisely at the point when Blake seems to have launched into a cloudy empyrean of his own fantasy that he is to be found on earth again, solidly approaching human experience from a fresh angle. These unpredictable twists and turns tempt one to speak, as he himself sometimes did, of his 'visions' rather than his 'vision'. The existence at once of so many diverse 'visions' (with corresponding changes of mode) and his seeming inability, perhaps unwillingness, to incorporate them into a single, comprehensive 'vision' make him at once the most attractive and the most exasperating of artists.

Small wonder, then, that some critics have chosen to see him consistently from one particular point of view. His realism, for example, has prompted a number of studies. We have had Blake the adversary of industrialism, Blake the prophet against the churches, Blake the apostle of free love. The two major ideologies of the contemporary world have both claimed him for their own. Not many years ago, an American scholar produced a study with the title, *Blake: Prophet against Empire*; and when, in December 1957, Russian writers, artists and others gathered at the Art Workers' Club in Moscow to commemorate the bicentenary of his birth, a speaker stated that recent Russian criticism 'saw in Blake's fantastic legends a new and original way of attempting to interpret the revolutionary upheavals of his time'.[4]

There is no need to deny the validity of any of these approaches to Blake. Each can be backed by evidence from within the writings themselves, each witnesses to Blake's preoccupation with the world in which he found himself. But this series of limited interpretations has led to a situation in which a reader may wearily remark that any book on Blake is utterly convincing—until you open the next book on Blake; or, indeed, until you return to the writings themselves. Let us glance, for example, at a specimen of Dr Bronowski's rhetoric as he depicts Blake, the voice crying against the evils of the Industrial Revolution:

> It is an astonishing vision. The reader must turn the pages of the last prophetic books himself, at random: and find everywhere the same sooty imagery, the air belched by industry. Men of letters, whom the machine keeps clean, have groped through this sulphurous rhetoric for the names tidily listed in the books of mystics. The names are there, and they are worth the finding. But Swedenborg the mystic had been an inspector of mines; Paine the deist planned iron bridges; Blake the poet lived in the Industrial Revolution bitterly in the decay of his engraver's craft. The oratory of *Vala or the Four Zoas*, of *Milton*, and of *Jerusalem* is loud with machines, with war, with law; with the cry of man preying on man; and with the rebellious mutter of working men.[5]

One would like to believe this. It would be refreshing to find a pristine critic of industry in Blake. But the reader who makes the experiment to which Dr Bronowski invites him will *not* find at every turn air that has been belched by industry or hear everywhere the rebellious mutter of working men. He will come across them from time to time, and be grateful to Dr Bronowski for having drawn attention to them. Their presence is a guarantee that Blake was no mere dreamer, removed from the issues of this world. But they do not give the dominating tone to the works, the tone which the reader most readily associates with them.

It is not even certain that engraving was so depressed a craft at this time. Blake earned a meagre living, but he seems to have had work always at hand when money was required. His complaint was not that he could not find employment, but that his patrons and employers would not let him do the work to which he felt himself impelled.

Blake was aware of the ills of his time, but his awareness was always supplemented by a belief that human ills are most surely dealt with by curing the 'mental' ills which lie behind them. Dark satanic mills arise in towns because men have dark satanic mills in their minds.

In the same way, assertions which are confidently made concerning Blake's views on other aspects of life will often be found to cancel each other out. It would be instructive, perhaps amusing, to promote a symposium in which scholars would be asked in turn to state simply Blake's opinions on religion, politics and sex. The many apparent self-contradictions in Blake's own work would immediately come to light: and the audience would be left wondering whether Blake was an orthodox Christian or an uncompromising rebel against religious forms; a preacher of free love, or a firm upholder of the marriage contract.

One attempt to deal with such contradictions was made by H. M. Margoliouth, who suggested that Blake, as the result of some sort of 'conversion' about the year 1799, was more orthodox in the religious beliefs of his later life.[6]

The case for some change in his beliefs is not unconvincing, but it can hardly be made in so clearcut a fashion. Many of Blake's most 'Christian' utterances occur before that time; many outspoken criticisms of orthodoxy, including *The Everlasting Gospel*, appear later. What happened at that time is more likely to have been one of many shifts of opinion as he tried to reconcile all the positive affirmations which he, the most positive of men, wished to make at one and the same time.

Alongside the various attempts to interpret Blake according to his realism, there have appeared a series of studies grounded in the supposition that he is, first and foremost, a symbolist poet.

The first long study of the kind appeared in the late nineteenth century, when symbolism was a new vogue. E. J. Ellis and W. B. Yeats produced a comprehensive edition of Blake's works, with extensive commentaries and large charts to set out his mythology in detailed and complicated schemes. In places the charts are useful and revealing; more often they disappoint and confuse the reader. If they are correct, one feels, Blake's symbolizing was so arid and arbitrary as to be largely valueless.

Most later attempts to organize Blake's symbolism are open to similar criticism. The studies by S. F. Damon, M. O. Percival and Northrop Frye, to name only three, contain much that is valuable and exciting to anyone who wants to discover what Blake was saying, yet the total impression is always unsatisfactory. Confident statements about the meaning of individual symbols in one study conflict with equally confident statements in another. Strong assertions, which seem to be leading to a positive conclusion, die out in a mass of associative imagery. Northrop Frye's exploration, for example, serves valuably to illustrate the weight of human experience in mysticism, folklore and literature behind some of Blake's images: one is given an unusually vivid picture of the lights and colours at play in his imagination. Yet in the end the wealth of images is more like a welter and we are left contemplating a landscape which is attractively coloured but not fully articulated.

The sort of irritation which assails the reader of such studies can best be indicated by quoting a sentence or two from H. M. Margoliouth's preface to his edition of *Vala*:

> . . . Vala is a veil between Man and reality. The actual genesis of the name may be before our eyes in the opening line of the Fragment on 71R . . .:
>
> Beneath the veil of Vala rose Tharmas from dewy tears.
>
> . . . If afterwards, as the drawing on 2R may suggest, he also thought of this world's vale, that would be quite like him.[7]

Such affectionate gestures ('that would be quite like him') get us nowhere. The combination of symbolisms involved in making the images of a vale on one hand and a veil on the other cannot produce anything but a blurred effect, since the two images do not readily assimilate together. And if we take either interpretation separately, we shall need to set it within a more fully organized structure of meaning—or Blake emerges as an arbitrary symbolist, for whom no higher status can be claimed than that of an inveterate fantasy-monger, unable to stop himself from playing continual little pranks on his readers.

A good deal of work in this tradition is more stringent—but even so, varying interpretations are too often reconciled by the useful phrase, 'different levels of meaning', without proper consideration of the conflicts which may still exist between such 'levels'.

Miss Kathleen Raine's work, which has not at the time of writing appeared in its final form, takes a particularly direct line with Blake's images. Where Frye would think in terms of Jungian archetypes, leaving open the possibility of various psychological interpretations, she asserts roundly that the images are metaphysically valid and reconcilable with the tradition of the Perennial Philosophy, which she sees as the major source of Blake's inspiration.

Here the answer to realist interpreters of Blake is developed to its fullest extent. Against their picture of Blake as prophet of humanism appears Blake as priest of the *philosophia perennis*, heir to the Neoplatonists and to the mystics of the centuries.

This is an extreme way of putting the argument. But if it appears at first sight a confined and local discussion of a single poet, reflection suggests wider implications. It is part of an important contemporary discussion, which both includes and stretches beyond most other arguments about the state of literature. The question ultimately at issue is this: whence does a poet derive the 'reality' in which his art is founded? From the world about him, or from the structuring of his own inward vision?

The underlying importance of this conflict in all modern criticism was shown by the argument which was provoked when Miss Raine produced some preliminary studies. Her assertion that Blake owed a still heavier debt than had been realized to his reading of Thomas Taylor was attacked by Mr W. W. Robson, who questioned many of her points in detail. As the

controversy developed, it became clear that the difference between the supporters and opposers of Miss Raine lay not in
points of detail but in questions of principle. Two different
views of the poet were involved. Thus Mr John Wain, in what
he perhaps thought to be a final and crushing attack on Miss
Raine's work, wrote simply,

> Isn't it, in fact, obvious that if a poet can't be shown to be
> important without bringing in all this lumber, then he *isn't*
> important?[8]

Somewhere behind this confident question one hears the echo
of a voice proclaiming, in the dawn of Romanticism, that a poet
is 'a man speaking to men'—but with the further implication
that since men do not normally concern themselves with the
metaphysical issues involved in Neoplatonism and mysticism,
the poet is automatically debarred from them, also.

There is yet another implication, again relevant to the issues
of modern criticism. It is tacitly assumed that the poem is the
text presented on the page, and that any attempt to go behind
that text in quest of further enlightenment is misconceived. If
the poet has not presented his full mind *there*, he has failed in
his task as an artist.

One admires the purity of this principle. A large amount of
clutter is automatically cleared away by its application. But its
supporters have been unnecessarily drastic in their dealings
with certain types of poetry, notably romantic poetry. D. W.
Harding, for example, has a sensitive essay on Blake's poetry,
implicitly following this principle, which is admirable so far as
it goes.[9] But it is notable that the poems which he holds up for
admiration are several from the *Songs of Innocence and of Experience*, together with some lyrical interludes from *Vala*. Such an
approach is likely to reduce to a very small compass the body
of Blake's work that is read and approved, however valuable
the discipline that it provides in dealing with them. Even in
connection with the *Songs of Innocence and of Experience* it may
cause the reader to miss some of the organization involved and
to be left with unanswered questions.

Writers of the analytical school, whom we may for the sake
of convenience call 'Aristotelians', have an important part to

play in criticism. They recognize that art is always a living and developing thing: that the most important art is that which is continually relevant to man in his total condition, speaking to him as a human being rooted in human society. But when it sets its sights too rigidly by these standards it becomes no more than a 'minimal' criticism, a criticism of the barricades. While the situation remains less urgent than that, we have leisure to look before and after and can enjoy the pleasure of projecting ourselves into ages which were not necessarily like our own. We may read Marlowe with an Elizabethan eye and listen to Mozart with an Augustan ear. Nor is it merely a luxury to do so. The health of civilization depends partly upon our ability to compare our own society with those of other ages which were built upon different presuppositions and fostered different attitudes.

It may be argued, moreover, that only a handful of masterpieces can communicate with men at all times and in all conditions. In most cases, the artist cannot possibly give all the information required. A good deal of his work will move by evocation of feelings and ideas common to his contemporaries— and that evocation may later be impossible without knowledge outside the work of art itself. To give a crude example, how can one respond adequately to the *Essay on Man* without some information which enables one to form an idea of the extent and limitations of the Augustan view of 'Nature'?

There is a further point to be made. If some knowledge of the 'inwardness' of the eighteenth-century mind is necessary before we respond properly to Pope, the need is still more pressing when we turn to the early romantics. For one of the main features of their achievement was precisely that so much in their minds could not be communicated to paper. The split between 'vision' and 'reality' was one of the chief problems with which they had to contend: as a result, their most sustained poetry was often written about the problem itself—poetry such as *The Prelude* or *Dejection* or *Milton*. To apply the Aristotelian principle is thus to blind ourselves to a great part of the achievement of Wordsworth, Coleridge and Blake and to leave ourselves fumbling with inadequate concepts.

In trying to escape the strait-jacket of the 'Aristotelians', however, it is not necessary to move to the opposite extreme. Blake's importance does not lie only in his relevance to the Perennial Philosophy. The Blake who reveals himself in his more personal writings is an obstinate, even pig-headed individual, who is not afraid to reject traditional concepts if he can find no validity in them, or to distort themes of the perennial philosophy if that is the only way of bringing them into line with his own vision. For this reason, Professor Frye's objections to the word 'mystic' as applied to Blake are wholly justified:

> If mysticism means primarily a contemplative quietism, mysticism is something abhorrent to Blake, a Selfhood-communing in Ulro; if it means primarily a spiritual illumination expressing itself in a practical and (in spite of its psychological subtlety) unspeculative piety, such as we find in the militant monasticism of the Counter-reformation, the word still does not fit him.[10]

The point is that Blake is an artist, and if we are to concede him artistic importance, another fact must inevitably be brought into play. We must approach him by way of his imagination. And because the imaginative achievement of Blake is so central to his work, I propose to use the word 'visionary' in discussing him. The word has a variety of associations, of course, and is often used pejoratively: if it implies a criticism of Blake, however, that criticism will need to be answered. It is, moreover, the word which he preferred to use in describing himself. It suggests a devotion to the imagination which not only exalts it to a dominant position, but is ready to give reasons for doing so.

The reasons for the high importance of the imagination to Blake have often been given. Men of the late seventeenth century, intoxicated by the discoveries of Newton, had conceived an exaggerated respect for the inter-related concepts of Reason, Nature and Law. By so doing they were, by default, debasing the place of emotion and imagination in human experience. Emotion was allowed for; but the idea that it might ever be a source of revelation was discouraged, as 'enthusiasm'. And imagination, cut off from direct and central play, began to subsist as a separate function, relieving man when he was tired from the exercise of reason by allowing him to indulge dreams of Gothic splendour and enjoy controlled spasms of pleasing terror.

Somewhere along the line, a factor essential to the health of art had withered away. Art had become steadily more civilized, yet despite its appeal to the enlightened sensibility its range had become more restricted. The philosophy of Locke and Newton, which set out simply to explain the workings of the universe, had become an imprisoning cavern. The abstract, intersecting lines which men plotted across the face of nature had assumed solidity and formed a net in which their vision struggled. As Blake's own powers developed, he became more and more aware of these enclosing forces. Nor was he the man to look for a way of compromise. Once he revolted against the world-picture of his time he must build a world-picture of his own and proclaim that in the teeth of his contemporaries.

Even Blake, however, could not claim exemption from the universal law that what men do determines what they become. If a man revolts against society he will grow a hard skin of defence against that society. Blake saw this clearly when he wrote: 'Cowper came to me & said. "... You retain health & yet are as mad as any of us all—over us all—mad as a refuge from unbelief—from Bacon Newton & Locke." '11

The man who wrote those words evidently had a much better idea of what he was doing than many of his critics. Indeed, Blake's consciousness of his own purpose, his sophistication, will be a constant theme in these pages. That his sophistication is not always recognized is partly his own fault: for his obstinacy in refusing to explain his symbols has led to insufficient and wrong explanations being applied to them. Yet the indications are that most of his symbols are rooted in organized thinking, even if the 'working' is sometimes left behind before they reach the presented page. Yeats used to insist that the poetic vision could not be sought simply for its own sake; rather, the poet must wrestle with the angel of inspiration and hope that when the struggle was accomplished the vision would be granted.12 One sees that much of Blake's best work came to him in this way—after the struggle was over.

There is great consistency in the vision. Confusion on this point springs from the fact that where a poet is so loath to declare his central principles, the reader is presented with a set of statements, from which the central ones have to be extracted.

He must decide which statements are merely subsidiary, which
are the ones that govern and judge their fellows. It is not surprising that individual sentences have been picked up and
regarded as central, simply because they give a clear statement,
while others, more obscure but more telling, are disregarded.
Moreover, single statements which can be regarded as truly
central are rare. Blake's philosophy consists rather of interlocking statements, each modifying the others. In consequence,
a whole nexus of ideas must sometimes be grasped before the
exact significance of single statements can be weighed.

To take a simple and basic example, there is at the heart
of Blake's attitude a twin belief in the essential humanness of
God and in the germ of divinity at the heart of human nature.
Traditional views of the transcendence of God and the un-
worthiness of man are thus both modified. Yet Blake has been
claimed as a more or less orthodox Christian by writers who
have extracted the various theological statements from his
writings and as a humanist by those who have extracted his
protests against dogma. In spite of his use of Gospel sayings for
the support of his position, however, Blake's fashioning of God
in the image of man could never be regarded as orthodox by
the Christian churches.

> Thou art a man God is no more
> Thy own humanity learn to adore . . .[13]

No theologian in the orthodox tradition of Christianity could
accept so uncompromising a statement. Similarly, those who
wish to claim Blake for the liberal humanist tradition will be
constantly bewildered by the stringency of his standards of
'humanity'. True humanity, according to him, is not to be
found by taking the average of the mass of mankind as we know
them. Rather, it is glimpsed whenever a man, anywhere, lives
by his own inward vision. From the fullness of that vision the
majority of men have fallen away. If Blake refuses to acknowledge the existence of original sin, his belief in the loss of
original vision provides him with a no less exacting yardstick
for the judgment of human conduct. It is in the means and
manner of human reformation that he differs significantly
from the Christian position.

The fact that so much of Blake's thinking falls into similar, individual patterns, justifies us in treating characterizations of him either as 'social critic' or 'mystic' with reserve. A more accurate word to describe him would be 'humanist'; but even then we should be forced to define our use of the term carefully. Blake's humanism differs from both the normal senses in which the word is used. Sixteenth-century humanism was an attempt to provide a synthesis between Reason and Faith: to make room for the best of paganism and classical literature within the more general truths of religion. By the nineteenth century, on the other hand, humanism had become an attempt to elevate reason over faith: it often had a strong anti-clerical flavour. The 'human' presupposed by Renaissance humanism was a Christian who deserved the enlightenment to be found in other cultures and in the exercise of Reason; in Victorian times he was more likely to be a rationalist agnostic who believed in the power of developing technology to create a better standard of living for all.

Blake would not have recognized either of these blue-prints for human nature. He was neither committed to orthodox Christianity nor yet willing to see human nature simply as a part of 'Nature'. He was of a select company (which includes figures as diverse as Coleridge, Dickens, Forster and Lawrence) who announce their belief in humanity yet refuse to accept any definition which is drawn from looking at the sum of human beings. Instead they insist that the key to understanding 'humanity' can only be found by an exacting look at the nature of the individual.

The view of the individual which emerges from Blake's writings is governed both by the power of Blake's own imagination and by his indignation at social injustices. The two qualities combine into a condition which might be described as that of 'visionary humanism'. In some of the prophetic books indeed, the power of his imagination is so overwhelming that it might be more accurate to call him a 'humanist visionary'. In the works to be commented on here, however, there is always a point of social or political relevance which gives the work a central theme, while still raising all the other questions.

This is no ordinary view of man; it begins by looking beneath the carapace of social behaviour in each human being to discover the energies which animate, the vision which controls. The point where reason and energy rise from their normal, unawakened state, touch one another and merge into an interanimating vision and desire is for Blake the central 'humanity' in each man. We cannot begin to understand his attitude unless we grasp the firmness of this belief that behind the characteristics of each man there exist the lineaments of the 'eternal man', most nearly apprehended when we see him possessed by his energies or radiant with his own imagination but even then glimpsed only fleetingly. This 'eternal man' may be sensed in the lineaments of another human being, particularly when he exercises energy, but cannot be focused and held by the senses. Nevertheless, many of Blake's paintings are attempts to suggest his elusive form.

Such a belief brought him into immediate conflict with the general eighteenth-century assumption that human nature is ultimately something which can be grasped as a single entity. His counter-assertion draws on the observation that a man is not the same man when he is reasoning as when he is exercising his energies (a point which was also observed by Hume); he is different again when he is in love—and yet again when he is momentarily possessed by inspiration. His identity alters, or grows.

The paradox is that for Blake the 'genius' that is in every man and is therefore eternal and universal also makes each man unique. When he thought about social and political questions it was the eternal man that was most present to him, the eternal humanity which stood in judgement on all acts of inhumanity and injustice and deplored society's failure to allow individual self-fulfilment. In the end, however, he returned to the individual artist as the one man who could express his 'genius' and so awaken the 'genius' of other men. The progress through political poems such as *The French Revolution*, *America*, and *Europe* culminates fittingly in *Milton*, where Blake is driven to assert that the 'essential' human being is the artist. That progress will provide a useful framework for the study that follows.

Blake's rejection of orthodox contemporary attitudes led him into immediate difficulties, the greatest of which was that of finding a tractable style. He could draw upon his experience of humanity and society in his own time; he could draw upon the more imaginative statements of the mystics; but neither furnished him with what he really needed. There was no visionary-realist 'tradition'. Bunyan at his most imaginative came near to it, but he was too interested in propagating a biblical pietism to indulge his gifts in this direction. The nearest approach to a tradition lay in the achievement of particular poets and artists, such as Chaucer, Shakespeare and Milton, or Michelangelo and Raphael. With each of these, however, the visionary achievement was only a part of the intention and effect: Blake looked for a pure line which would be central to his art.

The result of his search was a style which inevitably leans towards Platonism, while avoiding complete identification with the Platonic position. His work involves a search for the eternal images underlying the tricks and sports of time. But these eternal images are not placed outside man: they do not stand like Byzantine mosaics in eternal judgment upon the changes and chances of this world. Blake's realism demands that his images be relevant to the fact of change as well as that of permanence: his most successful images represent the lineaments of states through which men must pass, while also showing, within those lineaments, the lineaments of the eternal man.

A central statement of this dual position is to be found in his description of the picture entitled 'The Last Judgment':

> This world of Imagination is the World of Eternity it is the Divine bosom into which we shall all go after the death of the Vegetated body This World of Imagination is Infinite & Eternal whereas the world of Generation or Vegetation is Finite & Temporal There Exist in that Eternal World the Permanent Realities of Every Thing which we see reflected in this Vegetable Glass of Nature
>
> All Things are comprehended in their Eternal Forms in the Divine body of the Saviour the True Vine of Eternity the Human Imagination who appeard to Me as Coming to Judgment among his Saints & throwing off the Temporal that the Eternal might be Establishd . . .[14]

An artist who starts out with presuppositions such as these is
not likely to establish ready communication with either the
realists or the orthodox mystics of his audience. Neither those
who base their philosophy upon sense-perception nor those who
seek to escape from the tyranny of the senses will find immediate satisfaction in an art which is concerned with the inter-
penetration of sense-perception by inward vision. So little
established language exists for such communication, indeed,
that the most profitable way of understanding the full body of
Blake's work is to follow him, step by step, as he evolves one
symbolic pattern after another in successive attempts to express
his peculiar sense of the world.

To follow in Blake's tracks, however, is not always easy. So
quickly could his mind leap from one fact to another, stimulated
by the vision of the moment, that the connection must sometimes elude us. H. M. Margoliouth was recently able to show
how such a leap could be followed, by examining two diverse
works, the one verbal, the other pictorial.[15] The first was the
verse with which Blake concluded the small book of engravings
entitled *The Gates of Paradise*:

To the Accuser who is
The God of This World

Truly My Satan, thou art but a Dunce
And dost not know the Garment from the Man
Every Harlot was a Virgin once
Nor canst thou ever change Kate into Nan

Tho thou art Worshipd by the Names Divine
Of Jesus & Jehovah: thou art still
The Son of Morn in weary Nights decline
The lost Travellers Dream under the Hill[16]

The point here is not fully clear at first reading and demands
acquaintance with other statements by Blake about Satan.
Satan is to be identified with the fallen Lucifer, angel of light—
that is clear from the second stanza. But the nature of his fall
is purely Blakean. It lies in his fall from a grasp of individual
identities to a 'single' vision where all things are related and
made comprehensible only by means of formulated laws. It is
in this sense that Satan is worshipped by the names of Jesus and

Jehovah. Men think of Jesus as a further proclaimer of Jehovah's law, instead of seeing him as the revolutionary who comes in order that law may be no more.

The same point occurs in the first stanza, where Satan is charged with inability to tell the Garment from the Man, or to trace the enduring 'virgin' in the harlot, or to distinguish one individual from another. But why the first line—the use of the word 'dunce' or the opening 'Truly'? Why, for that matter, *should* Satan be unable to distinguish in this way?

The answer could be, of course, that Blake was indulging in a piece of pleasant fantasy without thinking very hard about what he was saying. But here it is not so. As Margoliouth pointed out, the first line is evidently complementary to a line in Young's *Night Thoughts*. The last line of Night VIII reads,

Thy Master, Satan, I dare call a Dunce.

Moreover (as Margoliouth further points out) when Blake came to this line while working on his illustrations to Young, he chose an unexpected image, showing Satan kneeling before Christ in the wilderness, holding out stones to be turned into bread. Blake evidently interpreted this particular temptation as a sign of Satan's essential failure to distinguish the living from the dead, the man from the garment. Yet were it not for the existence of this illustration, the full force of Blake's view of Satan, and the relevance of his first line to the rest of the poem, would be lost to us.

One purpose of the ensuing study is to carry further this process and, by following the development of Blake's mind, to nullify some nonsensical and contradictory statements which have been made about his ideas. Yet the present purpose is not so much to destroy as to fulfil. Most readers who take up one strand in Blake's philosophy and establish that at the expense of the others are right in their own way and according to their own vision. It would be unBlakean to deny them the validity of their own attitude. It is only right, nevertheless, that the artist himself should also be allowed to stand in his own, more complex identity.

Certain misapprehensions recur in the handling of Blake's symbolism. It is often supposed that each of his symbols, including his mythological personages, stands for one particular quality or object, such as 'anger', 'desire' or 'mercy'. His thinking is a good deal more subtle than such a series of static and conventional identifications would suggest. Symbols and personages alike commonly have their existence within a dynamic pattern of his ideas: it is important to grasp the pattern in order to approach the constituent symbol. Orc, for example, is often identified with 'sex', simply, or 'revolution', or 'desire'. If there is a quality with which he can be identified it is in fact 'energy'. But there is also an idea involved. 'God out of Christ is a consuming fire' is one possible formulation of it, 'love without light is lust' is another. Orc's very existence is involved with this idea which, in its turn, moves in a larger cycle of ideas.

Blake is a very literary poet. The extent of his debts to the Bible and to Milton is obvious at a first reading; he also shows awareness of many other English writers. Again, however, it would be wrong to identify 'influences' too closely. Blake's imagination has usually been at work before his reminiscence reaches the printed page: this is no passive importation of a symbol from outside but an integration into a new pattern, carrying its own associations and functions.

The subtlety and organization of Blake's ideas have been underestimated in another important respect. He lived at a time when dialectical thinking as we know it was in its infancy: one would not immediately think of associating such a new pattern of thought with work which seems to be basically 'unintellectual'. Yet a type of dialectical thinking is inherent in his work. He may have derived it from contemporary thought: Swedenborg, for example, constantly speaks of a lost 'living' sun, as opposed to the 'dead' sun of our universe, which has become partitioned into light and heat; and he uses the latter 'dialectical' state as an image of fallen man. But the origins may also be traced further back, in that eighteenth-century optimism about the universe which produced a conviction that, rightly understood, it was a harmonious whole, reconciling the apparent warring parts. In this sense, even Pope thought dialectically.

Blake took over and developed Swedenborg's hint that the

Fall was a division *within* man rather than a separation from something outside him. In a Fall which takes place by such division, *all* the powers are correspondingly diminished, withering in their isolation from the synthesizing whole which would allow them to grow together and nourish one another. Nor is it simply a matter of 'human' powers. Since, according to Blake, 'all deities reside in the human breast', the process of the Fall involves the 'deities' themselves. If God casts out Satan he will himself be diminished by the loss: it will appear to Satan equally that God has been cast out. This type of dialectic is so basic to Blake's thinking that lack of attention to it goes far to explain the fumblings of some critics when confronted with the resulting patterns in his symbolism.

Despite his devotion to dialectical thinking, however, it would be wrong to consider Blake as the mythologist of the technological revolution. Only one basic dialectic is recognized by the thoroughgoing technologist and that, the dialectic involved in the progress of science, is regarded as both desirable and invincible. In a society which is geared to such progress, belief in it is likely to furnish the goods which we associate with the dominant mythologies of history: security, assurance, an unquestioned set of dogmas by which all human experience is judged. Those who become sufficiently involved in the processes of technological improvement may not even perceive that a problem exists: they may live out a complete and useful lifetime within the machine that they are helping to service, secure in their conviction that whatever the apparent setbacks (wars between rival technological societies, the boredom and apathy of millions of workers) the pattern imposed is the only possible one.

For those who are concerned with the more strictly intellectual processes involved in science, the situation may not be so simple. C. P. Snow has indicated that many of the most conscious scientists that he has known have been, in their general attitude to life, pessimistic.[17] Their faith in the power of science has given them an optimistic view of society in general, but their awareness of the inexorable laws of the universe suggests to them that the plight of the individual human being is tragic. Their 'mythology' of the universe is ultimately structured in mathematically describable laws against which the single human being, at the mercy of chaotic forces from within and without, must necessarily feel himself an alien.

The Romantic artist stands away from the main current of scientific thinking in two important respects. His imagination, on the one hand, is highly developed: and it is of the nature of imagination to long for something eternally beautiful, set beyond the flux of circumstance. A hunger for eternity can never be satisfied by a civilization which is continually and totally preoccupied with the makeshift and temporary—the cartoon comment, the shifting fashion, the experimental structure.

On the other hand, the Romantic artist is also aware of the basic physical condition of man. Man is Adam, 'of the earth', unhappy when he is too far removed from the basic rhythms of life. His true grandeur and glamour depend upon his maintaining a link with the nature of which his body is a part.

Romantic art is often divided against itself, therefore. One of its functions, indeed, is to present to technological man a mirror for his own divided image, reminding him of the twin resources of earth and imagination from which he is isolating himself.

Imaginative vision and awareness of the physical condition of man are both strong in Blake, but the stress lies always upon the former. In his greatest poetry and art he reconciles the two: elsewhere visionary beauty seems to exist in separation from physical glamour, and sometimes suffers as a result. Yet it must be borne in mind that the Blake who constantly spoke of his desire to recall men to the Divine Vision also wrote a lyric which began,

> Dear Mother, dear Mother, the Church is cold.
> But the Ale-house is healthy & pleasant & warm;[18]

and when, many years later, he portrayed the Canterbury Pilgrims setting forth from their Southwark inn, he pictured the Tabard as a building in his favoured Gothic style and indicated his approval of it.

In later works the glimpses of a rich sensuous life occur more and more rarely, but they are there. They are noticeably vivid in the earliest works of all. Some critics are embarrassed to

account for the presence among them of verses such as the
following:

> This city & this country has brought forth many mayors
> To sit in state & give forth laws out of their old oak chairs
> With face as brown as any nut with drinking of strong ale
> Good English hospitality O then it did not fail[19]

There is an irony in this verse—it is put into the mouth of
the Lawgiver. But there is also a nostalgia, for the Lawgiver is
thus shown in pursuit of his own anti-self, yearning for the
generosity of true justice. The Blake who can seem so rarefied
and far from popular taste in his more abstruse prophecies can
also be seen pursuing to their source the elements in popular
art which, surviving in an etiolated form in calendars and fur-
nishings redolent of 'olde England', betray to this day a yearning for the rich and the grand. And as soon as we turn to his
pictorial illustrations of such states we see that he is protected
against vulgarity by his unique combination of irony and
innocence.

The only fault of irony is that it is a negative posture. In
Blake's time more positive gestures were difficult. When he
tried to make them they always involved, necessarily, a strong
sense of the separation within civilization as he saw it: and he
was so far a victim of the predicament described that his own
achievement tended towards fragmentation. Yet behind the
rhetoric of the Prophetic Books, caught in the lineaments of the
faces which he drew, there lies the vision of an integrated
human condition, both rich in sensuous apprehension of the
present and alive to its own intuitions of the eternal beauty
implicit in all living forms. The scope and intensity of that
vision go far to justify the title bestowed upon him by one of the
characters in *Point Counter Point*: 'the last civilized man'.[20]

2 A Fourfold Vision

Readers who come to Blake's work for the first time are often most impressed by isolated lines and phrases. Many of these are striking and memorable: from them, moreover, it is possible to build up a picture of Blake as a figure anticipating Nietzsche in his advocacy of desire and energy. It is true that in many of the works that we shall be examining the action is grounded in a conflict between reason and energy; it is also true that during the phase of his career when he was writing them he was at times exploring the idea that desire and energy might be the key to the universe. Some of his best art and poetry results from that exploration. But Blake's thought is more complex than this. Behind his delight in the forms of energy there exists an even more deeply rooted pre-occupation with Vision. From the time when, as a boy, he saw a tree at Peckham Rye 'starred with angels' he was always obsessed by the importance of such moments of possession; later experiences confirmed him in the belief in another order, set apart from the natural order investigated by the scientists: an order apprehended by the imagination.

Blake's humanism is idiosyncratic: it rests on the pre-supposition that all men possess an eternal form which subsists in the interplay between vision and desire. Eternal Man exists primarily by those two faculties, which nourish his genius and promote his generosity. But men as we know them have fallen from this estate. As a result, the fruitful dialectic between Vision and Desire is replaced by a warring and fruitless dialectic between Reason and Energy.

From the time of the French Revolution, Blake was working out the implications of his beliefs in relation to the political, religious and social conditions of his time. It is during this period that we witness the evolution of his own version of humanism.

Throughout the period he was fascinated by the figure of

John Milton. From his early reading in *Paradise Lost* to the point when he identified himself with the figure of its author in his poem *Milton*, he saw Milton as his most important predecessor in the path that he was forging for himself. In particular, *Paradise Lost* was a valuable stimulus to his thinking about the conflict between Reason and Energy.

His best-known remarks about Milton occur in *The Marriage of Heaven and Hell*: one aphorism, in particular, has become a commonplace of Milton criticism:

> Note. The Reason Milton wrote in fetters when he wrote of Angels & God, and at liberty when of Devils & Hell, is because he was a true Poet and of the Devils party without knowing it.[1]

The vividness of Blake's language is enough to convince many of his readers that they can understand what he is saying without difficulty: he is declaring himself a wholehearted supporter of Milton's Satan; he is a precursor of Byron and Shelley.

To turn Blake into a nineteenth-century Satanist without further qualification, however, is to underestimate the subtlety of his position. Even his other comments on *Paradise Lost* in the same section show that something more is involved than a declaration of allegiance to the forces of 'evil':

> Those who restrain desire, do so because theirs is weak enough to be restrained; and the restrainer or reason usurps its place & governs the unwilling.
>
> And being restraind it by degrees becomes passive till it is only the shadow of desire.
>
> The history of this is written in Paradise Lost, & the Governor or Reason is call'd Messiah.
>
> And the original Archangel or possessor of the command of the heavenly host, is calld the Devil or Satan and his children are call'd Sin & Death
>
> But in the Book of Job Miltons Messiah is call'd Satan.
>
> For this history has been adopted by both parties
>
> It indeed appear'd to Reason as if Desire was cast out, but the Devils account is, that the Messiah fell, & formed a heaven of what he stole from the Abyss
>
> This is shewn in the Gospel, where he prays to the Father to send the comforter or Desire that Reason may have Ideas to build on, the Jehovah of the Bible being no other than he, who dwells in flaming fire. Know that after Christs death, he became Jehovah.

But in Milton; the Father is Destiny, the Son, a Ratio of the five senses. & the Holy-ghost, Vacuum!

Whatever this means, it is not a simple realignment of *Paradise Lost* to make Satan the hero and God the villain. We shall not understand it at all, in fact, unless we grasp that in this reading of the story all the parties have fallen. It appears to the Devil that the Messiah fell and to Reason as if Desire were cast out: and if the Devil has the better of it the only reason is that the Messiah fell further. In the state of true humanity, desire exists within the bounding line of form. At the Fall, however, reason, which should be simply the outward running line of energy, turns into a restraining force—and so deprives itself of its proper nourishment. It falls: the Vision of Art becomes the analytical reason, forced to make a heaven out of what is given to it by the 'Abyss of the five senses'. And so in the Gospel when Christ prays for the Comforter, he is praying for the restoration of Satan, at present the raging Energy which raises itself against the will of God, but in his true stature the Desire which would restore Reason to the state of Vision. (And indeed when the Comforter arrives, it is in the shape of tongues of fire.) Without Desire, Jehovah exists in a consuming and destructive fire which he constantly strives to control by tyranny and law; when Christ dies, he also enters this state. In the Book of Job, likewise, the 'Satan' who tempts is, like Milton's Messiah, a figure who has restrained Desire until it is no more than a disease with which he tries to destroy the weak but persistent vision of Job. The pattern remains; but the protagonists are reversed.

This is no simple inversion of the 'moral' of *Paradise Lost*, therefore. Indeed, although Milton would not have agreed for one moment with Blake's analysis, he might well have acknowledged that Blake had laid bare certain elements in the 'meaning' of his poem, as he intended it, with unusual penetration.

In recent times there has been a tendency, in reading *Paradise Lost*, to apply the same standards that one would use for a realistic work of fiction dealing with moral issues. The characters taking part, and the morality of their actions, are examined as one would examine the actions of characters in a novel, each being regarded as of equal stature with the rest. Certainly, to anyone who reads the poem in this way, Satan emerges as the most vivid and sympathetic of the participants. It is not surprising if, for such readers, Blake's statements about Milton are simply a more forceful version of Dryden's assertion that Satan is the true hero of the poem.[2] Over a century ago, when the novel-form was widely used for the discussion of morality and the portrayal of character, such views were particularly popular. Walter Bagehot wrote in 1859 that the great error which pervaded *Paradise Lost* was that 'Satan is made *interesting*':

> The interest of Satan's character is at its height in the first two books. Coleridge justly compared it to that of Napoleon. There is the same pride, the same satanic ability, the same will, the same egotism. . . . Few Englishmen feel a profound reverence for Napoleon I. There was no French alliance in *his* time; we have most of us some tradition of antipathy to him. Yet hardly any Englishman can read the account of the campaign of 1814 without feeling his interest in the emperor to be strong, and without perhaps being conscious of a latent wish that he may succeed. Our opinion is against him, our serious wish is of course for England; but the imagination has a sympathy of its own, and will not give place. We read about the great general—never greater than in that last emergency—showing resources of genius that seem almost infinite, and that assuredly have never been surpassed, yet vanquished, yielding to the power of circumstances, to the combined force of adversaries, each of whom singly he outmatches in strength, and all of whom together he surpasses in majesty and in mind. Something of the same sort of interest belongs to the Satan of the first two books of *Paradise Lost*. We know that he will be vanquished; his name is not a recommendation. Still we do not imagine distinctly the minds by which he is to be vanquished; we do not take the same interest in them that we do in him; our sympathies, our fancy, are on his side.
>
> Perhaps much of this was inevitable; yet what a defect it is! especially what a defect in Milton's own view, and looked at with the stern realism with which he regarded it! Suppose that the author of evil in the universe were the most attractive being in it; suppose that the source of all sin were the origin of all interest to us![3]

Since Bagehot wrote, the moral standards which we apply to human actions have swung so far from those current in his day that Satan now sometimes commands support for his actions as well as for the personality which he displays. But the attraction

has always been there: one has only to look through the large
number of illustrations for *Paradise Lost* which were executed in
the Romantic period to see this. More recently, the case in
favour of Satan has been argued by both A. J. A. Waldock, in
Paradise Lost and its Critics, and by William Empson, in *Milton's
God*.[4]

It is difficult to deal with this position without entering upon
a long and detailed argument; the only point which needs to
be reiterated here is that some at least of the polemic in favour
of Satan and against God depends on a reading of the poem as a
straightforward moral narrative. And Milton, admittedly, has
encouraged such a reading by presenting his opening books in a
form which contains so much dramatic writing. Drama automatically suggests a tension between equals. Nevertheless,
there are elements in the poem which cannot be absorbed into
such a reading. Blake, with his visionary preoccupations and
nose for allegory, would fasten eagerly on such points which the
modern reader, brought up in a different tradition, hardly
notices. One of the first and most striking is Satan's encounter
with Sin and Death at the gates of Hell in Book Two. We are
told immediately afterwards that they are respectively his wife
and son—but any attempt to deal with this relationship
realistically only makes it ludicrous. At this point Milton ex-
pects his reader to respond as to allegory. His concern is with
the process by which sin and death came into the world, not
with Satan's domestic life.

The same point might be made concerning several other incidents in the poem, including the following:

> Eve's gazing at her own reflection in the pool just after her
> creation.

> The return of Satan to Hell and his attempt to celebrate the
> triumph over man with his fellow-devils, which is thwarted when
> they discover that they are turned into serpents.

> The ultimate fate of Paradise, carried down the river until it is
> no more than a desolate rock in the ocean.[5]

There is every indication that Blake took these and similar incidents and made them the basis of his own interpretation of
the poem. Where other critics have attacked Milton's moral

lved, Blake would
oem that was not

o those who argue
ne poem. Such a
us 'characters' in
aking: it assumes,
lling against God.
d a case. To quote

song and feast and
interesting than his

: subsumed into a
ls the interplay of
l his crew cease to
...ples. When he is
dealing with God's relations with Satan, Milton is stating not
what the ideal relationship between ruler and subordinate
should be, but what the relationship between good and evil
always is. Satan has many noble qualities as a fallen angel,
but the qualities that are always lacking between himself and
his associates are precisely those which Lewis mentions: light
and love. The devil may display great energy and considerable rhetorical talent, but God has all the light and the music.

The point could be argued more fully and at length; but it is
time to return to Blake. For, whether or not acceptable to
present-day critics, C. S. Lewis's idea of the Miltonic heaven is
also Blake's. He too visualized an organized light and harmony
which left no room for self-love. Whatever is to be said in
favour of fallen man, the final and unchanging point is that his
state is *unnecessary*. It is a ghastly mistake.

If one follows the critics to move beyond this elementary
position and examine the debates of the poem as though they
were debates between human beings, rather than between a
principle of harmonizing light and one of destructive energy,
our sympathies are soon aroused in favour of Satan and against
God. It must be observed, however, that although the critic's

charges against God may be connected, they contain two separate counts. The first is that God is a tyrant, the second that he is a logic-chopping pedant. The first is Shelley's ('One who in the cold security of undoubted triumph inflicts the most horrible revenge upon his enemy . . . with the alleged design of exasperating him to deserve new torments');[7] the second is Pope's ('And God the Father turns a school-divine').[8] The first argument is the one that has most occupied critics. By the natural development of Renaissance thought the Promethean predicament of man has come to the fore: if man is the prey of a cruel divinity who cares little for the fate of his creatures, the rhetoric of Satan emerges as a wonderful voicing of his natural protest. Blake's assertion that Milton was of the Devil's party without knowing it is seized upon as an exact statement of the truth.

Yet, as we shall see, Blake was not so preoccupied as later critics with the Promethean state of man. He would share Milton's belief that man is in this state not because of a legal disobedience, but because his very disobedience implies a voluntary self-exclusion from God's paradise. It was not the 'tyrannical' aspect of Milton's God that alienated him so much as the 'rational' aspect. God, already given a perfect case against Satan, emerges in his speeches as an ancient legalist, bound, to a ridiculous extent, by the laws of his own universe. The central being of a heaven of light and music and love reveals himself as a faceless idol of Necessity, caught within the cobweb of his own abstractions. Blake expressed his horror in a single sentence:

> But in Milton; the Father is Destiny, the Son, a Ratio of the five senses, & the Holy-ghost, Vacuum!

There was a sense, however, in which Milton had accurately expressed the spirit of his time. The God of Milton's poem was to be the God worshipped in eighteenth-century Europe. His rationalism would allow the inhumanities of Blake's England. The prophecy could be taken further: for rationalism coupled with political tyranny was to provoke, in the American and French Revolutions, a revolt not altogether unlike that of Satan and the rebel angels.

Blake's attitude to Milton involved making a simple distinction. He accepted Milton's Heaven and rejected Milton's God. To put it more precisely, he declared that God, as well as Satan, had fallen. Blake's heaven has no more to do with necessitarian rationalism than with unrestrained energy: nor can it exist in the absence of either visionary reason or the energies of desire. If either side is cast out, then both are automatically cast out, for the very existence of his heaven involves the maintenance of a dialectic between them.

But Blake, in rejecting Milton's God, was not simply turning *Paradise Lost* inside out. Milton would have argued that any apparent injustices on the part of God were justified by the complete and overwhelming goodness of the heaven for which he was fighting, compared with the evil and enormity of Satan's cause. Blake, on the other hand, would argue that nothing could justify injustice and that the tyrannies of God the Father were due to the fact that he had deprived himself of the energies of Satan. He reshuffled the values of Milton's poem. God the Father, as the embodiment of Reason, he assigned to the lowest place and, in *The Marriage of Heaven and Hell*, declared that the world of Satan was at least superior to *that*. But above these spheres he placed two more. Superior to both was the state of Milton's Paradise, the state of wedded happiness; and superior to all three was the world of Milton's Heaven, the world where music and light, love and life, conspiring, render unnecessary anything so mean as self-assertion and self-love.

Further realignments of Milton's universe followed. The world of Hell in which Satan is discovered in Book One became the world of the God of Reason. Satan really had no business in such a lifeless place and it was characteristic of his nature that as soon as he became himself again at the beginning of the poem he exercised his energies—first by building a palace and then by breaking out of Hell altogether. We glimpse here a Blakean paradigm—the serpent of energy which necessarily breaks out of the shell of Reason. But once this realignment is made, and the caves and dens of Hell assigned to Milton's God, Blake can follow Milton's depiction of Satan very closely. Because Satan is cut off from Milton's heaven, it follows that his energies must inevitably be debased, through lack of contact with their visionary source. The proud, plumed serpent of Eden will, by devotion to itself, inevitably become the mean, creeping serpent of earth, feeding on dust and ashes.

Blake also reinterpreted the Paradise sequences in Milton's poem, applying the same symbolism to sexual love. Many years later he reported to Crabb Robinson a visionary conversation between himself and Milton:

> '. . . I saw Milton in imagination and he told me to beware of being misled by his *Paradise Lost*. In particular, he wished me to show the falsehood of his doctrine that the pleasures of sex arose from the Fall. The Fall could not produce any pleasure.'[9]

Commenting on this, Northrop Frye has declared that it is best ignored.

> Blake is alleged to have complained that Milton was grievously in error in saying that the pleasures of sex arose from the Fall. Milton, of course, said nothing of the kind, as Blake, who made at least four illustrations of Satan watching the love-play of the unfallen Adam and Eve, knew very well.[10]

Milton did say something of the kind, however, and Blake may well have had in mind a specific passage in *Tetrachordon*, where Milton's attitude to sexual pleasure is made clear:

> . . . wisest Solomon among his gravest Proverbs countenances a kinde of ravishment and erring fondnes in the entertainment of wedded leisures; and in the Song of Songs, which is generally beleev'd, even in the jolliest expressions to figure the spousals of the Church with Christ, sings of a thousand raptures between those two lovely ones farre on the hither side of carnall enjoyment.[11]

The limitation of sexual pleasure to 'the hither side of carnal enjoyment' is evidently the point which Blake thought erroneous: and it is clear from *Paradise Lost* that while Milton allowed for physical pleasure in the raptures of Adam and Eve, he thought that 'carnal enjoyment' was the specific element in their love-making that arose after the Fall:

> but that false Fruit
> Farr other operation first displaid,
> Carnal desire enflaming; hee on *Eve*

> Began to cast lascivious Eyes, shee him
> As wantonly repaid; in Lust they burne. . . .[12]

These are the carnal pleasures which arise from the Fall in
Milton's eyes: Blake is simply arguing that if they are pleasures
at all then they must have existed before the Fall: 'The Fall
could not produce any pleasure.' It was impossible for him to
conceive of a sexual happiness in Paradise which did not contain within itself every sort of sexual pleasure.

As with the conflict between God and Satan, however, Blake
does not wish either to reject or invert Milton's statements but
to subject them to a subtle reinterpretation. He is not saying
that lustful desire is as good a form of sexual pleasure as any
other. On the contrary, he would willingly accept Milton's
analysis of the love-making between Adam and Eve after the
Fall. The imagery of this passage, with its constant reference to
'burning' and 'fire' suggests that their love-play is now a
microcosm of what has happened in the universe at large. The
fiery Satan has arisen to assume command within it. Blake
would see this as a description of what happens in love-making
when sexual energy is exploited at the expense of the containing
vision which unites the lovers. In a later poem, 'The Crystal
Cabinet', a love-relationship is described in precisely these
terms.[13]

In this way, the state of Paradise becomes closely linked with
the Hell of Energy and the ironically named 'Heaven' of
Reason, for its existence depends on uniting, precariously, the
forces of which these other two states are fallen relics: such a
union can be eternally consummated only in the true Heaven.

Blake has thus built up his own version of the universe described in *Paradise Lost*: its elements are now regrouped to form
the following ascending scale of states:

(1) The 'Hell' of Book One is really the 'Heaven' of Milton's
God. With its dens and bogs, illuminated by an ineffectual light,
it represents the state of Reason when cut off from all other forces,
including Energy.

(2) Satan's statement 'Myself am Hell' is literally true: Hell
exists wherever Energy is exercised without controlling vision—
whether in the building of an artificially lit palace or in a journey
through space intended for the destruction of others.

(3) Superior to both these states is the state of innocent wedded happiness as represented by Adam and Eve; but the fact that reason and energy are divorced within the world at large makes this state a precarious one, always liable to fail by the insurgence of energy. It is a 'Crystal House'.

(4) Only in true Heaven can the state precariously established in married happiness be permanent. Here reason and energy, now raised into vision and desire, exist as a fruitful dialectic instead of a warring division.

These states became for Blake four 'levels of vision': as such they formed an enduring paradigm for his thought (not to be confused with the 'Four Zoas'). The levels of vision may briefly be characterized as follows:

(1) The state of Darkness (Blake's Ulro) in which unilluminated Reason alone holds sway.

(2) The state of Fire, the state in which energy is freely exercised. A creative artist or a lover, purely by exercising his energies, enters this state, which is later called Generation. Another symbol for it is the destructive sun.

(3) The state of 'Light' (paradise) often called by Blake Beulah (from Isaiah, where the word is translated 'married' and from Bunyan, where it is the country from which the pilgrims can see the city to which they are travelling). Blake sees this state as one in which the first two ('Heaven' and 'Hell') are 'married'. It also expresses his idea that sexual love can give a brief revelation of that eternal light which belongs to the state of full vision. Its symbol is the moon.

(4) The state of full Light or Vision, which reconciles all the others. It is recaptured only rarely—by the Genius in his moments of full inspiration, for example. Its symbol is the lost sun of vision described by Swedenborg, in which heat and light are reconciled.

Although Blake objectifies these states in his prophetic books, he thought of them primarily as psychological categories. He described them as levels of vision: single, twofold, threefold and fourfold respectively. His most important reference to them comes in a letter of 1802:

Now I a fourfold vision see
And a fourfold vision is given to me

Tis fourfold in my supreme delight
And three fold in soft Beulahs night
And twofold Always. May God us keep
From Single vision & Newtons sleep[14]

The existence of these states, and the relations between them, is an indication of the subtlety and sophistication of Blake's attitude. His humanism may sometimes seem to be best expressed by his delight in energy, sometimes by his feeling for suffering humanity and his tenderness towards the innocent. Either might serve as a sufficient attitude for a lesser writer. But Blake's feelings in both these spheres are always tempered by his ultimate respect for the supreme vision and for poetic genius. According to him, we may exist, minimally, as human beings when we exercise our gifts of analysis and reason; or, more strongly, when we express our energies in indignation or creativity; or, better still, when we exercise love and compassion. But we only exist fully in our humanity when we live by our own genius and acknowledge the individual genius of other men.

Blake's humanism, like his vision, is fourfold.

An appreciation of Blake's various 'levels' of vision, with their respective symbols, is of assistance in unravelling the meaning of difficult passages in the poems. Apparent contradictions are reconciled when the warring elements are seen to belong to different levels in the structure of his vision. Blake uses his symbols in a sophisticated manner, relating them to the spheres of reason, energy or love respectively and then exploring the relationship between those spheres.

About the visionary experience itself he is less sophisticated. The organization of his universe of symbols is carried out against a conviction that the exercise of vision corresponds to man's profoundest insight into reality. It is as though within each man there resides an eternal being who is brought into play in the moment of vision. This, his 'eternal self', will finally be released at the moment of death.

This conviction of Blake's, the most permanent feature of his thought, can be linked with the visionary experiences of his youth. It was probably confirmed as a central and organizing belief by his experience at the deathbed of his brother Robert, whom he saw at the moment of death rising from the bed and disappearing through the ceiling, clapping his hands for joy.[15] Two years later the signatures of William and Catherine Blake were added to the resolutions of the 1789 Swedenborgian Conference which included the affirmation that

> immediately on the Death of the material body, (which will never be reassumed,) man rises again as to his spiritual or substantial body, wherein he existeth in perfect human form.[16]

It is against this belief about the outward and inward natures of human beings that Blake's interest in earlier mystical philosophers must be viewed. He more than once acknowledged a debt to the writings of Paracelsus and Boehme, for instance, whom he regarded as predecessors of Swedenborg. In the writings of both these men he found the doctrine of the inner forms of nature, the 'signature' borne by all natural objects.

Desirée Hirst has recently drawn attention to some of the passages in Paracelsus which express a conviction that there exist two natures in man.

> . . . every man is composed of two, viz.: of a material and of a spiritual body. The materiallity gives body, blood and flesh; but the spirituality gives hearing, feeling, smelling, touching and tastings. . . . In this therefore are the great wonders of God to be known, that there are two bodies, viz. an Eternal and a Corporal . . .[17]

As she points out, another distinctive feature of Paracelsus's doctrine is the great stress which is laid on imagination. Other thinkers had spoken of the dual nature of man, but it was rare to find the imagination so firmly regarded as the central human faculty in perceiving spiritual reality.

> Imagination is Creative Power. Medicine uses imagination fixed. Phantasy is not imagination, but the frontier of folly. He who is born in imagination discovers the latent forces of Nature. Imagination exists in the perfect spirit, while phantasy exists in the body without the perfect spirit. Because Man does not imagine perfectly at all times, arts and sciences are uncertain, though in fact they are certain and, obtained by means of imagination, can give true results. Imagination takes precedence over all. Resolute imagination can accomplish all things.[18]

This association between the imagination and the spiritual may well have influenced Blake's thinking. His phrase, 'Corporeal Understanding', a faculty which he opposes to the 'Intellectual Powers', may equally derive from Paracelsus' use of the Latin word 'corporeus' to describe the reasoning of those who are not alive in their spiritual nature.[19]

Blake's enthusiasm for Swedenborg was evidently at its height in the year 1789; afterwards he was to decide that Swedenborg's belief in a 'real' universe behind the world of appearances was not accompanied by any true imaginative power or insight into the human condition. Although there is a recognizable Swedenborgian element in his subsequent writings, therefore, it is always Swedenborg reinterpreted. This is nowhere more true than in the case of Swedenborg's humanism. Swedenborg had declared in *Divine Love and Divine Wisdom* that

> God is very Man. In all the Heavens there is no other Idea of God, than that of a Man . . .

Blake annotated this emphatically:

> Man can have no idea of any thing greater than Man as a cup cannot contain more than its capaciousness But God is a man not because he is so perceivd by man but because he is the creator of man[20]

As he read on in Swedenborg's works, however, Blake decided that such statements masked a contempt for the world and humanity which corresponded to much in eighteenth-century orthodox devotion. His own conception of the relation between the human and the divine would give more weight to the importance of the human.

Blake's sense of an inward, more real, human nature is an essential element in all his work. But he is rescued from simply providing another version of the former mystical traditions by two things: the strength of his imagination and the depth of his insight into human nature. It is these two features of his work which give it its unique appeal to readers of all ages. Blake's humanism differs from many previous mystical philosophies by allowing the imagination to act as intermediary between the outward and inner natures of man. In his eyes man is not a divided being, body and soul, with little hope of reconciliation between them; he is a being of contraries. These contraries can be reconciled by the imagination, which both gives him a sense of his eternal nature and teaches him how to live fully in his mortal body.

It is this that gives Blake's humanism and his art their peculiar qualities. Their obsessive and private nature derives from his determination not to be lured into either unworldly mysticism or worldly materialism. Their positive achievement results from his unerring sense of imaginative form. Blake's imagination seeks that midpoint between mysticism and materialism where matter reveals its eternal form: a form which has no merely static or allegorical existence but which makes itself known by the presence of energy. He is more attracted to children at play than to the contemplation of a Chinese jar; more interested in the patterns woven by insects than in the study of geometry. His art and poetry alike find their natural pitch at the point where eternal identity and organic change meet in the running line of energized form.

Such are the permanent ideas and convictions by which Blake lived and organized his art. At the end of the eighteenth century they served for a time as the framework for his concern with the pressing question of liberty, sexual, political and religious.

3 The Energies of Desire

At the time when the death of his brother Robert was confirming Blake in his early conviction of the importance of vision in human experience, the outbreak of the French Revolution, and its impact on English life and thought, gave him a new and urgent concern with the question of social and political freedom. Liberty, long cherished by the English as an ideal, now seemed to be spreading to other nations as a fact. Human nature, it seemed, was less irredeemable than had been imagined: a renewal of humanity in England might yet lead to the full establishment of liberty in the country which had produced so many prophets of freedom.

Political abuses were not the only ills to be rooted out. Disaffection within nations, or between one nation and another, could be matched by the failure of love between individual human beings. The same oppressive laws which had caused the American peoples to break away from England and the French to rise against their rulers could be found at work throughout society, even in the family. The hindering of the brotherhood of man in the world at large was paralleled in the basic social organism, where the imposition of the moral law upon the love of individual men and women led to their love being stifled by jealousy and self-limiting enclosure.

Political tyranny and human jealousy were, Blake felt, subtly interrelated. Restraint was in each case the cause, and even if the two types of restraint might seem very different, the mechanisms which they set in motion corresponded closely. In both cases men found themselves caught in the toils of a conflict between reason and energy. This had been the theme of his early poems *Tiriel* and *The Book of Thel*: and, without giving up the positions which he had assumed in those books, he now proceeded to refine upon his basic pattern. The lost integration of Vision and Desire was now kept in the background, though always presupposed as the ideal condition of humanity;

the practical implications of the separation were examined more closely in terms of human life as it is lived.

In order to express his political and social ideas in poetic form Blake introduced certain mythological figures of his own creation.* The pattern of ideas involved is straightforward, but it involves a re-working of certain ideas which he had already used in earlier works and which must be briefly mentioned here. *The Book of Thel* had contained mention of a figure of lost love, an absent sun-god of vision, whom he named Luvah. *Tiriel* had involved an adaptation of the allegory of *Paradise Lost* to fit this conception of lost vision. Adam and Eve, instead of being rejected from Paradise, were supposed to have remained there in an innocence which, unrenewed by energy, degenerated into the foolishness and aged childishness of the characters Har and Heva. Har, the fainéant father and law-giver, was all that remained of Adam the visionary. In this paradise, which had been 'lost' not by sin but by a fatal separation between vision and desire, man and serpent had fallen together into a state of impotent reason and destructive energy respectively. The mercurial and hypocritical spirit of fallen energy was represented by the hero of the poem, Tiriel. The most positive figure left in this fallen world was the protagonist of simple honesty and righteous indignation, Ijim.

This simple reordering of Milton's allegory gives way, in the specifically social and political poems, to a development of the basic mythology which involves a more subtle organization. The place of Har is now taken by Urizen, Blake's most important mythological creation, the spirit who controls and limits all human energies, maintaining his power by the imposition of laws. The cruelty and despair which result from such activity had both been part of Tiriel's personality but Blake now divided them, assigning them respectively to two sons of Urizen. Tiriel's imposition of harsh laws, which turns limitation into repression, is now the function of Bromion, the tyrant; while his lack of vision is taken over by a character named Theotormon.

---

* Since it may not be easy for a reader new to Blake's mythology to keep the significance of the various figures in his mind, a brief summary of the patterns which dominated his myth-making is given for purposes of reference in Appendix One.

In this way, Blake moves away from his original simple
design, in which Adam and Satan were paralleled respectively
by Har and Tiriel. Organized as simply as that, the pattern
had afforded little scope for developing a detailed mythological
interpretation of human affairs. Something more than a simple
opposition between reason and energy was required. Under
the rearranged scheme, therefore, the limited structure of
Tiriel was replaced by the following:

	Urizen		Leutha
	(spirit of restraint)		(sexual freedom)
Bromion		Theotormon	Oothoon
(tyranny of law)		(visionless doubt)	(spirit of desire)

More ramifications followed, but it is likely that this particular form was evolved at a particular time, since four out of
the five names involved have a Greek origin, which can be
briefly intimated as follows:

Urizen   from οὐρίζειν 'to limit' (Dorothy Plowman)[1]
Bromion   from βρόμιος 'roaring' (Frye), 'Bacchus' (Damon)[2]
Theotormon from Θεός 'God', τόρμος 'gap'.
Leutha   from ἐλευθερία 'freedom.'[3]

Under this new alignment of Blake's ideas, the two main contending principles in the universe are those of restraint and
liberty; while the three components of Tiriel, his tyranny, his
lack of vision and his vague energy, are divided out, the first
two being given to Urizen's two sons, while the third is assigned
mainly to the sphere of Leutha.

These new forces are deployed in Blake's prophetic book,
Visions of the Daughters of Albion (a natural sequel to *The Book of
Thel*). The name Oothoon is the only one in the book which
does not have a Greek origin. Professor Northrop Frye has
pointed out that the setting of the poem recalls Ossian's
Oithona,[4] but feels that the story, which is about a romantic
heroine's preference of death to dishonour, has little to remind
us of Blake. His parenthetical remark that Blake might have
been protesting against such a code may well point to the truth,
however, for Oothoon and Oithona are alike victims of the
moral law.

Oothoon resembles the earlier heroine Thel in that she faces

entry into the state of experience. Whereas Thel, a dweller in
the vale of Har, could approach the earth only under the law,
however, experiencing desire as restraint and therefore fleeing
from it, Oothoon, dwelling in the vale of Leutha, experiences
desire as freedom, and so responds to its delight. But Oothoon's
exploitation of freedom in this way immediately involves her in
the far greater conflict between freedom and restraint, so that
the whole force of the moral law is at once bent against her in the
person of a tyrannical avenger who attacks her, while her
visionless lover can do nothing for her. Hence Oothoon's complaint, which furnishes the 'Argument' at the beginning of the
poem:

> I loved Theotormon
> And I was not ashamed
> I trembled in my virgin fears
> And I hid in Leutha's vale!
>
> I plucked Leutha's flower,
> And I rose up from the vale;
> But the terrible thunders tore
> My virgin mantle in twain.

Her story now unfolds. And although the poem is, throughout, a story of oppression by the moral law, Blake immediately
suggests the link between moral and political restraint by
making a connection between Oothoon and America:

> Enslav'd, the Daughters of Albion weep: a trembling lamentation
> Upon their mountains; in their valleys, sighs towards America.
> For the soft soul of America, Oothoon wanderd in woe,
> Along the vales of Leutha seeking flowers to comfort her . . .

Although, by implication, a political symbolism runs through
the rest of the poem, specific political reference ends soon after
this point. Blake has now introduced a theme more vital to his
present purpose. His Thel wandering in the garden was dimly
aware of a presence missed, a God who once walked in the
noonday heat of the garden but is now heard only as a voice in
the evening. So Oothoon now walks, her search for 'comfort'
immediately recalling Rachel weeping for her children or Mary
Magdalen weeping outside the empty tomb. No visionary god
appears to restore Oothoon to happiness, however. Instead,

she devotes herself to the 'bright Marygold' of Leutha's vale, which tells her that if her flower is plucked another will spring in its place, because 'the soul of sweet delight / Can never pass away'.

As soon as Oothoon has overcome her hesitations and plucked the flower, however, she finds herself in the grip of the forces which have usurped the land in the absence of the true god. She is attacked by Bromion, fierce agent of the moral law, who both assumes possession of her and brands her as a harlot. Where the Elizabethan lover could cry, in delight, 'O my America, my newfound-land!'[5] Bromion cries,

> Thy soft American plains are mine, and mine thy north & South . . .

He tells Theotormon that he may marry her, now that she is his harlot, and protect the child which she will bring forth. Theotormon can respond only in jealousy, leaving Bromion and Oothoon bound back to back as 'terror and meekness', while he weeps at the threshold. As he does so, cries are heard from a whole landscape of oppression, where misery and lust flourish because Theotormon has failed to rise to his proper stature:

> . . . beneath him sound like waves on a desart shore
> The voice of slaves beneath the sun, and children bought with money,
> That shiver in religious caves beneath the burning fires
> Of lust, that belch incessant from the summits of the earth

The yearning for love which rises up from this whole landscape is also localized in Oothoon. Since Theotormon insists on devoting himself to ideals of purity and holiness, she calls on him to act upon her, if only in the strength of his holiness. Her real need is that he should descend as the winged god of Love, but in her terror at his jealousy she visualizes his wings as those of eagles. She therefore calls upon him to descend and tear her flesh, that she may reflect the image of Theotormon on her 'pure transparent breast'. As the Eagles do so, Theotormon smiles severely and she reflects the smile

> As the clear spring mudded with feet of beasts grows pure & smiles.

This line, which can be linked to the lyric 'The Clod and the Pebble' in *Songs of Experience*,[6] reflects a favourite theme of Blake's. Innocence is both self-giving and inviolable.

In the moment of vision which follows this experience, Oothoon calls upon Theotormon to rise in his true glory. Even as she does so, she recognizes that the eagle is a bird that only looks to the sun, without possessing its glory. If Theotormon rose it would be in the more visionary form of a sun-god:

> . . . arise O Theotormon for the village dog
> Barks at the breaking day. the nightingale has done lamenting.
> The lark does rustle in the ripe corn, and the Eagle returns
> From nightly prey, and lifts his golden beak to the pure east;
> Shaking the dust from his immortal pinions to awake
> The sun that sleeps too long.

She goes on to explain how in the past she has been taught to think of herself as a prisoner of her five senses and how her head and heart were divided, respectively, into enervated light and dark heat.

> And they inclos'd my infinite brain into a narrow circle.
> And sunk my heart into the Abyss, a red round globe hot burning
> Till all from life I was obliterated and erased.

But her longing for the sunrise that would restore her to true life is disappointed:

> Instead of morn arises a bright shadow, like an eye
> In the eastern cloud: instead of night a sickly charnel house . . .

The favourite eighteenth-century device showing the 'eye of God' looking out of the heavens comes in conveniently here as a symbol of the moral law, with the charnel-house as a symbol of its victims.

Oothoon justifies her plea by pointing to the many animals that show signs of possessing another sense beyond the five of man—the bee forming its cells, the chicken avoiding the hawk. Is there not a similar mystery in man: 'the thoughts of man, that have been hid of old'? She could be happy if only Theotormon would turn his eyes upon her.

Theotormon does not respond as she hopes. The illustration (Fig. 31) shows him completely shut up, while she hovers over him, chained in her flame of desire. He breaks his silence with a long speech expressing his doubts about the very points which Oothoon has been raising.

> Tell me what is a thought? & of what substance is it made?
> Tell me what is a joy? & in what gardens do joys grow?

As he closes his long catalogue of doubts, Bromion comes in with his scientific knowledge to point out that there are indeed things which flourish upon the earth to gratify senses unknown —namely those phenomena which can be perceived only by the microscope or the telescope or by voyagers to undiscovered countries. Having replied to Oothoon's assertion with a statement that betrays his subservience to the five senses, he continues with questions of his own which demonstrate his bondage still further:

> Ah! are there other wars, beside the wars of sword and fire?
> And are there other sorrows, beside the sorrows of poverty?
> And are there other joys, beside the joys of riches and ease?
> And is there not one law for both the lion and the ox?
> And is there not eternal fire, and eternal chains?
> To bind the phantoms of existence from eternal life?

Such questions are fraught with still more irony than Theotormon's: for we know that Blake's answer would be in each case the one that Bromion does not expect—that there *are* wars of eternity in which men exercise their warlike arts without destroying, sorrows and joys that make up the human condition without involving material loss or gain, a separate law for the lion and the ox and an eternal fire which, instead of binding from, is the gateway to, eternal life.

Oothoon's reply, echoed by the daughters of Albion, takes the argument a stage further back. Instead of Bromion and Theotormon she addresses the Creator who is their master:

> O Urizen! Creator of men! mistaken Demon of heaven:
> Thy joys are tears! thy labour vain, to form men to thine image.
> How can one joy absorb another? are not different joys
> Holy, eternal, infinite! and each joy is a Love.

She develops the point, asserting that glorious differences exist between different animals, between different men, and between different emotions in the same man. As she does so,

however, she thinks of some 'different' men who illustrate her
theme—but in another way:

> With what sense does the parson claim the labour of the farmer?
> What are his nets & gins & traps. & how does he surround him
> With cold floods of abstraction, and with forests of solitude,
> To build him castles and high spires. where kings & priests may
>   dwell.

This picture of a fortified church for the protection of
abstractions and privilege leads on to a picture of the family
brought up in the bondage of this visionless world—the mother,
forced to 'drag the chain / Of life, in weary lust', her child
brought into line and perverted from its natural joy by the
physical coercion of its elders.

Returning to her theme (which amplifies Tiriel's final
moment of truthful vision) she speaks of the varying gifts of
different animals—and reiterates Thel's question ('Does the
Eagle know what is in the pit? / Or wilt thou go ask the Mole?')
in a form which explains its significance still further:

> Does not the eagle scorn the earth & despise the treasures be-
>   neath?
> But the mole knoweth what is there, & the worm shall tell it thee.
> Does not the worm erect a pillar in the mouldering church yard?
> And a palace of eternity in the jaws of the hungry grave
> Over his porch these words are written. Take thy bliss O Man!
> And sweet shall be thy taste & sweet thy infant joys renew!

Her speech reflects a favourite theme of Blake's: all things in
the earth, even the death and burial of human beings, minister
to fresh life. And the joy of the worm, innocent in itself, reflects also the joys of sexual intercourse, acting as an *exemplum* to
man to take his bliss also. The reflection leads into Blake's
longest panegyric in praise of the fulfilment of desire, which includes also his severest strictures on concealment and shame:

> The moment of desire! the moment of desire! The virgin
> That pines for man; shall awaken her womb to enormous joys
> In the secret shadows of her chamber; the youth shut up from
> The lustful joy. shall forget to generate. & create an amorous
>   image
> In the shadows of his curtains and in the folds of his silent pillow.
> Are not these the places of religion? the rewards of continence?

The self enjoyings of self denial? Why dost thou seek religion?
Is it because acts are not lovely, that thou seekest solitude,
Where the horrible darkness is impressed with reflections of desire.

Oothoon blames concealment for the failure of Theotormon and her own consequent fading, 'wailing on the margin of non-entity'. She renews her charges against the possessiveness of self-love, claiming that she herself would be glad to seek out new girls and new delights for Theotormon. In opposition to the miser and his secret joys she places the animals that find their joy even while they possess nothing—simply by fulfilling their natural functions:

The sea fowl takes the wintry blast. for a cov'ring to her limbs:
And the wild snake, the pestilence to adorn him with gems & gold.
And trees. & birds. & beasts. & men. behold their eternal joy.
Arise you little glancing wings, and sing your infant joy!
Arise and drink your bliss, for every thing that lives is holy!

As the poem concludes Theotormon is still refusing to listen. But the true point of the poem lies in this paean, with which Blake begins to reach the heights of his visionary style. Nature is shown subsisting for ever in its myriads of different forms, holy in the individuality of each; man, equally, is holy in the lineaments of each human emotion. This is the positive which consummates the dialectic of Vision and Desire and, in destroying false 'holiness', redeems the contraries of Reason and Energy. Among the poems written under the spell of this newly awakened vision are some of Blake's greatest achievements, such as *The Marriage of Heaven and Hell* and the *Songs of Experience*.

The Marriage of Heaven and Hell follows in a direct line from *Visions of the Daughters of Albion*. 'The Devil' is introduced as spokesman for views which, in the other volume, are associated with Leutha. Having also introduced there the two negative figures of Bromion and Theotormon to characterize Law and Doubt, the negative intellectual forces at work in his age, he now presents a positive figure, Rintrah, who personifies that 'honest indignation' which characterized Ijim in *Tiriel*. Subsequently he will provide a partner for Rintrah, Palamabron, to represent another positive force in the contemporary world.

Between them Rintrah and Palamabron represent, respectively, the prophetic and priestly characters. Owing to the loss of vision in the age, their field of activity is restricted, so that Rintrah is limited to the expression of indignation, while Palamabron may appear, not as the minister of pity but as the hypocritical priest, accusing of sin. Nevertheless, for all their shortcomings, the lineaments of the sublime prophet and the merciful priest persist somewhere within these two figures.

In the 'Argument' of the *Marriage* Rintrah is shown as an angry thunder-god, louring in heavy clouds. For simple goodness, which could formerly flourish apart from the fashions and foibles of civilization, is no longer even a straightforward quality.

> Once meek, and in a perilous path,
> The just man kept his course along
> The vale of death.
> Roses are planted where thorns grow.
> And on the barren heath
> Sing the honey bees.

This is one of Blake's best pictures of the progress of the honest man through the world of twofold vision. He uses images of the 'guardian spectre': the rose of twofold vision guarded by its thorns, the bee of twofold vision guarded by its sting. This is the image of the creative worker as Blake conceived himself, persevering in his lonely and difficult path, at one and the same time innocent yet ready, if attacked, to defend his innocent vision. And this he sees to be the position of all honest men. The figure of the 'traveller', which Blake uses constantly for his approved way of life, probably owes something (as does also the landscape in the section) to Johnson's *Vanity of Human Wishes*:

> The needy traveller, serene and gay,
> Walks the wild heath, and sings his toil away.
> Does envy seize thee? crush th'upbraiding joy,
> Increase his riches and his peace destroy;
> Now fears in dire vicissitude invade,
> The rustling brake alarms, and quiv'ring shade,
> Nor light nor darkness bring his pain relief,
> One shews the plunder, and one hides the thief.[7]

In other places Blake develops his own version of the dangers which beset the honest man, seeing them as created by the doubter and the accuser of sin. At this moment, however, he is preoccupied by a different danger. There may come a time when even the limited fruits of the wilderness, cultivated by the just man, will attract the fraudulent and thieving: the dishonest man, seeing that honesty pays, will begin to ape the manners of the just and the honest for his own ends. At such a time, the just man, driven even from his hard and dangerous way of life, will be made to exchange for the rigours of the wilderness the barrenness of the desert. Instead of enjoying a hard but productive toil, he will be forced into a stance of protest and anger:

> Now the sneaking serpent walks
> In mild humility.
> And the just man rages in the wilds
> Where the lions roam.

The roaring of the lion is another symbol of twofold vision—but there is a further development. Not content with the defensiveness of the rose or the bee, twofold vision is turning to the counter-offensive. Blake now feels impelled to attack the hypocrisy of the present age. *The Marriage of Heaven and Hell* represents an attempt to let the fire of twofold vision burst through the clouds of single vision that infest his world.

The work, which contains many half-satirical imitations of Swedenborg's style, corresponding to Blake's ambiguous feelings about him, begins with an open and aggressive assertion of dogma.

> As a new heaven is begun, and it is now thirty-three years since its advent: the Eternal Hell revives. And lo! Swedenborg is the Angel sitting at the tomb; his writings are the linen clothes folded up. Now is the dominion of Edom, & the return of Adam into Paradise; see Isaiah XXXIV & XXXV Chap:

Blake is making the most of a striking coincidence: 1757, the year announced by Swedenborg as inaugurating a new dispensation with the Last Judgment,[8] was also the year of his own birth. If Swedenborg's writings lie like the linen clothes by the tomb, the fact that they are there indicates that the visionary

figure whom they enshrined has risen from his verbal-dog-
matic prison and is walking abroad. Blake probably regards
himself as this Risen Man, but his use of the term 'the Eternal
Hell' also indicates a controlling irony. If he has arisen from
the dead it is because he represents the Poetic Genius, the Prophetic Character which must forever arise against any tyranny
of Reason. Damon is probably right in thinking that the
'dominion of Edom' carries a reference to Esau, and Bloom in
further drawing attention to the 'redness' of Esau in the Old
Testament (the redness of energy and eventually of Orc).[9]
Blake regards himself as the rough honest character now called
upon to re-assert the dominion of energy and overcome the
smooth rogueries of Jacob-like deceivers.

In this militant context it is not surprising that he announces
the necessity of dialectic more openly than he has done before.
The oppositions which have been described in previous poems
are now openly affirmed:

> Without Contraries is no progression. Attraction and Repul-
> sion, Reason and Energy, Love and Hate, are necessary to Human
> existence.
> From these contraries spring what the religious call Good &
> Evil. Good is the passive that obeys Reason   Evil is the active
> springing from Energy.
> Good is Heaven. Evil is Hell.

The contraries between these pairs of qualities correspond
to the contraries between single and twofold vision. And here it
is necessary once again to insist on the presence of irony. When
the Devil speaks in the following pages he is to be regarded as
speaking in the person of Blake only to the extent that Blake, as
an artist, considers himself to be constantly in a state of twofold vision. But Blake is always aware of other levels of vision.
Threefold vision makes a fleeting appearance in the book; and
fourfold vision, although not specifically mentioned, looms in
the background to support the lower three levels and to
confirm the possibility of making permanent that marriage
between Heaven and Hell which is adduced briefly in threefold
vision. The insistence on twofold vision here has an element of
paradox: Blake has found a convenient stick to beat the men of
single vision, a basis of comparison by which they can be

laughed out of court. To imagine that his proclamation of the gospel of energy and its superiority to the gospel of reason, together with the many statements which he uses to support it, puts him in the same category with those who proclaim Strength through Joy is to ignore the full content of Blake's vision. When he states, for example, that the cut worm forgives the plough, the statement has to be taken in conjunction with Thel's equally cogent affirmation:

> That God would love a Worm I knew, and punish the evil foot
> That wilful, bruis'd its helpless form . . .[10]

Thel speaks with the voice of Beulah and threefold vision; her love is as far above the devil's cultivation of energy as that is above the dead world of Reason and single vision.

Against this reservation, of course, we must place the argument which Blake himself used about Milton. As an artist, he was naturally a dweller in twofold vision—'of the devil's party'. He is therefore at ease when writing in this vein. Nevertheless such an artist is also at odds with his own condition as a human being: and Blake's exploitation of the other levels of vision shows recognition of the point.

The Voice of the Devil is now heard, putting his view of the matter. He begins by redefining Good and Evil, attacking the view that evil comes only from the body and good only from the soul. What the religious imagine to be good and evil are in fact contraries, necessary in order that there shall be progression. That which they take to be the soul is nothing of the sort. They see only the reason that furnishes the bound or outward circumference of energy; the true soul is something which is revealed by the body and its energies. Reason seems superior to the energy which it contains only when perception is restricted to the limitations of the five senses. Once aware that the body is not so contained we shall see that the soul is a more splendid form of energy, and is eternal delight.

In formulating this conception Blake is assisted by his idea of the universe. In the cosmos, too, there is an opposition between reason and energy. The sky, dark and void, is a physical manifestation of reason; the sun is a mass of energy. In the heavenly state, as described in the Book of Revelation, there would be no

need of a sun, for God himself would be present. Blake pre-
sumably interprets this as meaning not that the sun will be replaced, but that it will at last appear in its true form. Instead
of its energy being contained in a single orb, it will be transmitted through the whole universe as a living, humanized
light: the deficiencies which result from the restriction of
energies will disappear in a world where life is set free. Instead
of being contained by the unnatural limited circular form of the
sun, light will flow in living forms which provide their own
control.

Thus the struggle between reason and energy among mankind, only finally to be resolved by the achievement of fourfold vision, can be seen reflected in the heavens, where the
opposition between void and energy is reinforced by man's insistence on emphasizing the laws that govern the heavens at the
expense of responding to their glory. Instead of seeing the sun
as a containment of life and energy, rational man draws
mathematical lines across the heavens until he is enmeshed in a
spider's web of mathematical analysis.

Blake continued to insist on the importance of this opposition
for the rest of his life. In 1825, he spoke of one of his 'visionary
experiences' (whether actual or symbolic) to Crabb Robinson:

> 'I have conversed with the Spiritual Sun—I saw him on Primrose
> Hill. He said: "Do you take me for the Greek Apollo?" "No," I
> said. "That" (and Blake pointed to the sky)—"that is the Greek
> Apollo. He is Satan." '[11]

In the *Marriage* Blake continues by commenting on *Paradise
Lost* and the Book of Job in terms of the philosophy which the
Devil has been expounding.

> Those who restrain desire, do so because theirs is weak enough to
> be restrained; and the restrainer or reason usurps its place &
> governs the unwilling.
>   And being restraind it by degrees becomes passive till it is only
> the shadow of desire.
>   The history of this is written in Paradise Lost. & the Governor
> or Reason is call'd Messiah.

This worst of all possible worlds, in which reason is not
merely a restricter and container of desire but actually takes its

place, results, as we have seen, in the corruption of Milton's
Satan from a glorious to a fallen state and brings Sin and Death
into the world. Reason is also the disease with which Job is
smitten: from being rich and generous, he is reduced to a
shadow of his former identity.

Against the pale world of restriction which he has been
painting, Blake now sets the superior world of Hell, which
exists as soon as the energies of twofold vision are cultivated.
Although appearing like torment and insanity to the 'Angels'
who exist in single vision, the fires of Hell are the enjoyments of
Genius to those who have learned to walk among them.
Returning home, Blake finds himself crossing the 'abyss of the
five senses' which separates the two worlds. On this abyss a
devil is writing two lines (adapted satirically from Chatterton)[12]
which sum up the philosophy of Hell and its worship of energy:

> How do you know but ev'ry Bird that cuts the airy way,
> Is an immense world of delight, clos'd by your senses five?

The soaring energy of the bird is a fitting symbol of the view
that energy is the real link between man and the infinite, that
twofold vision is the key to fourfold.

This basic, poised assertion is a key to the meaning of the
'Proverbs of Hell' which follow. Even the title possesses a
certain irony, for these sayings are more like anti-proverbs.
Conventional proverbs are usually counsels of prudence—that
Prudence which is, according to *these* Proverbs, 'a rich, ugly
old maid courted by Incapacity'. Blake's, on the other hand,
are counsels *against* prudence, on the grounds that the exercise
of Desire may lead to that central knowledge which will not be
revealed to the self-imprisoned:

> The road of excess leads to the palace of wisdom.

> If the fool would persist in his folly he would become wise.

As Blake develops this central insight, his proverbs reveal a
delight in those individualities which each reveal an essential form
of creation. They are less a series of proverbs than a growing
hymn of creation, a paean to all forms of energy and delight.

> A fool sees not the same tree that a wise man sees.
> He whose face gives no light, shall never become a star.
> Eternity is in love with the productions of time.

Yet the further sense is always pressing, and the full series can only be understood in its light. An aphorism such as the following is not a curious form of hyperbole but a precise statement:

> The roaring of lions, the howling of wolves, the raging of the stormy sea, and the destructive sword, are portions of eternity too great for the eye of man.

One needs to keep the more basic aphorisms in *There is no Natural Religion* constantly at hand to explain such mysterious statements.

> I.   Mans perceptions are not bounded by organs of perception. he perceives more than sense (tho' ever so acute) can discover . . .

> VII.   The desire of Man being Infinite the possession is Infinite & himself Infinite
> Application. He who sees the Infinite in all things sees God. He who sees the Ratio only sees himself only.[13]

Blake's present conviction that twofold vision tells of eternity more intensely than any other form of human experience not only makes him see the wrath of wild beasts as a portion of infinite energy, but also leads him towards symbolism:

> When thou seest an Eagle, thou seest a portion of Genius. lift up thy head!

The eagle suggests Genius by the power of its energies; its love of the sun extends the symbolism: the genius who is apparently exploiting the potentialities of twofold vision is really seeking the lost fourfold. One of Blake's illustrations shows an eagle with a serpent in its talons: if the serpent represents the ambiguities of energy, the spread wings of the eagle suggest a vision which can either stoop to rational analysis or soar to the sun.

If the deepest point of the 'Proverbs of Hell' is to be found in *There is no Natural Religion*, the next section derives in part from a companion plate entitled *All Religions are One*. This, like the other, was presented in the form of an argument. Accepting the rationalist plea that the true method of knowledge must be by experiment, Blake proceeds to argue that the true faculty of knowing must therefore be the faculty which experiences. But he is able at this point to turn away from the philosophy that would confine experience to sense-experience by arguing that the central experience of each man is his experience of the Poetic Genius. Just as all living things derive their forms from their inner genius, so man derives his true form from the Poetic Genius, which is common to all human beings. All sects of philosophy are adaptations of the Poetic Genius to the weakness of individuals, all national religions derive from varying receptions of it. Even the Old and New Testaments are products of it, made necessary by the limitations of the bodily senses. All Religions are one and find their ground in the true Man.[13]

This argument is continued in the next section of the *Marriage*. The ancient Poets used to ascribe Gods and Geniuses to every city and country, but there came a time when the deities concerned were abstracted from the objects to which they had been attached and set up as beings in themselves. Thus began the tyrannies of Priesthood, imposing abstract forms of religion upon mankind: men forgot that 'All deities reside in the human breast'.

The point is brought home in another Memorable Fancy, a witty account of a dinner-party at which Blake questions the prophets Isaiah and Ezekiel about their inspiration. Isaiah explains that he did not actually hear or see God with his senses. But since he did perceive the infinite in everything and since (like Rintrah) he believed that honest indignation was the voice of God, he wrote without caring about the consequences. He wrote from a firm persuasion, as did all poets in former times.

Ezekiel takes up the explanation. It was the eastern nations that first taught the principles of human perception, but they disagreed concerning the source of those principles. The prophets of Israel differed from the rest in holding that it was the Poetic Genius: and, holding this belief, they despised the Priests and Philosophers of other countries. They maintained that all other deities would eventually be proved to originate from their own, the central revelation of their religion being in their poetry, the psalms. And so firm was their persuasion that in the end it came to pass, for now all other nations do indeed bow down to the Jews' god and their moral code. His own privations were undertaken with the aim of 'raising other men into a perception of the infinite'.

Blake now advances to the central image of his twofold
vision. The earth, he asserts, is about to be consumed by fire,
as has always been prophesied. But the result of these fires will
be not destruction but a cleansing: as the creation is consumed it
will appear infinite and holy instead of finite and corrupt. The
fires of twofold vision will cleanse the doors of perception and
man, at present imprisoned within a cavern, will see everything
in its infinite nature.

This use of fire will correspond to the method which Blake
has perfected in his own engraving: the idea leads him to
another Memorable Fancy in which a Printing house in Hell is
depicted, to show the way that knowledge is transmitted from
generation to generation. The various human beings and
animals mentioned all suggest twofold vision. The theme of infinity is also present—an Eagle 'caused the inside of the cave to
be infinite'. One purpose of the description is to contrast the
common idea of making a book (the mental labour, the intricate
technical processes) with the inward process involved. The true
end of printing is that infinite energy shall be transferred from
the artist to the apprehension of his fellow human beings, who
otherwise lie imprisoned in the cavern of their five senses.
There is also, as Desirée Hirst has pointed out, a reference to
one of Swedenborg's 'Memorable Relations' in which the
sound of a 'Mill' leads him to explore a passage that brings him
to an apartment where he 'saw an old Man sitting amongst
Books, with the Word before him, and collecting out of it
Passages in support of his Doctrine . . . in the next Room there
were Scribes who collected the Papers, and copied them in a
Book'.[14] Blake's idea of the transmission of knowledge is
different.

He now returns to the opposition between the Prolific and
the Devourer, which corresponds to that between Energy and
Reason. The Energies of this world, which seem everywhere to
be in chains, are more important than the rational powers which
contain them. They permit such devouring activities only
because they themselves would cease to be prolific if the
Devourers ceased to receive the excess of their delights.

Blake probably has in mind here the opposition between the
Nile of Egyptian mythology and the sterile sea that receives it

(one form of the relationship between Osiris and the usurping Typhon, according to Plutarch).[15] If the sea did not receive its excesses, the Nile would overflow and the land would be deprived of the good that its waters bring. But no one would therefore argue that the sea is more important than the Nile.

The reasoning at this point is subterranean, relying partly on the fact that the Osiris of the Nile is also the lost sun-god, while the Typhon of the sea is also, in the heavens, the usurper who has taken possession of the sun and now perverts its energies.

In the next Memorable Fancy, Blake is enabled to depict the opposition between single and twofold vision over a wider area. Now it is an Angel of single vision that comes to him and pleads with him to forsake his foolish ways before he finds himself plunged into a burning dungeon for ever. Blake asks to see his eternal lot, in order that he may compare it with that which the angel is preparing for him. The angel conducts him through a stable and through a church, then down into the church vault, at the end of which is a mill; through the mill they pass into a cave and down the winding cavern until a void as boundless as the nether sky appears beneath their feet. This progression of landscape is perhaps intended to represent the decline of Christianity, from the visionary moment in the stable when the divine and the human were reconciled, through the organization of a church to enshrine this vision, to the point where man is imprisoned by the system which has been established and lives in the cavern of his senses—his world dominated completely by the mill of analytic thinking, the starry skies no more than a vast sphere for the employment of disembodied reason. Certainly when they reach the 'nether sky', it is a Newtonian universe that greets their eyes.

> By degrees we beheld the infinite Abyss, fiery as the smoke of a burning city; beneath us at an immense distance was the sun, black but shining; round it were fiery tracks on which revolv'd vast spiders, crawling after their prey; which flew or rather swum in the infinite deep, in the most terrific shapes of animals sprung from corruption. & the air was full of them, & seemd composed of them; these are Devils. and are called Powers of the air. I now asked my companion which was my eternal lot? he said, between the black & white spiders

Against this vivid spider's web of mathematical analysis, however, a threat appears (not unlike the roaring of waters which assailed the world of sensibility and Euclid's *Elements* in Wordsworth's well-known vision).[16] The abyss turns into a raging sea and a monster appears.

> . . . we saw a cataract of blood mixed with fire and not many stones throw from us appeard and sunk again the scaly fold of a monstrous serpent.   at last to the east, distant about three degrees appeard a fiery crest above the waves   slowly it reared like a ridge of golden rocks till we discoverd two globes of crimson fire, from which the sea fled away in clouds of smoke, and now we saw, it was the head of Leviathan, his forehead was divided into streaks of green & purple like those on a tygers forehead: soon we saw his mouth & red gills hang just above the raging foam tinging the black deep with beams of blood, advancing toward us with all the fury of a spiritual existence.

What is happening here is the uprearing of uncontrolled Energy against the waste of a world controlled only by Reason. It has been pointed out that the 'three degrees' correspond to the longitudinal direction of Paris from London,[17] and that the monster could therefore refer directly to the French Revolution. This may well be: but in any case Blake is describing what he takes to be an eternal process. Single vision will inevitably provide a void into which will rush the forces of twofold.

At this point the Angel leaves him, and he finds himself immediately removed from this terrifying scene. Instead, he is sitting on a bank by a river in moonlight, listening to a harper who sings to the harp, 'The man who never alters his opinion is like standing water, & breeds reptiles of the mind'.

The respective attitudes of Blake and the Angel are here thrown into relief. Earlier Blake had proposed that they should commit themselves to the Void: an attitude which the Angel had rejected as presumptuous. Now, when the Angel leaves him, so does the terror of the scene. Instead, he finds himself translated into a landscape of threefold vision, where the energies of man are controlled by harmony—where Heaven and Hell are 'married'.

The Angel, when found, is surprised at Blake's escape; Blake replies by proposing to show the Angel *his* lot. First he flies

with him into the body of the sun. Having thus brought him
into the full power of genius, he escorts him to a point between
Saturn and the fixed stars, where he shows him the world prepared for him by opening the Bible in the church which they
visited earlier. This turns out to be a deep pit with houses in
which monkeys and baboons feed upon one another: 'and here
& there I saw one savourily picking the flesh off of his own tail'
(the combination of urbane wit and cockney humour, rare in
Blake's more serious works, reminds us that he belongs to the
London which also produced Charles Dickens). When the
stench is too much for them they re-emerge into the mill,
where the skeleton of one of the bodies, brought by Blake,
turns out to be Aristotle's Analytics.

> So the Angel said: thy phantasy has imposed upon me & thou
> oughtest to be ashamed.
> I answerd: we impose on one another, & it is but lost time to
> converse with you whose works are only Analytics

Once again, the world of Energy is shown triumphing over
the world of Reason. The illustration (Fig. 30) at this point
shows the monster Leviathan struggling, and apparently
drowning, in the sea. Although energy is by nature superior to
reason, any submission to the sea of the five senses and single
vision causes it to be swallowed up in its own coils.

So far Blake's attitude to Swedenborg has remained ambiguous; in the next section, however, he attacks Swedenborg the
man and declares that he lacked originality: any man might
construct from the writings of Paracelsus and Behmen works of
equal value, while Swedenborg himself, possessing, as an
intellectual, the attitude of an 'Angel', was too conceited to
learn from the Devils.

There follows another Swedenborgian 'Memorable Fancy'
which continues the theme with an argument between an
Angel and a Devil. The Devil stands before the Angel and proclaims his gospel:

> The worship of God is. Honouring his gifts in other men each
> according to his genius. and loving the greatest men best, those
> who envy or calumniate great men hate God, for there is no other
> God.

The positive philosophy of the *Marriage* is here summarized: since it is through Genius that one knows God, one worships God best by honouring the individual genius of each man. On hearing this, however, the Angel becomes almost blue—'but mastering himself he grew yellow, & at last white pink & smiling, and then replied . . .' His reply takes the form of an assertion that Christ sanctioned the ten commandments, and that all other men are 'fools, sinners, & nothings'. The Devil retorts with the observation (which Blake was to develop in a later poem)[18] that Christ himself had broken all the restrictions contained in the ten commandments. 'Jesus was all virtue, and acted from impulse, not from rules.'

When he hears these words, the Angel, convinced, stretches out his arms, embraces the flame of fire and is consumed to arise as Elijah. The seriousness of this event, the passing of a rational spirit into the prophetic state, from single vision to two-fold vision, is immediately lightened by a resumption of the witty tone:

> Note. This Angel, who is now become a Devil, is my particular friend: we often read the Bible together in its infernal or diabolical sense which the world shall have if they behave well.
>
> I have also: **The Bible of Hell**: which the world shall have whether they will or no.

On this gay note, the argumentative part of the work comes to an end, rounded off by a drawing of Nebuchadnezzar eating grass. The degradation of the rational tyrant is further emphasized by a repetition of Blake's saying,

> One Law for the Lion & Ox is Oppression.

Blake has reached another of his peaks. Honouring the genius of each man and creature has been raised to the level of a religious act. He concludes *The Marriage of Heaven and Hell* with a Song of Liberty.

Such a conclusion demonstrates that he has now reconciled the two great experiences of his youth. The outbreak of the French Revolution and the death of his brother had constituted a double revelation, each modifying the other. Because of what he had learned from his brother, he would never allow his enthusiasm for liberty to draw him into commitment to any particular political movement. Liberty remained his ideal: but true freedom could not be brought about by political means. Only when men learned to exercise their own genius and to honour the genius that was in others would they find true freedom—and then political freedom would follow automatically.

Blake's developed thought is thus of twofold application. He has evolved a political interpretation of human history and a view of the personal problems of his contemporaries, both of which follow a similar pattern. Organized groups of men behave like individual human beings, since they suffer from the same lack of vision on a larger scale.

In the next two chapters these two themes, the social/moral and the political, will be isolated and considered separately. But the two streams run together: they spring from the central statements of *Visions of the Daughters of Albion* and *The Marriage of Heaven and Hell*. The coalescence of Vision and Desire in a world where men dared to live by their own inward genius and to delight in nature as a fountain of living forms would remove at one stroke both the tensions between individual men and women and the sterile struggles for power in larger groups.

Blake had not finally solved his chief problems in these works. Rather, he had found a central position from which he could continue to reflect on them. This central position was in itself a creative one. The two works that we have examined witness to its potency: their exuberance is their beauty. Its force was present in the making of other lyrics, which both extend Blake's central themes and exert a vivid appeal on the common reader by reason of their own inward form and genius. The total intellectual and visionary effort involved in his longer works had liberated the full resources of his creative imagination.

4 The Lion and the Rose

One major problem confronting all Romantic poets is that no adequate rhetoric exists for the most important things that they wish to say. This has always been true, but never more so than in the age of the French Revolution, when a century's devotion to law, intellectual, political and moral, had left men without a language of the imagination. So we find Wordsworth using, even for imaginative work such as his accounts of dreams, an adapted form of the Miltonic diction. Coleridge, likewise, succeeds in making his central statement only when his higher consciousness is eliminated. Only then can his subconscious bring his major symbols together in a pattern—which still remains beneath the surface of his poem. *Kubla Khan* is at surface level an achievement of the imaginative sensibility rather than of the pure imagination. When these poets wish to write imaginatively, they regress to simpler poetic forms—Wordsworth to the lyrics of the Lucy poems, Coleridge to the ballad-forms of *The Ancient Mariner* and *Christabel*.

Blake was in a similar predicament. In his most satisfactory statements, those of indignation and satire, his rhetoric could draw upon the tradition which had included the genius of Swift. But despite his gift for harnessing wit to honest indignation, Blake was not content to remain a satirist. A positive vision must be offered, to counter the rationalist orthodoxy of his day. Since no strong visionary tradition existed in his society, he had sought one within the human mind itself, using paradigms derived from Milton and Boehme to assist his interpretation. Yet if it was difficult to create such a pattern, it was harder still to find a language adequate for it. It is not surprising that he, too, fell back on simple lyric forms. And since his genius flowered with unusual purity within them, he is best remembered today not, as he hoped, for an epic achievement, but for several lyrics of a few stanzas each.

The universal appeal of these lyrics is not difficult to demonstrate.

Tyger Tyger, burning bright,
In the forests of the night;
What immortal hand or eye,
Could frame thy fearful symmetry?

In what distant deeps or skies
Burnt the fire of thine eyes!
On what wings dare he aspire?
What the hand dare sieze the fire?

And what shoulder, & what art,
Could twist the sinews of thy heart?
And when thy heart began to beat,
What dread hand? & what dread feet?

What the hammer? what the chain,
In what furnace was thy brain?
What the anvil? what dread grasp,
Dare its deadly terrors clasp?

When the stars threw down their spears
And water'd heaven with their tears:
Did he smile his work to see?
Did he who made the Lamb make thee?

Tyger, Tyger burning bright
In the forests of the night:
What immortal hand or eye,
Dare frame thy fearful symmetry?

G. K. Chesterton says somewhere that no one can read the lines,

There has fallen a splendid tear
From the passion-flower at the gate

and then maintain that Tennyson is not a poet. Blake's lyric has a similar immediate and striking effect. And the sensationalism is admirably controlled, the imagery, in particular, being handled deftly. At the turn of a line an image from just before will blend into a new one which both echoes it and points in a new direction.

When the stars threw down their spears
And waterd heaven with their tears:

Did he smile his work to see?
Did he who made the Lamb make thee?

The stars are here redeemed from their normal Blakean associations of coldness and abstraction by being personalized. Even the fact that they have been fighting is muted: they are pictured in a moment of regret. Their hardness and glitter, on the other hand, are sustained in the image of 'spears'. The glitter, in fact, persists through to 'tears', even if the hardness is modified on the way by the words, 'and watered heaven', with their full import of pity and the pastoral. Meanwhile, however, the sense of the stanza has turned on its axis: softness and pity have now become dominant and the glitter only a subordinate brightness within the new image of a grave smile on the face of a creator who might seem to have expressed his nature more properly in creating the lamb. The swing of this axis confirms a swing in the poem as a whole which might have been guessed at from the change of movement at the beginning of the stanza. The vivid, urgent questionings are replaced by a nostalgic pair of questions which in their turn mute the repetition of the first questions in the last stanza, leaving them, also, distant and mysterious.

Such brilliance and control make the poem supreme by any standards. Yet even here, at the height of Blake's poetic achievement, all is not clear. How, for example, would one answer the questioner who asked bluntly (as a questioner did on one occasion) 'But when *did* the stars throw down their spears?' One might dismiss such an approach as brutal and irrelevant, for we are used to an evocative use of imagery which works by suggestion rather than statement. Yet Blake has a disconcerting habit of sounding as though he means what he says. And the question might pose itself in our minds again once we had glanced through the literature on Blake and read some interpretations of the tiger itself, the central symbol of the poem:

> The problem of *The Tyger* is, quite simply, how to reconcile the Forgiveness of Sins (the Lamb) with the Punishment of Sins (the Tyger).   S. F. Damon[1]

> The tiger is itself a mirror image of man in his fallen state. He lives in a forest of darkness, a womb of nature. His identification

and confrontation by Blake and Los is his symbolical leap from
the forest into the light of day.   Hazard Adams[2]

Christ is become the Tyger, symbol of energy burning in a
darkening world.   J. Bronowski[3]

Whichever meaning we associate with the tyger in this poem,
it is clear that a symbolic connotation is intended. The tyger of
revolt burns in the forests of oppression. A hand seizes this fire as
the fire of revolt is seized in *A Song of Liberty*. Or the tyger is the
burning ferocity of the lustful 'king of night', which is seized and
fixed within the frame of mortality. Both meanings are acceptable, and both may be present.   Stanley Gardner[4]

These definitions differ bewilderingly when placed side by
side. Yet their respective authors are in closer agreement about
the poem than they might seem to be from these isolated statements. They are aware that the tyger is related to basic Blakean
ideas such as those of wrath, energy and the desire for liberty.
What they do not agree about is Blake's attitude to his own
basic ideas. Does he approve or disapprove of energy—
especially when it takes the form of political or sexual revolt?
If critics do not deal with the apparent contradictions involved
in Blake's work, they are unlikely to agree about the meaning
even of such a central image as that of the tyger.

It is at this point that the fourfold paradigm helps to unravel
the issues involved, by exposing the ambiguity of twofold
vision. The uncontrolled energy of twofold vision which
threatens destruction, is also necessary to the fourfold, an isolated element of it. Although the threefold pastoral landscape
of pity and pathos is nearer to the infinite fourfold, the tyger
displays a feature of fourfold vision of which the lamb knows
nothing.

The most succinct commentary on the poem, as Damon has
also seen, is the inscription which Blake placed on one of his
pictures:

God out of Christ is a consuming fire.[5]

But some acquaintance with the structural dynamics of Blake's
speculations is needed to see just *why* it is such a complete
comment.

Investigation of this sort of point involves a problem that has
been touched on before, for it can lead to conflict with those
critics who maintain that there is a direct and obvious 'meaning'
to the poem, evident at once to the intelligent and responsive
reader. D. W. Harding, for example, offers the following
exposition of the fifth stanza:

> Blake asks, with scarcely believing awe, whether the Creator
> smiled with satisfaction in what he made when in fact its ferocious
> strength was so appalling that even the stars abandoned their
> armed formidability (the spears suggested by their steely glitter)
> and broke down in tears.[6]

A close look at this interpretation, however, suggests that it is
not nearly as 'obvious' as it looks. Professor Harding has
interpreted the syntax of the stanza in a particular way in
order to establish his sense: 'when' is now not simply a statement
of time but is involved with the second half of the stanza, carrying a partial meaning of 'although'. But this changes the tempo
of the stanza. Where the 'naïf' reader could be expected to
linger over the first and second lines, hearing the note of distant
sadness in them, Professor Harding's interpretation, forcing a
strong stress on 'stars', throws the second line into a hasty
parenthesis before the questioning is resumed. In this way the
chief musical attraction of the stanza, the relaxing of the rhythm
to create a mood of nostalgia and introduce naturally the note of
sadness that pervades the question in the second pair of lines,
is lost. What purports to be a plain, straightforward interpretation turns out to have saved the 'sense' of the poem at the expense
of throwing away some of its essential beauty.

Since so much is lost in the process, we are justified in asking
whether the sense that has been saved is the only one available.
Our acquaintance with Blake's thought suggests a different
possibility. His conception of the fall from fourfold vision,
which is evidently involved here, is not of a succession of events
at the beginning of time but of a single complex and eternal
event, in which all the components are interrelated. Pity,
wrath and fallen reason were and are created at one and the
same time, at the disintegration of fourfold vision into separate
light, fire and darkness. In this cosmic disaster, the fading of
vision creates strife, strife involves the separation of energy in

the shape of wrath, and, as wrath separates, only pity is left to weep over the tragedy. Yet the answer to the question 'Did he who made the lamb make thee?' is still 'yes', if one is thinking of fourfold vision. It is the *isolation* of energy that was not willed by the Creator.

Professor Harding has spoken out against the introduction of meanings from outside the poem as presented on the published page. Writing of Joseph Wicksteed's interpretation of the poem he says,

> The objections to this kind of writing as comment on Blake are first that it imports into the poem intellectual meanings that are too remotely and indirectly derived from the words, if they can claim to derive from them at all, and second that the parish-magazine quality of sentiment it expresses is totally foreign to the tautness and strength of the state of mind Blake invites us to share.[7]

If it is Wicksteed's interpretation that is at stake, one is inclined to sympathize with Professor Harding. But a much wider principle of interpretation is involved. And even if one takes one's stand on 'faithfulness to the text', with Harding, disagreement remains. The crucial question is not merely whether a proposed meaning derives from the words, but whether it *fits* them, harmonizing with the effects created by rhythm, tone and imagery. Professor Harding's interpretation wars with this 'total' verbal impact of the poem; the main virtue which it claims, that of allowing the poem to do its work un-hindered, it does not properly possess.

For the impact of the poem is not one of 'scarcely believing awe'. The emotion aroused is rather one of mingled delight and horror. It is because the horror is controlled by the harmonized energy of the poem that it appeals so strongly to children, who enjoy the experience of controlled terror. To adopt Blake's terminology, even while the twofold imagination in us is recoiling from the threat of the tiger, the lost fourfold in us is responding to the attraction of its energy and brightness. Blake's total mythology is here in tune with his emotional effect.

If there is any point at which Blake's intention might be said to war with the immediate impact of his poem, it is at the level of immediate realism. Real tigers, seen in captivity, impress the observer by the elasticity of their movements, the feline sensitiveness that controls their ferocity, the softness that sheathes their threat. Blake's poem is rather about the idea of a tiger. His effect relies upon establishing the tiger within a visionary framework of burning and brightness and fearful symmetry. Only when our attention has been fully focused upon its dazzling lines and burning eyes are we ready to imagine a quintessential furnace and a cosmic smith.

The full import of these cues must be picked up, therefore. To see the tiger as a literal tiger and not as an articulation of energy is to pitch the end of the poem into a key of extravagance and hysteria. The final questions are not rhetorical gestures, however, but the vivid formulation of a controlled ambiguity.

The same point applies even more strongly to Blake's drawing of a tiger at the end. The design, which comes as a disappointment to many readers, takes the sense a step further, by endeavouring to combine the facial lineaments of a tiger with those of a human being; the same motif occurs in his first illustration to the *Inferno*, where the wild beasts which encounter the poet are shown as embodiments of his own passions.[8]

The tiger is only one of the symbols of twofold vision in *Songs of Experience*. A full list would include also the lion, the serpent, the sunflower and the rose. Moreover, each of these symbols brings out some particular aspect of twofold vision. If the tiger represents it in its pure form, energy burning in and for itself, with no reference to other levels of vision, the lion represents the link with fourfold vision, for its pride and beauty give it an aspect of infinity. The serpent, on the other hand, points in the opposite direction, towards single vision: its energy is an energy that can creep and lick the dust. And if the rose, with its thorn, suggests the defended pride of twofold vision, proof against all except the subtle worm, the sunflower suggests the constant yearning of twofold desire for fourfold infinity.

Blake's dialectic is to be found everywhere in his *Songs of Innocence and of Experience*. The 'contrary states of the human soul' are a dialectic in themselves. The human child is born into the tender state of threefold vision, but the growth of its own energies brings about the challenge of twofold vision. It can either accept the challenge and walk through the flames of twofold vision towards a more organized form of the threefold, illuminated now by infinity, or follow the tenour of the world around, refuse to accept energy and drift down towards the darkness of single vision.

A grasp of Blake's dialectic also clarifies the relationship between companion poems in the two collections. As J. D. Jump once remarked, the poem beginning 'Little Lamb, Who made thee?' would be hardly bearable were it not for our knowledge that in the parallel collection there is a poem about a tiger. Similarly, we do not have to agree with David Erdman that the two poems about Charity Schools, the one admiring the children flowing into St Paul's 'like flowers of London Town', the other expressing indignation that children should be reduced to being fed by 'cold and usurous hand' in a land that is rich and fruitful, necessarily presuppose a process of disillusionment between the composition of the two sets of lyrics.[9] Blake at the age of twenty-seven was perfectly capable of knowing that the same scene might be viewed in two different ways according to the mood of the observer, and that the impossibility of entertaining both views at the same time did not necessarily invalidate either.

Another poem which gains by such juxtaposition is *The Little Boy Found*, which appears immediately after *The Little Boy Lost* in *Songs of Innocence*:

> The little boy lost in the lonely fen,
> Led by the wand'ring light,
> Began to cry, but God ever nigh,
> Appeard like his father in white.

The stanza gains on being read in the light of the Swedenborgian insistence that God can only appear in human form, or Blake's own assertion that 'God only acts and is in existing beings and men'.[10] If taken as a simple assertion of divine benevolence, however, it would suffer from our knowledge that God does not always intervene to rescue little boys who are lost. The previous poem, ending

> The night was dark no father was there
> The child was wet with dew.

The mire was deep, & the child did weep
And away the vapour flew.

makes clear that Blake is more concerned about two different
conceptions of the relationship between God and man: the one
which abstracts God until he is no more than a vapour, and
the one which sees him in action whenever a father rescues his
child.

It has to be acknowledged, however, that the strength of
many of these poems is precarious, since they rely not on the
existence of a corresponding tension in the mind of the reader
but on success in communicating to him a state of inward
vision. Dr. Tillyard has made a valuable comparison between
the opening of Goldsmith's *The Deserted Village* and Blake's *The
Ecchoing Green*.

The extract quoted from Goldsmith is as follows:

How often have I loitered o'er thy green,
Where humble happiness endeared each scene!
How often have I paused on every charm,
The sheltered cot, the cultivated farm,
The never-failing brook, the busy mill,
The decent church that topt the neighbouring hill,
The hawthorn bush, with seats beneath the shade,
For talking age and whispering lovers made!
How often have I blest the coming day
When toil remitting lent its turn to play,
And all the village train from labour free
Led up their sports beneath the spreading tree,
While many a pastime circled in the shade,
The young contending as the old surveyed;
And many a gambol frolicked o'er the ground,
And slights of art and feats of strength went round;
And still as each repeated pleasure tired,
Succeeding sports the mirthful band inspired.

Blake's 'Ecchoing Green' is placed in comparison with it:

The Sun does arise,
And make happy the skies.
The merry bells ring
To welcome the Spring.
The sky-lark and thrush,
The birds of the bush,

Sing louder around,
To the bells chearful sound.
While our sports shall be seen
On the Ecchoing Green.

Old John with white hair
Does laugh away care,
Sitting under the oak,
Among the old folk.
They laugh at our play,
And soon they all say
Such such were the joys,
When we all girls & boys,
In our youth-time were seen,
On the Ecchoing Green.

Till the little ones weary
No more can be merry
The sun does descend,
And our sports have an end:
Round the laps of their mothers,
Many sisters and brothers,
Like birds in their nest,
Are ready for rest;
And sport no more seen,
On the darkening Green.

Dr Tillyard describes the second as 'an oblique statement of the joys of gratified desire' and proceeds to make the two poems exemplify his distinction between Poetry direct and oblique.[11] The distinction which he is making is valuable and fundamental, but the terms employed are ambiguous. The first poem communicates through an agreed language of sensibility, the second demands a response of the reader to the vision *behind* the poem, after which the words will automatically fall into place. Either poem could therefore be described as 'direct' or 'oblique', depending on whether the language or the underlying emotion was in question.

We cannot explore this question fully: it will be enough to say that 'communication by way of inward vision' is a more common poetic experience than one might suppose from reading many critics. In *Songs of Innocence* not only 'The Ecchoing Green' but 'Nurse's Song' and 'Holy Thursday' rely on this mode. The reader must offer a willing response—must, indeed, have had something of the experience described—if he is to enjoy the poem to the fullest extent.

The method is a dangerous one, since it contains no built-in discipline to restrain the poet. Several poems in the collection descend dangerously near to sentimentality. Their uncertainty of level is matched at times by an unevenness of technique which suggests that although Blake is known to have revised his poems, he would not be alive to every error. 'Warbled out these metres meet' is one unhappy line, while

> Besides I can tell where I am use'd well,
> Such usage in heaven will never do well.

is painfully lame (but see p. 205). On the other hand Blake can be over-fastidious. In reading the last line of a stanza of *The Tyger*, for example,

> And when thy heart began to beat,
> What dread hand? & what dread feet?

only a pedant would point to the obscurity. Yet Blake felt the force of potential criticism at some point, for in one copy he altered the line to read

> What dread hand form'd thy dread feet?[12]

His second thoughts are manifestly wrong: the rhetoric of the first version speaks more directly to the reader than the rectified syntax of the second.

The *Songs of Innocence* are more open to the danger of banality because, with one notable exception to be examined presently, their keynote is threefold vision, little reference being made to other forms of experience. Most of them are constructed round images of pathos or the pastoral—the lamb, the lily, the tear or the river. The human virtues celebrated are simple: Mercy, Pity, Peace and Love. Blake's triumphs here lie in his ability to achieve a complete psychoscape to express such qualities. He manages to create a world possessed by human virtues, by the simple process of evoking the world as children see it in imaginative moments. The structuring of the landscape is informed by visionary dynamics until it glows with its own inward light: and the use of echoing effects in the verse suggests that the scene is also self-contained within its own harmonies.

To achieve such an impression of harmony and innocence is the most difficult of artistic tasks. In the *Songs of Experience*, on the other hand, the scope is widened: symbols from one level of vision are constantly pitted against symbols from another. In *The Clod & the Pebble*, for example, the clay of threefold vision is contrasted with the pebble of single vision: the one malleable to the feet of cattle, the other serving only as an obstruction to the free-flowing waters of the brook. The Clay (which summons up the world of Thel) symbolizes the selflessness of Love, the pebble the possessiveness of Love. Such are the contrary states of the human soul at their extreme.

In those *Songs of Experience* which are concerned with the exploration of single vision there is less of a hit-or-miss effect. Blake is there able to rely upon his command of satire and invective, which is more readily summoned than the state of innocent vision.

The Human Abstract shows the ease with which he wields these powers. It begins with an ironic stanza, outlining the reasoning by which human injustices might be defended:

> Pity would be no more,
> If we did not make somebody Poor:
> And Mercy no more could be,
> If all were as happy as we;

The reasoning seems sound enough: mercy and pity are elements of threefold vision which rise to meet the demands created by the oppressions of single vision: to abolish those injustices would be to abolish mercy and pity. But we cannot go on to argue that threefold vision would be abolished with poverty. Blake says elsewhere that if fourfold vision were firmly established threefold would still exist as a place of rest from its fierceness: pathos is always needed to balance the sublime.

The following stanza contains the next step in the line of reasoning. Political theory suggests that peace can be established simply by creating a balance of forces, so that one fear cancels another. But it ignores the fact that so negative a state of affairs must lead to further corruption and deterioration.

And mutual fear brings peace;
Till the selfish loves increase.

The growth of self-love leads to cruelty, and cruelty to the rise
of Humility, followed by Mystery and Deceit. The whole
process is summed up in the image of the Tree of Mystery. For
this Blake draws on the tradition of the Upas tree, that mysterious poison plant which appeared constantly in the literature
of his time. The Upas tree was confidently supposed to exist in
some parts of the East, poisoning the area around it for some
distance. There was one major obstacle to belief in the tale,
however: no one stated that he himself had actually seen one.[13]
For Blake, adept in mythology, the fruitlessness of the quest
involved no mystery whatever:

The Gods of the earth and sea,
Sought thro' Nature to find this Tree
But their search was all in vain:
There grows one in the Human Brain

Blake, in his later illustrations, often portrays such a tree, leaning over man to hide true vision from him. The tree of his
paradise, on the other hand, is a slender, lofty tree which carries
its leaves and fruit above mankind, but presents no obstruction
to light.

Tree-symbolism is again active in *A Poison Tree*, which
begins with a succinct statement of the difference between
action undertaken in two-fold vision and that undertaken in
single vision:

I was angry with my friend:
I told my wrath, my wrath did end;
I was angry with my foe:
I told it not, my wrath did grow.

In succeeding stanzas the poison continues to grow in the shape
of a tree which eventually bears an apple of deceit. The enemy
steals it in secret and dies and the speaker, in his single vision,
is glad that it should be so.

Succeeding songs describe how the guardians of single vision
worship Mystery for its own sake until they turn into tyrants. *A
Little Boy Lost* is about a boy who argues, with Cordelia-like
honesty, the impossibility of loving another as oneself, since
thought cannot know anything greater than itself: the only love

possible to him is that of the little bird which picks up crumbs at the door. The Priest immediately holds him up for condemnation as one who 'sets reason up for judge / Of our most holy Mystery' and condemns him to be burnt. *A Little Girl Lost* describes a girl in the Age of Gold who enjoys the delights of love, forgetting her fears, only to be met by the reproaches of a snowy-bearded father:

Ona! pale and weak!
To thy father speak:
O the trembling fear!
O the dismal care!
That shakes the blossoms of my hoary hair

This father is not, like the priest of the previous poem, cruel. He is kind and full of love for his daughter. But he makes her tremble none the less, for he is a creature of single vision, unable to regard what she has been doing as anything but a crime. He resembles the old father of 'Aged Ignorance' in *The Gates of Paradise* who busies himself with cutting the wings of a young cherub.[14] It is the tragedy of his etiolated threefold vision that his innocence can do nothing to help the girl pass through the fires of twofold experience that confront her.

A few other poems may be considered with this group. *A Divine Image* (etched but not included by Blake) is a counterpart to *The Divine Image* in the previous collection. To the assertion that Mercy, Pity, Peace and Love have human lineaments it replies that Cruelty, Jealousy, Terror and Secrecy also have human lineaments. *The Chimney Sweeper*, likewise, sets against the simple piety of the sweeper in *Songs of Innocence* the hypocrisy of those who put the sweeper to his toil and yet 'are gone to praise God & his Priest & King.' *London*, finally, seems to be, as Professor Pinto suggests,[15] a reply to that pious children's hymn by Isaac Watts which begins,

Whene'er I take my walks abroad,
How many poor I see,
What shall I render to my God
For all his gifts to me?

It is hard to agree that the speaker in Blake's poem is also a child, however—if he is, he must be as precocious as Watts's is smug.

I wander thro' each charter'd street,
Near where the charter'd Thames does flow,
And mark in every face I meet
Marks of weakness, marks of woe.

This is not the voice of a child.

The poem is perhaps the least controversial of all Blake's
works. The poet speaks so directly to his fellow-men that no
knowledge of his personal vision is necessary to assist the understanding. The voice of Blake's indignation is always his clearest
voice: and the imagery of this poem is both subtle and completely self-contained.

But most thro' midnight streets I hear
How the youthful Harlots curse
Blasts the new-born Infants tear,
And blights with plagues the Marriage hearse

From this poem we may turn to one, equally fine, which
contrives in the course of its two stanzas to raise the problem of
interpretation in an unusually sharp form.

Ah Sun-flower! weary of time,
Who countest the steps of the Sun:
Seeking after that sweet golden clime
Where the travellers journey is done:

Where the Youth pined away with desire,
And the pale Virgin shrouded in snow:
Arise from their graves and aspire,
Where my Sun-flower wishes to go.

Here is a poem which can make, by way of its imagery, a direct
impact upon the imagination which differs from any literal
'meaning'. The atmosphere which is created for the reader who
responds directly to the words of the poem without looking at
them too closely is one of a drowsy summer afternoon, full of
richness and heat. He may also feel the presence of a sleazy
but attractive corruption. If the reader's approach is to seize
on the opening image as the keynote and to allow the other
imagery to work as it will, such a response is both natural
and legitimate.

The reader who is steeped in Blake's writings, on the other
hand, will read the poem in a different way. He will respond

to the sun as an image of eternity, as well as of physical attraction, and will feel the ache of spiritual yearning in 'pined away
with desire' and 'shrouded in snow'. He will see that the sunflower is used here to link twofold vision with fourfold. G. M.
Harper, in a valuable article,[16] has pointed out that Blake
almost certainly derived the image of the sunflower from Neoplatonic sources. ' . . . All things pray, and compose hymns to
the leaders of their respective orders . . . Hence the sunflower,
as far as it is able, moves in a circular dance towards the sun'
(*Hymns to Orpheus*). Yet Blake has contrived to make the image
his own. The image of the flower, slowly and imperceptibly
turning to keep its face toward the sun in the heavens, is a
perfect image of the yearning for eternity in creatures of time.
The element of yearning is made more poignant by being related to the 'steps' of the sun and so to the 'traveller's journey'
which makes the 'weariness' human. But now there is a modula-
tion into another run of imagery, still associated with the flower
and the sun, so that the sun-face of the flower, bright yet
impotent vegetation compared with the brightness and energy
of the sun that it resembles, is made to symbolize the youth and
the virgin, who carry within themselves the lineaments of fourfold vision, yet by their enforced abstinence are deprived of
that fulfilment of their earthly desire which would reveal the
nature of the eternity that they long for. At this point Blake is
moving beyond his Neoplatonic sources and exploiting the
image of the sunflower more fully. His handling of symbolism
in the poem is wonderfully deft and economical; and the avail-
ability of an alternative meaning to those who read the poem
without such considerations adds to its attractiveness.

From this tiny masterpiece we may turn to the 'Introduction'
of the *Songs of Experience*, which presents similar problems of
interpretation over a longer space. Dr Leavis has offered a
detailed exegesis of the poem, which may be reprinted in full as
an example of the 'Aristotelian' approach to Blake at its best:

> Hear the voice of the Bard!
> Who Present, Past, & Future sees
> Whose ears have heard,
> The Holy Word,
> That walk'd among the ancient trees.

Calling the lapsed Soul
And weeping in the evening dew;
That might controll,
The starry pole;
And fallen fallen light renew!

O Earth O Earth return!
Arise from out the dewy grass;
Night is worn,
And the morn
Rises from the slumberous mass.

Turn away no more:
Why wilt thou turn away
The starry floor
The watry shore
Is giv'n thee till the break of day.

Attempted paraphrase of this poem would be brought up
against awkward questions—would turn, in fact, into interpretation and comment. In spite of the semi-colon at the end of the
second line, we find ourselves asking whether it is the Holy Word
of the Bard that is calling the 'lapsed soul'. There is clearly a
reference to the voice of God in the Garden calling Adam, but is
it God that *might* control the starry pole?—though it could hardly
be the Soul (an interpretation permitted by punctuation and syntax) that might? And surely 'fallen light' is Lucifer? When we
find in the next two lines that Earth has fallen too we cannot help
associating her with Lucifer, though she is clearly the 'lapsed
soul', and is also associated with the 'dew' ('dewy grass'—'evening dew') with the Holy Word (or the Bard); and by then it has
become plain that prose paraphrase is an inappropriate enter-
prise. Interpretation is not a matter of deciding, here and there,
which of two or more possible readings gives the right sense.
Blake, by his own poetic means, which essentially disdains the
virtues of prose, is defining his own peculiar intuition of evil, dis-
harmony and a general fall.

Looking back at the first stanza we can see how Blake *uses* the
Christian theme and subdues it completely to his own unorthodox
purpose. The opening line of invocation is Druid and pagan in
suggestion (how utterly remote from Gray's Bard Blake's is!) and
'Present, Past and Future' suggests Fates, Weirds or Norns—suggests, in fact, anything but a distinctively Christian sense of Time
and Destiny. So that when the 'Holy Word' comes it enters into a
strongly non-Christian context of associations, the total effect

being something that (it might be said) is neither Christian nor pagan. The 'ancient trees' among which the 'Holy Word' walks, are, growing though they may in the Garden, Druid and are immediately evocative of a religious awe.[17]

This criticism constantly asks the right questions; it also shows exceptional sensitiveness to the implications of Blake's language. In doing so, however, it explicitly denies to Blake the 'virtues of prose'. His communication, it is suggested, is essentially poetic—not in the sense of being vague or woolly, but in making up for any syntactical ambiguities by a precision in the handling of imagery and association, and so producing a 'whole sense' of a different kind from that which we associate with plain prose.

The presuppositions of this argument need not be dealt with again here: it will be sufficient to point out that the rejected method of 'prose paraphrase' can be carried further than it is in Dr Leavis's first paragraph.

To begin with, the ambiguity as to *who* is to 'control the starry pole' may be resolved if one decides that Blake was here remembering the *Second Anniversary* of Donne:

Shee to whose person Paradise adher'd,
As Courts to Princes, shee whose eyes ensphear'd
Star-light enough, t'have made the South controule,
(Had she beene there) the Star-full Northerne Pole . . .[18]

This is precisely the sort of image which would strike Blake, and recur to him when he was thinking of the fallen woman to whom Paradise no longer 'adheres'. If so, it is very definitely the 'lapsed Soul' that 'might control the starry pole'. And as we examine the symbols of the poem as a whole and relate them to the speculative thought which we have traced through Blake's writings, the poem can be made to yield a more precise meaning in other cases also. For example, 'The opening line of invocation is Druid and pagan in suggestion . . . ' Blake himself would have made a clear distinction so far as the Druid associations of his poem are concerned. In the sense that 'Adam was a Druid'[19] only the Bards and Gothic artists preserved the pure Druid tradition. The Druids of history would be nearer to the 'Starry Jealousy' of the next poem. And if it is argued that

such distinctions are not important for our reading of this particular poem, we can reply that they are important precisely
because Blake wished to *exclude* certain Druid associations from
his invocation. The trees, the starry pole and the 'stony dread'
of the next poem are all to be associated with the Druids who
built Stonehenge and offered human sacrifice. 'The "ancient
trees" among which the "Holy Word" walks are . . . Druid and
are immediately evocative of a religious awe.' Even so: but the
'religious awe' must be specifically dissociated from 'religious
mystery' (which is Druid in the cruel sense) and associated instead with the religious vision, which is Bardic.

Further interpretations can be made, which refine upon the
intuitions which Dr Leavis offers and make more possible a
total response to the poem. Blake *is* 'using the Christian theme
and subduing it completely to his own unorthodox purpose'.
But what is that purpose? Dr Leavis is rather imprecise here,
reflecting that the total effect is 'neither Christian nor pagan',
and that the ancient trees are Druid and 'immediately evocative of a religious awe.'

This hint of an explanation does not carry us very far: with
the clues at our disposal, it is possible to define Blake's position
more exactly. The 'Holy Word' is not the God of Genesis who
walked in Eden after the Fall, for that God was not weeping but
calling sternly for Adam, as he hid himself. Blake's myth is
different. There is no separate God, no embodied principle of
justice who searches out the disobedience of man and pursues
him with his vengeance. Blake's Word walks weeping for the
lapsed soul. Nor has Blake simply substituted a God of mercy
and love for the stern God of the Old Testament. The conception is more complicated: this figure is both God and Adam;
existing in the pity and love of threefold vision he weeps over a
Soul that has fallen towards the darkness of single vision. But
he does not call her to his own state of pity and love—for he too
is fallen, and weeps for himself as well as for her: rather he calls
her to rejoin him in the state of fourfold vision, which he cannot
regain without her aid.

Behind the figure of the Holy Word looms Blake's vision of
the original state of Man, a Spirit walking in the Garden. This
cosmic man was of glorious majesty: his crowned head reached

to the heavens and formed the true 'Pole' of the universe. (Cleopatra's imagery to describe her lost Antony, ranging from her cosmic conception of him to her bare statement, 'The soldier's pole is fallen'[20] may have played its part in this picture). In this unfallen state, a constant dialectic exists between the man of fourfold vision and the woman of threefold vision— between the Spirit and the Garden. The Fourfold is eternal in his truly human, supersolar splendour, but needs to be constantly renewed by association with the Threefold: the cyclic echoing fountain in the paradise garden, the moon in the night.

The Bard knows all this well: and because he understands why the Holy Word weeps, he takes up the same appeal, calling on Earth to rise from her fallen state and resume her true sphere of dominion—so helping to bring about the daybreak, the return of the Lord of Vision whose coming will shine with the glory of the sunrise.

But in the fallen state, the Vision has become separated from the Love which should sustain it: the two have fallen apart. As a result, the proud head of vision in the Heavens has degenerated to a mere pinhead of light, a cruel pole-star of Law, fit object of worship for later Druids. Equally, the garden of love has fallen away from its former happy state, as the Bard discovers when he calls upon Earth to rise 'from out the dewy grass'. 'Earth's Answer', the next poem, explains why she cannot respond to his call:

> Earth rais'd up her head,
> From the darkness dread & drear.
> Her light fled:
> Stony dread!
> And her locks cover'd with grey despair.
>
> Prison'd on watry shore
> Starry Jealousy does keep my den
> Cold and hoar
> Weeping o'er
> I hear the Father of the ancient men
>
> Selfish father of men
> Cruel jealous selfish fear
> Can delight
> Chain'd in night
> The virgins of youth and morning bear. . . .

The poem continues with the same complaint, echoing closely the cry of the Daughters of Albion to Urizen.[21] But the main point has already been made. Earth cannot rise, because the only lord whom she can recognize is the god of Law and Jealousy. Like Oothoon, she is chained to a rocky shore; her eyes, like Tiriel's, are stony orbs of lost vision. So Blake brings together the image of Andromeda, bound to the rock, and Medusa, freezing to stone everything which she sees, in a single image of bondage and loss of vision. The Perseus who would free her would restore her vision: for the 'Gorgon' within her is also the instrument of her bondage. The cyclical fountain in the garden is now an ocean that beats the shore; the former garden is a rocky strand: the lost, light-giving lover has shrunk to a pattern of stars in the heavens. The Holy Word who walked among the ancient trees had already fallen in becoming Word rather than Vision, but his fallen state was nothing compared with that of the tyrant, 'starry Jealousy', who as Law now rules the heavens, binding that Love which ought to be free.

Earth and her Lord are mutually trapped. The tyrant cannot be the true light because he lacks the love that would renew his vision; Earth cannot give him true love because she is held by the dark iron law of jealousy. The twin images of the cold distant pole-star and the dark rocky shore depict the fallen state of man at its lowest, without vision and without love. Only the Bard can appeal to them by his ancient knowledge of the sun-god and the garden which they dimly shadow. Only he offers hope of a break in the vicious dialectic.

The meaning which thus reveals itself in the two poems may be complicated, but it is also satisfying in the fuller range of imagery which it offers and in its resolution of verbal ambiguities. The overt pessimism and bitterness of the poem is balanced by hints of a happier landscape, mediated by such images as 'starry pole' and 'fallen light'.

The basic pattern of paired images which is used here, the Spirit and the Garden, the Word and the lapsed soul, the starry pole and the rocky shore, can be seen to reverberate through the remainder of *Songs of Experience*. Later, Blake matches the dark statement of the opening two poems with two poems that strike a more optimistic note—beginning with stanzas which prophesy the ending of the alienation between Earth and her lord:

In futurity
I prophetic see,
That the earth from sleep,
(Grave the sentence deep)
Shall arise and seek
For her maker meek:
And the desart wild
Become a garden mild.

With this enunciation of his theme, Blake confronts one of the most thorny problems for a romantic writer. If innocence is the desirable state, from which men have fallen to experience, how can their paradise be restored? Is not the state of experience, once established, permanent?

The two poems, *The Little Girl Lost* and *The Little Girl Found*, set out to answer these questions. A girl in a state of innocence is shown actually redeeming her parents in their state of experience. Here there is a parallel with Coleridge. Just as Blake's Tiriel resembles Cain in *The Wanderings of Cain*, so the Lyca of this poem resembles Cain's small son, Enos, in the same poem. Lyca is a child of nature, like Coleridge's 'lovely boy' who is plucking fruits in the wilderness.[22] She has a complete trust in nature—and has indeed lost herself by listening to the songs of wild birds. When she is weary, she is disturbed only by the knowledge that her parents are weeping for her, which makes sleep difficult. Nevertheless she invokes the moon of threefold vision to help her to sleep.

Frowning frowning night,
O'er this desart bright,
Let thy moon arise,
While I close my eyes.

When she falls asleep, wild beasts come to her. But instead of attacking her, they fall under the spell of her complete trustfulness and retained innocence:

The kingly lion stood
And the virgin view'd,
Then he gambold round
O'er the hallowd ground:

Leopards, tygers play,
Round her as she lay;
While the lion old,
Bow'd his mane of gold,

And her bosom lick,
And upon her neck,
From his eyes of flame,
Ruby tears there came;

While the lioness,
Loos'd her slender dress,
And naked they convey'd
To caves the sleeping maid.

There is a striking resemblance between these lines and a similar incident in *The Faerie Queene*:

It fortuned out of the thickest wood
A ramping Lyon rushed suddainly,
Hunting full greedie after salvage blood;
Soon as the royall virgin he did spy,
With gaping mouth at her ran greedily,
To have attonce devour'd her tender corse:
But to the pray when as he drew more ny,
His bloudie rage asswaged with remorse,
And with the sight amazd, forgot his furious forse.

In stead thereof he kist her wearie feet,
And lickt her lilly hand with fawning tong,
As he her wronged innocence did weet . . .[23]

Blake has entered fully into the spirit of Spenser in his lyric—in fact his own verse is the more illuminated. He has also taken over some of Spenser's symbolism and moulded it according to his own pattern. If he saw Una with her lamb and lion as emblems of the honest human soul with its guiding 'emanation' and defending 'spectre' (to use his own expressions), he would evidently see the lion as also representing the Experience which Una needs to face if her lover is to be saved. But Blake works out this implication of the lion image more fully. The 'hallow'd ground' around the sleeping Lyca is related to the Ecchoing Green of *Songs of Innocence*, while the 'lion old' with 'his mane of gold' represents vividly the richness and timelessness of twofold experience at its best. The 'ruby tears' of the lion, which follow, are one of the happiest symbolic strokes in all Blake's work. As tears, they represent the tender pathos of threefold vision, as *ruby* tears, they have the sublime, eternal beauty of fourfold vision. The flame from the lion's eye, his most threatening feature, has become a tear, the melting pathos of which burns also with the inward fire of the ruby. It is a telling stroke, which in two words contrives to suggest how the energies of twofold vision, when combined with innocence, can point the way to the nature of the true and eternal fourfold vision which alternates between the sublimity of Vision and the pathos of love. Yet despite its heavy charge of meaning, the image has the immediate imaginative appeal of an enchanted castle in a fairy tale.

The story of Lyca is clearly allegorical. As Kathleen Raine and William Empson have pointed out in defence of those who look for a hidden meaning, a lost child in real life would be glad to think that its parents were anxious and weeping, for that would show concern for its rescue.[24] Equally, one may add, a child who was really lost would be unwise to trust too readily to the benevolence of wild beasts, in spite of stories which tell of their care for the young. As usual with Blake, this is not a story for the literal-minded. It is a story of innocence facing experience, and turning its threatening energies into powers which will guard and fulfil the Divine Image latent in every man.

The Little Girl Found goes on to extend the parable to Lyca's parents. In their search for their daughter they wander far, over the deserts of single vision. At length they too are confronted by the lion, who bears them to the ground and stalks round them, 'smelling to his prey'. But to their surprise, he goes on to lick their hands: and when they look at him again he is seen in a different guise:

> They look upon his eyes
> Fill'd with deep surprise:
> And wondering behold,
> A spirit arm'd in gold.
>
> On his head a crown
> On his shoulders down
> Flow'd his golden hair.
> Gone was all their care.

Follow me he said,
Weep not for the maid;
In my palace deep,
Lyca lies asleep.

As in the previous poem, the energy of twofold vision reveals the eternal glory of fourfold. But this time the vision is fuller: the fourfold is revealed as the spirit who walked in the garden, a crowned figure with golden hair, an Apollo. And he leads them to find their child asleep 'among tygers wild'.

To this day they dwell
In a lonely dell
Nor fear the wolvish howl,
Nor the lions growl.

For them the lesson is the same as for Lyca. The energies of experience are not to be feared; rightly handled, they are charmed into the very forces by which innocence is transformed into eternal vision. Yet this will happen in the midst of a fallen world: the dell of the final stanza is reminiscent of the 'wilderness' of the honest man in the Argument to *The Marriage of Heaven and Hell*.[25] Their grasp of the truth about life forces Lyca's parents to live apart from the world.

The illustration to the first poem has troubled some critics, who have pointed out that the Lyca who is specifically stated to be seven years old is shown embracing a youth, and manifestly older. It has even been suggested that the drawing was really intended for the poem with the similar title of *A Little Girl Lost*. A simpler explanation is that it reflects the idea contained in the opening stanzas, that Earth will arise to seek her maker in open-hearted love. The happy paradisal love depicted is the 'organized innocence' to which man will return.

In these poems Blake has succeeded in one of his chief aims, creating an art that will appeal vividly to any child, yet will carry a weight of meaning ('Grave the sentence deep') to the discerning reader. He has taken one of the oldest and most attractive of nursery tales, the story of Beauty and the Beast, and while allowing it to retain all the enchanted atmosphere of a nursery tale, has given it a detailed symbolic organization that relates it to the full body of his speculations.

At different times, he included this pair of poems in both the

Songs of Innocence and the *Songs of Experience*. It is not difficult to
see the reason: this is one of his most serious attempts to reconcile the two states of the human mind which are the subject of
those collections. Many of the Victorians were to grapple with
the same problem: and when they failed it was because they
could not in the long run see experience as anything but a corruption of innocence. In consequence, Innocence could never
redeem experience—it could only create a state of remorse.
Yet long before them, Blake had dealt with the same problem
more successfully by portraying innocence as a state of mind, a
fundamental identity, which could never be radically affected
by anything that happened to its possessor.

> Every Harlot was a Virgin once
> Nor canst thou ever change Kate into Nan

True innocence must pass through experience before it can be
fully confirmed: and this is the way that 'experience' is redeemed.

In these two poems, the threatening Spectre is potentially a
guardian angel. In other poems, however, Blake shows the
ambiguity of the Spectre working another way. What began
as a defence turns into a corruption. This descent from twofold
to single vision is several times portrayed by the image of the
rose and the thorn, which has already appeared in the Argument to *The Marriage of Heaven and Hell* to suggest the guardianship of honesty. Now, in the brief poem *The Lilly*, it is compared to the sheep with its horn (another favourite symbol of
twofold vision for Blake) and both are contrasted with the Lily
of threefold vision:

> The modest Rose puts forth a thorn:
> The humble Sheep, a threatning horn:
> While the Lilly white, shall in Love delight,
> Nor a thorn nor a threat stain her beauty bright

The point is made more strongly in *My Pretty Rose Tree*, where
the narrator refuses 'such a flower as May never bore' in favour
of his own rose tree, only to find that his Rose

> turnd away with jealousy:
> And her thorns were my only delight.

In *The Garden of Love,* the thorns are entirely separated, to become symbols of single vision. The narrator goes to the Garden, only to find that a chapel has been built on the green and
' "Thou shalt not" writ over the door'. In the garden itself
there are tombstones and graves,

> And Priests in black gowns, were walking their rounds,
> And binding with briars, my joys & desires.

The finest of these poems is *The Sick Rose.* Here the contrast
between twofold and single vision is established in the images
of the rose and the worm:

> O Rose thou art sick.
> The invisible worm,
> That flies in the night
> In the howling storm:

> Has found out thy bed
> Of crimson joy:
> And his dark secret love
> Does thy life destroy.

The worm, usually a symbol of innocent sexual love, not un-
related to the caterpillar that can turn into a chrysalis and then
a butterfly, is here an emblem of corruption. The change is
wrought by the fact that it is an 'invisible' worm, with 'dark
secret love': shame and single vision are responsible for this
destructive lust that preys on true love instead of nourishing it.

The poem is another of Blake's triumphs. Its immediate and
striking collocation of images, each enriching the other, makes
it fine by any standards. Knowledge of Blake's mind simply
helps to define the imagery more closely, and show how his use
of it differs from that of his predecessors. The cankered fruit or
flower is a familiar emblem, which occurs in Bunyan's *Book for
Boys and Girls,*[26] and frequently in the eighteenth century.
Professor V. de Sola Pinto has drawn attention to two of Mrs
Barbauld's *Hymns in Prose,* in one of which she describes the
downfall of a stately tree (because 'the worm had made its way
into the trunk, and the heart thereof was decayed, it mouldered
away, and fell to the ground') and in another the transient
beauty of the rose.[27] Another source, closer to the imagery of
the poem as we have it, can be found in Young's *Night Thoughts:*

> Death's subtle seed within,
> (Sly treacherous miner!) working in the dark,
> Smil'd at thy well-concerted scheme, and beckon'd
> The worm to riot on that rose so red,
> Unfaded ere it fell; one moment's prey![28]

As always in his reading of Young, Blake's creative imagination is at work. He turns the sense of the lines inside out, making the rose itself the point of attention and identifying the worm with 'Death's subtle seed within'. Where Young was simply creating an image of sudden death, and probably intended the rose and the worm to represent the fate of the body *after* death, Blake reshapes the image-pattern to produce a less literal sense, in which the secrecy of sudden death and the corruption of the feeding worm come together in an unforgettable picture of possessive lust. (When Blake illustrated Young's lines some years later, he kept strictly to Young's sense and avoided any reference to his own—an example of his readiness to discipline himself to another man's meaning when appropriate.[29])

Another image of this corruption appears in a manuscript poem which begins 'I saw a chapel all of gold ...'[30] None dares enter this place of mystery; when, finally, a serpent comes and forces its way through the doors, it drags its slimy length along the pavement and vomits its poison upon the bread and wine. As always, Blake's disgust is a disgust at the *misuse* of sexual faculties. If the chapel had not been turned into a place of mystery it would not have been defiled.

Blake's fullest treatment of the connection between his levels of vision and the various forms of sexual experience occurs in the poem entitled *The Crystal Cabinet*.[31] The narrator tells how he was caught by a maiden, who locked him in her crystal cabinet. Here he had a threefold vision of the world:

> This Cabinet is formd of Gold
> And Pearl & Crystal shining bright
> And within it opens into a World
> And a little lovely Moony Night
>
> Another England there I saw
> Another London with its Tower
> Another Thames & other Hills
> And another pleasant Surrey Bower

Another Maiden like herself
Translucent lovely shining clear
Threefold each in the other closd
O what a pleasant trembling fear

O what a smile a threefold Smile
Filld me that like a flame I burnd
I bent to Kiss the lovely Maid
And found a Threefold Kiss returnd . . .

Blake presents the height of Vision as it is given to man in his
sexual relationships—a delight to be enjoyed, but also to be
recognized for what it is, a passing revelation, and relinquished
without regret. The lover of his poem is not content to do this,
however. Having burned in twofold vision and come into a
state where threefold vision points towards fourfold, he will not
leave that final vision to exist freely in its own form, but tries to
snatch and possess it. Like Prometheus he wants the final
secret, and the status of a god.

I strove to sieze the inmost Form
With ardor fierce & hands of flame
But burst the Crystal Cabinet
And like a Weeping Babe became

A weeping Babe upon the wild
And Weeping Woman pale reclind
And in the outward air again
I filld with woes the passing Wind

The Promethean action breaks the threefold vision: possessiveness exiles both lovers into the world of single vision, depriving
them of the higher forms of vision which might otherwise have
possessed them.

This poem shows how closely the forms of sexual experience
and the four levels of vision were linked in Blake's mind. Its
shape also helps towards an interpretation of the most difficult
of all his lyric poems: *The Mental Traveller*.[32]

The latter poem is deliberately dialectical throughout. The
stage is held by the figures of a man and a woman, whose
relationship differs continually. Their identity is never revealed, but it seems evident that the man represents the Divine
Image, while the woman stands always in close relationship to
human Law—whether as agent or victim.

The Divine Image, unlike normal human babies, is begotten in woe and born in joy. But he is born into a world which has no place for him and fears the strength of his powers. So he is delivered to the Law, in order that he may be held in restraint.

> And if the Babe is born a Boy
> He's given to a Woman Old
> Who nails him down upon a rock
> Catches his shrieks in cups of gold
>
> She binds iron thorns around his head
> She pierces both his hands & feet
> She cuts his heart out at his side
> To make it feel both cold & heat
>
> Her fingers number every Nerve
> Just as a Miser counts his gold
> She lives upon his shrieks & cries
> And she grows young as he grows old . . .

Several traditions combine here. Christ was the victim of tyranny by the established powers from the time of the cruelty of Herod until his crucifixion; Dionysus, as Kathleen Raine has mentioned, suffered the cutting out of his heart.[33] Against the divine victim Blake sets the woman, who destroys him by her cruelty and by the rationalism of single vision ('Her fingers number every nerve').

But 'God out of Christ is a consuming fire': the result of binding the Divine Image is to release its Energy in fierce destruction. Instead of the fourfold god, there emerges the two-fold youth of Revolt who attacks the Woman—now, by the operation of the Moral Law, become a Virgin:

> Till he becomes a bleeding youth
> And she becomes a Virgin bright
> Then he rends up his Manacles
> And binds her down for his delight
>
> He plants himself in all her Nerves
> Just as a Husbandman his mould
> And she becomes his dwelling place
> And Garden fruitful seventy fold

In this possessive state, the visionary element of the Divine Image has been destroyed, giving way to the energies of Desire.

But his humanity remains untouched, so that his state is that of Charity without fourfold Vision. His cottage is filled with gems and gold:

> And these are the gems of the Human Soul
> The rubies & pearls of a lovesick eye
> The countless gold of the akeing heart
> The martyrs groan & the lovers sigh.

The Male Image is full of good works: he is a repository of all those yearnings after the Eternal Vision which are expressed in the sigh of the lover or the groan of the martyr. But he can only relieve suffering, not cure it. As a result a new female figure is produced—the perfection of Love without Vision. This figure has all the beauty of the infinite without any of the generosity and selflessness that inhere in Vision. She is the perfection of the Female Will, worshipped by men and utterly egoistic. Like Lear's daughters, she exiles the man who once represented the Divine Vision:

> Till from the fire on the hearth
> A little Female Babe does spring

> And she is all of solid fire
> And gems & gold that none his hand
> Dares stretch to touch her Baby form
> Or wrap her in his swaddling-band

> But She comes to the Man she loves
> If young or old or rich or poor
> They soon drive out the aged Host
> A Beggar at anothers door.

The Aged Man, now deprived of both vision and love, wanders away until he can find another maiden. But in his reduced state, his embrace can be no more than the Promethean gesture of the lover in *The Crystal Cabinet*. Instead of inducing threefold vision, it produces a single vision which destroys even the world that he has known.

> The Cottage fades before his sight
> The Garden & its lovely Charms

> The Guests are scatterd thro' the land
> For the Eye altering alters all

> The Senses roll themselves in fear
> And the flat Earth becomes a Ball
>
> The Stars Sun Moon all shrink away
> A desart vast without a bound
> And nothing left to eat or drink
> And a dark desart all around

The imaginative brilliance of these lines invites comment. Blake conveys with a few deft touches the creation of a scientific world-picture as a refuge from lost Vision. When Man can no longer see himself as a Spirit walking in the Garden, he becomes obsessed instead by the nature of the universe at large, pursuing his quest through ever-increasing waste tracts of space: and his body becomes attuned to the universe which it sees. The 'hedgehog' image by which Blake links the fear of the senses without vision to their reliance upon knowledge of the shape of the earth to give them a solid resting-place, is particularly good. Instead of the Spirit in the Garden, there appear only isolated figures of light: sun, moon and stars; instead of the 'ecchoing green', a 'desart vast without a bound'; instead of nourishment, starvation; instead of human companionship, a 'dark desart'. The psychoscaping of single vision is wonderfully represented in these images, which give the stanza the visionary structure of a nursery-rhyme verse such as

> These little babes, with hand in hand
> Went wandering up and down
> But never more they saw the Man
> Approaching from the Town.

In this state of single vision the only activity left for the man and the maiden is a desperate love-making: succeeding stanzas describe their pursuit of each other through the desert. This activity, however, begins to create a state of energy there, even if it is only that of a wilderness 'where roam the Lion, Wolf & Boar.' The Man grows younger and younger in his pursuit, the Woman older and older, until, as at the end of *The Crystal Cabinet*,

> he becomes a wayward Babe
> And she a weeping Woman Old
> Then many a Lover wanders here
> The Sun & Stars are nearer rolld . . .

Since the energy of their love-making is bringing them into the world of twofold vision, they automatically begin to approach the region of lost Paradise. As they do so, they pass through the history of civilization. After the expulsion from paradise, man was supposed to have passed through the pastoral state represented by Abel and then to the building of cities as initiated by Cain. So the presence of the lovers brings mankind through these stages in reverse:

> The trees bring forth sweet Extacy
> To all who in the desert roam
> Till many a City there is Built
> And many a pleasant Shepherds home

But this is still only twofold and threefold vision. The Paradise of fourfold vision remains lost; anything which formed a part of it is a subject of fear. When men come to it at the heart of the energy of twofold vision, therefore, they find there only the 'frowning Babe', and are stricken by terror:

> They cry The Babe the Babe is Born
> And flee away on Every side

> For who dare touch the frowning form
> His arm is witherd to its root
> Lions Boars Wolves all howling flee
> And every Tree does shed its fruit . . .

The last image, as Miss Raine has pointed out, has an apocalyptic ring.[34] For, Blake would argue, whenever the Divine Image is discovered at the heart of twofold vision there is a Last Judgment. Faced with the infinite at the heart of their experience and possesing no means of approach to it, men fear it as an isolation of energy which threatens to destroy them. (Uzzah's arm was withered to the root when he touched the Ark—in a biblical incident which Blake once painted.)[35] They leave the energy of twofold vision to be dealt with by the impersonal forces of Law, which can be relied upon to bind it down by force and by visionless analysis—

> And none can touch that frowning form
> Except it be a Woman Old,
> She nails him down upon the Rock
> And all is done as I have told

So complicated and allusive is Blake's sense throughout this poem that one sympathizes with those critics who have stated that they would prefer *not* to know its meaning. The vividness of the poem can be relied upon to create patterns of imagery in the reader's mind which provide an authentic poetic experience, whether or not he concerns himself with its symbolism. Yet it would be a bold critic who would lay his hand on his heart and declare his ability to read the whole poem simply, at its face value, without his enthusiasm flagging at any point. Once Blake's symbolism is grasped, on the other hand, the cyclical nature of the sense becomes clear, and the poem, yet another of Blake's attempts to produce a general mythical pattern against which individual items of human experience can be measured and interpreted, controls its own imagery.

Blake's poetic gifts are usually at their best when devoted to the production of small nuggets of lyrical verse, and *The Mental Traveller* is long enough to forge a link between the concentrated poetic achievements of the *Songs of Innocence and of Experience* and the wider scope of the Prophetic Books. Whereas in the *Songs* he sets one level of vision against another to interpret a particular facet of human experience, he has tried here to involve all the levels of vision, and so briefly to indicate the full range of that experience.

The process which we have here followed in miniature is elsewhere carried out on a larger scale. In the lyrics he concentrates on individual human beings and tries to generalize from their situations; in the Prophetic Books he takes the political and social scene of humanity at large and tries to trace within it a mythical pattern, cyclical, like that in *The Mental Traveller*, and involving themes and symbols against which even the most revolutionary international events can be understood. This process begins concurrently with the exploration of the states of Innocence and Experience in his lyrics. The key to it is to be found in his reaction to the French Revolution.

5 The Genius of Revolution

At the end of his youth Blake had lived through a succession of events which irrupted into the quiet of the eighteenth century like a series of thunder-claps. The American and French Revolutions marked the end of an era as surely as did the 1914–18 war a century later. The latter event lacerated the European psyche more cruelly, by the sheer weight of physical suffering involved. The impact of the earlier revolution, particularly in England, was mental rather than physical. Awe at the power of events was matched by an exciting intellectual ferment: young men were torn between anxiety at the overturning of an established order, and attraction towards the new horizons of liberty.

Blake's basic sympathies lay with the revolutionaries. According to tradition, he paraded London wearing the red cockade of the Revolution, and warned Thomas Paine to escape just before he was due to be arrested.[1]

At the same time, the strength of his revolutionary fervour can easily be overestimated. An enthusiast of enthusiasts, he was attracted more by the idea and the promise of liberty than by the physical force which was used to achieve it. Terrors and bloodshed could give him no pleasure: moreover, the violence inherent in the revolutionary activities was more evident in France than in America, where the forces of order had been less firmly entrenched.

Blake needed both to explain the events of his time and to express his own complex attitude: sympathy with the revolutionaries combined with awareness of the dangers inherent in the use of force. One result of his speculations was the early poem *The French Revolution*—which might have been entitled *A Vision of the French Revolution*. Only one book has survived, and it seems likely that the project was abandoned as a result of the publisher's fears of Government action. The statement that all twelve books were finished may be true, but is more likely to have been a piece of enthusiasm on the part of the original advertiser.

The one book which does survive reveals the method which Blake adopted for his work. Points of historical detail did not concern him greatly. Anyone who wishes to see how much he changed such details in this first book will find an excellent chapter on the subject in David Erdman's study.[2] But it is important to note that the reasons for his changes were not ideological but artistic. He wished to set the events against a perspective of landscape and symbolism that would indicate their true significance: and in constructing the pattern he did not concern himself with small details that might work against the artistic effect.

The resulting poetry was not fully successful. Blake made the mistake of overloading it with imagery of a strong, melodramatic character. It has been observed, for example, that the word 'cloud',[3] in one form or another, occurs no less than thirty-six times in the course of three hundred and sixty lines. As usual, however, the melodramatic effect is less marked when one looks into the poem more closely to examine its symbolic content. Many images which seem little more than heavy ranting turn out to be playing a part in a pattern of thought which reduces or removes their sensationalism.

To begin with, the poem is written in favour not of revolution but of liberty. The distinction is important. Blake was no headlong supporter of political revolution. As he had pointed out in *The Marriage of Heaven and Hell*, however, the flames of energy were at least better than the dark restraints of Reason; in a world devoid of Vision they were bound to rise up continually and eventually to prevail. Behind the revolutionary events there lay a 'mental' struggle—a struggle devoted to the achievement of true liberty, which would be, not a political order, but a visionary order with necessary political and social consequences.

This central belief of Blake's is conveyed by the device of relating the events of the Revolution against a visionary background mediated by the imagery. The King of France, for example, is described with frequent references to the sun. Blake has taken over the Tudor image of the king as the sun, the central harmonizing orb of his kingdom. In the case of this king, however, the central sun-like power, already almost extinguished, is deadened by the nobles who surround him. By them, as by clouds, his light is hidden, only heat coming forth:

> Then the King glow'd: his Nobles fold round, like the sun of old time quench'd in clouds;
> In their darkness the King stood, his heart flam'd, and utter'd a with'ring heat, and these words burst forth. . . .

> . . . He ceas'd, silent pond'ring, his brows folded heavy, his forehead was in affliction,
> Like the central fire. . . . .

The theme of this book, as so often in Blake's work, is that of a broken dialectic. The King ought to be the sun of the nation, but is prevented by his nobles from shining. His true complement, which would enable him to appear in full splendour, lies beyond them—

> For the Commons convene in the Hall of the Nations; like spirits of fire in the beautiful
> Porches of the Sun, to plant beauty in the desart craving abyss.

Here are the true energies of the nation. Meanwhile, the counsel of the nobles to the king is full of perverted vision. The King himself, when not roused to his proper stature, is a creature of single vision. Even his sceptre is too heavy for him to wield, for cruelty or any other purpose. At first he does descend to consult with Necker, a Rintrah-like figure among his nobles who expresses the popular will: but pressure from the other nobles forces him to exile even Necker.

The horrors of the Bastille which are now described remind one of Blake's many references to man as imprisoned within his five senses—manacled and diseased, they are reduced to horrific shapes. First and foremost, however, they are victims of injustice. When Necker is exiled, it is his sense of justice that is stressed.

> Like a dark cloud Necker paus'd, and like thunder on the just man's burial day he paus'd;
> Silent sit the winds, silent the meadows, while the husbandman and woman of weakness

And bright children look after him into the grave, and water his
    clay with love,
Then turn towards pensive fields; so Necker paused . . .

One polarity of the poem is established in this image: justice
is ranged against injustice, the innocent husbandman and his
family against those who enslave and oppress them.

The other polarity is between complete darkness and complete vision.

Darkness obsesses the King as he anxiously tells the nobles of a
vision in which the spirits of ancient kings shiver over their
bleached bones, while their counsellors look up from the dust
crying that the prisoners have burst their dens and urging each
other to hide from the living in bones, in the hollow skull, in
stones or among the roots of trees. The King's fearful vision is
answered by the Duke of Burgundy. Specially created by Blake
(David Erdman points out that the line of Burgundy had died
out in 1714),[4] this figure brings into play a run of images, such
as vineyards, mountains and war, associated with the region,
which enables Blake to exploit subtly the traditional relationship between blood and wine. In this way, Burgundy becomes a
rich, fierce, not altogether unsympathetic character:

The fierce Duke hung over the council; around him croud, weep-
    ing in his burning robe,
A bright cloud of infant souls; his words fall like purple autumn
    on the sheaves.
'Shall this marble built heaven become a clay cottage, this earth
    an oak stool, and these mowers
'From the Atlantic mountains mow down all this great starry
    harvest of six thousand years?
'And shall Necker. the hind of Geneva, stretch out his crook'd
    sickle o'er fertile France,
'Till our purple and crimson is faded to russet, and the kingdoms
    of earth bound in sheaves,
'And the ancient forests of chivalry hewn, and the joys of the
    combat burnt for fuel;
'Till the power and dominion is rent from the pole, sword and
    scepter from sun and moon,
'The law and gospel from fire and air, and eternal reason and
    science
'From the deep and solid, and man lay his faded head down on
    the rock

'Of eternity, where the eternal lion and eagle remain to devour? . . .'

This opening to his speech is loaded with Blakean irony from
end to end. As on other occasions, however, the irony does not
simply point one way. Burgundy's great desire is for solidity and
permanence. He wants to live in a world that exists beneath
marble heavens and law-bound stars. He is appalled that the
world might become a harvest to be cut down by the 'mowers
From the Atlantic mountains' (the American revolutionaries);
that it might have the transience of a simple farm, a clay
cottage with its oak tree and its crops.

So far, Blake's irony is clearly pointing against Burgundy. It
is only pride that makes man unwilling to accept his status as a
creature of earth or to see that the world in which he lives finds
its own most natural symbol in the clay cottage and the yearly
harvest. But the irony becomes more subtle as Burgundy tries
to justify himself. Along with revolution, he foresees the collapse
of everything that holds the world together. Power and
dominion will be rent from the pole, sword and sceptre from the
sun and moon, law and gospel from fire and air, reason and
science from the deep and solid.

The universe that Burgundy lives in consists of the following
hierarchy:

                    Pole
            Sun   Moon
      Fire   Air   Water   Earth

This universe of power is dominated by Reason, its firm point
the pole star that shines, distant and inhuman, upon a night-
scape of human bondage. Within this framework sun and moon
are directly related to the sword and sceptre, the means by
which men are ruled inexorably, according to fixed laws; while
the four elements diversify this universe only a little, by sub-
dividing the symbols of its organization into law and gospel,
reason and science. We are back with four figures whom we
met earlier: Rintrah (prophetic justice), Palmabron (the gospel
of mercy), Theotormon (non-visionary reason) and Bromion
(scientific knowledge). These descriptions suggest their status

as they would be in an ideal world, however. In Urizen's world each is diminished—Rintrah to a fiery indignation, Palamabron to a mild hypocritical priestcraft, Theotormon to doubt, Bromion to rocky, opaque scientific analysis. Burgundy is anxious that these energies should continue to be so restrained and anchored, like the physical elements, within the firm structure of Urizen's law.

Burgundy's defence would be accepted by many thinking men. He struggles for the survival of all that is solid and permanent in the physical universe that he knows.

Once we see that Burgundy is essentially a creature of twofold and single vision, however, the guns of Blake's irony swing silently into position. Burgundy eliminates threefold vision by his contempt for the pastoral ideal, and tacitly acknowledges the loss of fourfold vision by his reference to man's 'faded head'. He is left with the argument that unless man resists these attacks upon his order he will simply be left on the rock of Eternity for the lion and eagle to devour.

His blindness stands exposed. If he were able to see more clearly, he would perceive, first that the 'harvest' brought about by the revolutionaries was, like all earthly harvests, not permanently destructive but a means of renewal of life and reconciliation with the earth; and secondly that the 'order' which he worshipped was a perversion of the true one. Ideally Law would be replaced at the centre of things by Man, so that instead of the pole-star shining on a distant shore, the Spirit would walk in his garden, resplendent with his sun of sublime power and moon of tender pathos: exercising the energies of justice, mercy, reason and science in the full light of freedom. In that condition, the energies of the lion and eagle, fearful to dwellers in single vision, would freely exercise themselves as energies of the sublime.

Burgundy, however, unable to see beyond the limits of twofold vision, demands that the energies of the King and nobles be devoted to war. He uses the imagery of *The Tyger*:

> 'Thy Nobles have gather'd thy starry hosts round this rebellious city,
> 'To rouze up the ancient forests of Europe, with clarions of loud breathing war . . .'

As he calls for this exercise of naked energy in war, his concluding words, ' " . . . the eagles of heaven must have their
prey" ' indicate the ultimate impotence of his arguments.

It is at this point that the King orders Necker to depart, declaring that Burgundy has spoken like a lion, but at the same
time admitting that

> '. . . dark mists roll round me and blot the writing of God
> 'Written in my bosom.'

His surviving consciousness of the proper function of a king
makes him confused in his arguments, uneasily aware of the
terrors which he is unleashing:

> '. . . and cries of women and babes are heard,
> 'And tempests of doubt roll around me, and fierce sorrows, be-
> cause of the Nobles of France . . .'

Nevertheless Necker goes, worshipped and kissed on the way by
those same women and children. Meanwhile, the nobles become more serpentine as their discussion continues, like the
debates in Milton's Hell. The Archbishop of Paris arises

> In the rushing of scales and hissing of flames and rolling of
> sulphurous smoke.

Burgundy, although restricted to a limited form of the twofold vision, had argued logically from his mistaken point of
view. The Archbishop is of a lower order. He sees what is to
come and responds with fear. Blake's irony is again used
skilfully, to suggest through his horror the refraction of a state
which a more enlightened observer would see as beneficial. The
Archbishop hears the voice of an aged man, hovering in mist:

> '. . . Nobles and Clergy shall fail before me, and my cloud and
> vision be no more;
> 'The mitre become black, the crown vanish, and the scepter and
> ivory staff
> 'Of the ruler wither among bones of death; they shall consume
> from the thistly field,
> 'And the sound of the bell, the voice of the sabbath, and singing
> of the holy choir,
> 'Is turn'd into songs of the harlot in day, and cries of the virgin
> in night.

> 'They shall drop at the plow and faint at the harrow, unre-
> deem'd, unconfess'd, unpardon'd;
> 'The priest rot in his surplice by the lawless lover, the holy beside
> the accursed,
> 'The king, frowning in purple, beside the grey plowman, and
> their worms embrace together.'

That the priest should rot in the same earth as the lover, the
King with the ploughman, would be a fate not without poetic
justice in the eyes of the Blake who wrote that prisons are built
with stones of law, brothels with bricks of religion. But the idea
horrifies the Archbishop and the nobles, now sunk in single
vision:

> . . . a damp cold pervaded the Nobles, and monsters of worlds
> unknown
> Swam round them, watching to be delivered; When Aumont,
> whose chaos-born soul
> Eternally wand'ring a Comet and swift-falling fire, pale enter'd
> the chamber.

Aumont brings a message that the Abbé de Sieyes has come
from the Nation's Assembly. He has walked through the army,
preceded by 'a dark shadowy man in the form/Of King Henry
the Fourth'—a great popular monarch who, according to
Paine's *Rights of Man*, had planned to abolish war in Europe by
forming a republic of nations.[5]

At this news the Dukes of Bretagne, Borgogne and Bourbon
are on their feet ready to fight. Blake's irony again pervades
Bourbon's statement:

> 'What, damp all our fires, O spectre of Henry,' said Bourbon; 'and
> rend the flames
> 'From the head of our King! Rise, Monarch of France; command
> me, and I will lead
> 'This army of superstition at large, that the ardor of noble souls
> quenchless,
> 'May yet burn in France, nor our shoulders be plow'd with the
> furrows of poverty.'

Now, however, Orleans rises, 'generous as mountains'. This
new image marks the appearance of the two positive values of
the poem, justice and vision: 'generous' is a word that always
bears positive value in Blake's writings. At the point when

Orleans rises the Archbishop tries to speak—to find, like Satan
at a celebrated moment in *Paradise Lost*,[6] that he can only hiss.

Orleans preaches the gospel of generosity. If the nobles are
princes of fire, their flames are 'for growth, not consuming'. He
paints a picture of man informed by fourfold vision, his brain
and heart fountains which 'cast their rivers in equal tides
through the great Paradise' while his hands, head, bosom, feet
'follow their high breathing joy'. Each part of the human body
follows its own joy without obstruction from the rest—

> 'And can Nobles be bound when the people are free, or God weep
> when his children are happy?
> 'Have you never seen Fayette's forehead, or Mirabeau's eyes, or
> the shoulders of Target,
> 'Or Bailly the strong foot of France, or Clermont the terrible
> voice, and your robes
> 'Still retain their own crimson? mine never yet faded, for fire
> delights in its form.
> 'But go! merciless man! enter into the infinite labyrinth of
> another's brain
> 'Ere thou measure the circle that he shall run. Go, thou cold
> recluse, into the fires
> 'Of another's high flaming rich bosom, and return unconsum'd,
> and write laws . . .'

Blake's attack on the eighteenth-century world view is intense in these last three lines, the first of which criticizes the
analytical Urizen who leans out of his illuminated circle to
divide and limit, the second the cold moral god on his snowy
mountain, writing his code of cruel laws. The devotees of such
gods are hereby offered a more generous alternative, a vision of
man which sees him as greater than the laws by which he is
analysed and governed.

At the conclusion of his speech the King rises to command
that the 'Nation's Ambassador', the Abbé de Sieyes, be called
in. After the intimations of sublimity in the speech of Orleans,
this man speaks with a quieter voice, asking for pity on the
distressed.

> '. . . Hear the voice of vallies, the voice of meek cities,
> 'Mourning oppressed on village and field, till the village and field
> is a waste.

'For the husbandman weeps at blights of the fife, and blasting of
trumpets consume
'The souls of mild France; the pale mother nourishes her child to
the deadly slaughter . . .'

Like Burgundy, he rises to cosmic imagery, but for a different
purpose. Burgundy had used the heavenly order as an established symbol of the permanence of sword and sceptre. The
Abbé, in contrast, sees the establishment of those heavens as a
cosmic disaster, when true vision was cut off from the people.

'When the heavens were seal'd with a stone, and the terrible sun
clos'd in an orb, and the moon
'Rent from the nations, and each star appointed for watchers of
night,
'The millions of spirits immortal were bound in the ruins of
sulphur heaven
'To wander inslav'd . . .'

The key to this image lies in the words 'seal'd with a stone'.
The story of the Resurrection is made a myth of the state of
Man. When Man is shut in a cave, and a great stone rolled
against the door, then his place at the heart of creation is
usurped by the 'marble heavens' of which Burgundy spoke,
while the energy and vision which should be harmonized within
him are separated into the heat of the sun and the light of a
separate moon and distant stars. Under this false, non-human
order, the multitudes of men wander beneath the heat of the
sun in an Egypt of the soul, like the enslaved children of Israel,
'black, deprest in dark ignorance, kept in awe with the whip,/To
worship terrors . . . ' Eventually, however, the dawn of Resurrection will come. Man will 'raise his darken'd limbs out of the
caves of night':

'. . . his eyes and his heart
'Expand: where is space! where O Sun is thy dwelling! where thy
tent, O faint slumb'rous Moon.'

In this moment of true Vision, the limited forces under which
energy and light are manifested to the senses will be swallowed
up in the Desire and Vision which will possess all men. The
Abbé breaks into a picture of humanity restored to liberty: the
soldier embracing the peasant, the nobles throwing away the

instruments of tyranny, the priest blessing instead of cursing. He concludes with 'the first voice of the morning'—a request that the army be withdrawn ten miles from Paris.

At these words there is a movement of contention among the Nobles, and after grim portents the voice of the Duke of Burgundy is heard delivering the King's command. He declares that if the Bastille moves into the country ten miles, then and only then will the army be disbanded. Otherwise the Nation's Assembly must learn that army and prison alike are the bands by which the kingdom is held.

In the Nation's Assembly, however, Burgundy's message is received with indignation and Mirabeau ('A rushing of wings around him was heard as he brighten'd') calls for the General of the Nation. As he obeys, Fayette, the General, becomes, however dimly, a representative of the lost light ('The aged sun rises appall'd from dark mountains, and gleams a dusky beam/ On Fayette . . . ') while in a cloud about him appear the consequences of his action:

> Like a flame of fire he stood before dark ranks, and before expect-
> ing captains
> On pestilent vapours around him flow frequent spectres of re-
> ligious men weeping
> In winds driven out of the abbeys, their naked souls shiver in
> keen open air,
> Driven out by the fiery cloud of Voltaire, and thund'rous rocks
> of Rousseau,
> They dash like foam against the ridges of the army, uttering a
> faint feeble cry.

The use of cloud and rock imagery to describe the activities of Voltaire and Rousseau suggests a flaw in the cause of the people. They are against injustice, but they do not possess Vision: they will be as cruel in the cause of liberty and reason as the King has been in the cause of tyranny. This lies in the future, however.

The army begins its move. In the palace, the King is left to the coldness of death, expressed in images of newts, snakes, damp toads and crowned adders. When at last a faint heat revives the King and the peers they go forth to see Paris quiet and without a soldier while 'the Senate in peace, sat beneath morning's beam'.

We do not know whether Blake worked on the poem beyond the end of the first book. The visionary symbolism of this one is, however, rounded and complete: it may be that with the conclusion of it his inspiration failed for the time being. If so, the importance to him of the symbolism is merely confirmed. A knowledge of its working helps to disperse the rather heavy effects of the imagery. The many cosmic images and images of violence work quite differently in the mind of the reader when they are seen as precise symbols to interpret and explain the behaviour of the various protagonists in a national drama.

Blake probably felt some dissatisfaction with *The French Revolution*. The fact is that its cosmic imagery, however precisely deployed in the pattern of its symbolism, is also there as part of the narrative: its effects at a 'realistic' level cannot therefore be discounted. Blake may well have taken the method from the Debate in Hell in *Paradise Lost*, where imagery is used to a similar effect: but what is satisfactory in describing daemons for one episode is less satisfactory in describing the chief actors in a longer work. In addition, more speeches are constantly demanded in order that the myth may be advanced at all.

During succeeding years, Blake explored other ways of creating a relationship between history and an interpreting mythology. He would sometimes, for example, express the visionary dimension visually, by means of illuminations to his etched plates or by providing a pictorial frontispiece and title-page to a work. One important work of the time culminates in a more direct expression of his beliefs. *The Marriage of Heaven and Hell* concludes with 'A Song of Liberty', in which the struggle between single and twofold vision is cast into a political form.

'The Eternal Female groand!' it begins. The reason for her groaning is that she is about to bring forth a child of Energy. This new force is an emblem of hope, for it is infinite. To the visionless of this world, however, it is merely terrifying. The male-tyrannic England is sick at the sight, the female America faints in virgin fear. 'Shadows of Prophecy' meanwhile prophesy the overthrow of kingly tyranny in France and priestly tyranny in Spain and Italy.

The 'newborn terror' stands on the mountains of true vision ('those infinite mountains of light now barr'd out by the atlantic sea') confronting the 'starry king'. Like Pharaoh confronted by Moses, Herod confronted by tidings of a 'king of the Jews' or Milton's God confronted by Satan, this established tyrant of snowy cold and dark clouds cannot endure the idea of a fiery rival. He is an amalgam of the moral God of the Old Testament ('a jealous god') with the intellectual God of Newton's universe. The 'jealous wings' wave over the deep, 'the hand of jealousy among the flaming hair' goes forth, and the new-born wonder is hurled through the starry night of Urizen's universe. But as he falls into the western sea, it flees away; simultaneously the king and his councellors and weapons of war plunge down into ruins. The story of Reason casting out Desire, only to find that it, too, automatically falls, is thus repeated in terms of the story of the Exodus, when the sea parted to admit the Israelites but the pursuing Egyptians were destroyed. The Exodus story continues as a basis for the next verses, but its elements are re-formed according to Blake's own ideas. Instead of Moses, figure of Liberty, leading his people away from Pharaoh, the Urizen-tyrant, Urizen himself re-emerges to protect his universe of Law by leading his people through the wilderness away from Vision

> With thunder and fire: leading his starry hosts thro' the waste wilderness he promulgates his ten commands, glancing his beamy eyelids over the deep in dark dismay.

The God who gave the Ten Commandments to Moses is an ally of Pharaoh: for tyranny has many ways of establishing its dominion; the 'new born wonder' opposed to him, on the other hand, is identified with the visionary side of Moses, the prophet who stood in the fire of Sinai and later broke the tables of the law:

> . . . The son of fire in his eastern cloud, while the morning plumes her golden breast,
>   Spurning the clouds written with curses, stamps the stony law to dust, loosing the eternal horses from the dens of night, crying

EMPIRE IS NO MORE! AND NOW THE LION & WOLF SHALL CEASE.

The Song ends with a Chorus in which Blake once again turns on the hypocrisy of priests and tyrants, concluding with his favourite doctrine:

For every thing that lives is Holy

The confrontation which dominates the Song of Liberty is the germ of the next political writings. The 'new-born wonder' or 'new-born terror' is now given the name of Orc,[7] while the snowy tyrant assumes his familiar name of Urizen. Wherever revolution appears in the name of liberty, these two antagonists will be seen at the basis of the conflict. There is also a sexual implication, so far only distantly implied in the sickness of 'Albion's coast' and the fears of the 'American meadows'. We have seen how in *Visions of the Daughters of Albion*, Oothoon was called the 'soft soul of America' while Bromion cried 'Thy soft American plains are mine!' The political implication now moves into central place, to become the prime *motif* of *America*.

Blake's interweaving of his sexual and political doctrines is well shown in a fragment which he etched on a plate and later cancelled. It runs as follows:

As when a dream of Thiralatha flies the midnight hour:
In vain the dreamer grasps the joyful images, they fly
Seen in obscured traces in the Vale of Leutha, So
The British Colonies beneath the woful Princes fade.

And so the Princes fade from earth, scarce seen by souls of men,
But tho' obscur'd, this is the form of the Angelic land.[8]

The pictorial illustration in the plate can be divided into two parts. The one shows the figure of a mother and child, familiar to us as symbols of threefold vision and closely resembling the image of liberty in *Visions of the Daughters of Albion*; the other shows a man, his head buried in his lap, while above him the branch of a tree is thrust across, imprisoning him. Blake's editors have not usually tried to trace a relationship between words and design, suggesting rather that the two were made on separate occasions.

The relationship, which is indeed obscure, has to do with a curious piece of folk-lore which was still current in England in the eighteenth century. It was supposed that a jelly-like substance called Nostoc, sometimes found on the ground in the early morning, was connected with the appearance of shooting stars. In modern discussions on the subject, however, it is not explained *why* this curious association of ideas should have arisen. In order to find out, we may turn to Van Helmont's *Paradoxes* of 1650, where Nostoc is described, simply and plainly, as 'The nocturnall Pollution of some plethoricall and wanton star'.[9]

This clue helps to reveal the meaning of the whole fragment. Blake is reiterating his theme that among the men of his day the images of desire too often remained only images: they were not realized physically. The male who could have brought about a consummation of desire remained a lonely dreamer; Vision and Desire were separated.

This is true politically also. The relationship between Albion and America is compared directly with that between Theotormon and Oothoon. Because no full relationship has grown up between the two nations, America being exploited and used as a harlot by the tyranny that rules England, the chance of true political union has been lost. Britain, bound and shadowed by concepts of law and dominion, has become lost in fruitless and selfish dreams: as a result 'The British Colonies beneath the woeful Princes fade'. Yet the rift that has developed between the two countries is of no use to mankind. A full and fruitful marriage, on the other hand, would advance the cause of liberty and peace in the rest of the world: 'tho' obscur'd, this is the form of the Angelic land.'

When we turn to the prophetic book entitled *America*, we find this theme still active. Indeed, the Frontispiece (Fig. 28) is composed in the same style as the illustration to the fragment, an imprisoned male representing England, a mother and child representing America. The symbolism is here further developed. The male, who still has his head buried in his lap, is now depicted as an angel, obscured by the folding of his giant wings. The mother and child are not the joyful figures of the earlier design: the face of the mother, turned vaguely towards the angel, is anxious and careworn, while that of the child expresses an energy which is on the point of turning into lust and rebellion.

This design points to a development in the use of the image.

The separation between self-enclosed male and liberated mother and child appeared static. The separation between the 'failed angel' and the anxious mother with her lusty child, on the other hand, suggests a process in motion. Because the male has lost his true vision, the mother is deprived of the support which should be hers, while the child lacks a controlling pattern for the development of its natural energies. When it has grown stronger, it will break out in open, destructive revolt.

This idea is caught up in the Preludium to the poem, which introduces the new force of energy, 'red Orc', and confronts it with the 'shadowy Daughter of Urthona'. Orc expresses the revolutionary fervour which rises in America against the cold hand of British rule, while the 'shadowy Daughter' is woman at the ultimate point of her neglect. She still nourishes desire for her lost lover—is still wailing for the visionary glory which she subconsciously knows him to possess—but in his absence will yield instead to the fierce energies of Orc. She is depicted as a caricature of Britannia, a pestilential goddess of the waning moon:

> Crown'd with a helmet & dark hair the nameless female stood;
> A quiver with its burning stores, a bow like that of night,
> When pestilence is shot from heaven: no other arms she need:

The Preludium which introduces these two figures does not, as one might suppose, describe events which take place before those described in the rest of the poem. Its function is to provide another form by which Blake can gear history to mythology: he has isolated the fragment of his longer mythology which is relevant to the events about to be described.

An examination of the doctrines in the Preludium should warn us against accepting too readily the arguments of critics who would make us see *America* as a single-toned trumpet blast in favour of the American Revolution. Inasmuch as revolution is praised it is for the same reason that the Devils are praised in *The Marriage of Heaven and Hell*: twofold vision is always better than single. But the exercise of energy alone leaves many problems, which can only be resolved by reference to higher levels of vision.

The ambiguity of revolutionary activity is already present in the imagery. Orc has been chained to the rock by his father Los, the 'spectre' of Urthona.

This is our first introduction to Los, who plays an important part in later writings. At this stage in his writing, Blake evidently needed a figure to express more permanently the attitude of Burgundy in *The French Revolution*. We have already seen how the Spirit in the Garden, diminished by the loss of vision, becomes no more than a distant light, shining on a rocky shore. This polarity Blake expresses as the opposition between Urizen, principle of law, and Urthona, spirit of earth. Urthona is represented as having withdrawn, leaving only his spectre Los, who guards the lost vision without actually possessing it. Los is therefore another of Blake's ambivalent figures. He has the ambiguity of the sons of Cain who, according to tradition, built cities and wrought in metals. The name 'Cain' means a smith; it is as a smith that Los appears. Other myths are also relevant: he stands in a generic relationship with the Loki of northern mythology and the Vulcan of Roman lore. The fact that the mythological smith is sometimes represented as lame, moreover, falls in with Blake's idea that Los is only half in contact with the earth. Like the sons of Cain, he is building and making in an attempt to recreate the vision which is lost to man: in consequence his creativity will often take the form of blind construction, a desperate attempt to bind nature to the service of man. In terms of the mythology of the heavens Los is a sun-god of an unusual kind: his task is to beat the infinite energy at large in the universe into a single, blazing orb which can replace (if only as a poor substitute) the true sun of eternity. His most spectacular performance is also his most characteristic: always, in every conceivable way, for good or ill, he must be setting infinity on the anvil.

The conception of Los was to develop and expand in Blake's mind. To the end he remained morally ambiguous, but as Blake came to accept the limitations of the universe, Los became more and more a heroic figure. He was increasingly identified with the artist as the true redeemer of fallen human nature.

In *America*, however, Los is simply a jealous father, a Zeus to his son's Prometheus, determined to keep Orc bound to the rock of the law. His Urizenic loss of vision is stressed. The energies of Orc respond to their bondage by pressing down roots into the world of the law and then breaking forth, destroying and consuming that world as they do so. At present, however, Orc remains bound and the 'shadowy female' is appointed to bring him food in baskets of iron. She is clothed in iron; her very tongue is iron; she represents the transmutation of Urthona's realm of earth into a kingdom of single vision.

Orc speaks. He tells her how his energies are stirring within him—the energies of an eagle in the sky, a lion on the mountains, a whale in the fathomless abyss, a serpent folding 'around the pillars of Urthona, and round thy dark limbs . . . ' (the energies of twofold vision, expressed in terms of the four elements). When she brings his food, he says, he howls his joy, but he cannot see her because she is hidden by the clouds (of single vision).

Now he slowly breaks his fetters and seizes her loins: as he does so there is an image of clouds being transformed into lightning. Simultaneously, following the image, the Daughter changes from the virgin of single vision into the harlot of twofold vision. With her 'first-born smile' she regains something of her lost character as an earth-goddess:

> . . . she put aside her clouds & smiled her first-born smile:
> As when a black cloud shews its light'nings to the silent deep.

She sees him as a part of the image of her lost Angel—

> Thou art the image of God who dwells in darkness of Africa;
> And thou art fall'n to give me life in regions of dark death.

When Phaethon fell, according to Ovid, the Ethiopians turned black;[10] it was in Ethiopia, too, that the sons of God were said to have descended to make love to the daughters of men.[11] Both pieces of lore are at work, aiding the suggestion that the fallen angel expresses himself in his energies alone.

The same energies that Orc felt earlier are now felt by the shadowy female in the form of revolutionary movements in various parts of the world: the serpent in Canada; the eagle in Mexico; the lion in Peru; the whale in the South Seas. To her, however, they are not delights but rending pains: they are pangs not of birth but of death:

> O what limb rending pains I feel. thy fire & my frost
> Mingle in howling pains, in furrows by thy lightnings rent;
> This is eternal death: and this the torment long foretold.

Her words strike the necessary warning note. The energies of
revolution may remind man of his lost state; in themselves they
produce only destruction and pain.

The text of the poem proper now begins. Three pages with
which the poem originally began were cancelled, to be replaced
by those which now stand there. One possible reason for the
cancellation is that use of the actual name of George III in an
inflammatory context made it more liable to prosecution as
seditious. On the other hand, the 'King of England' is still
mentioned in the final text.

The original page 3 also has a number of manuscript correc-
tions, for example the following:

> silent stood the king breathing (with flames *del.*) (hoar frosts *del.*)
>   damp mists
> And on his (shining *del.*) aged limbs (*&*c)

In each case, a word which has to do with heat or light has been
changed to one which either denotes clouds, cold or darkness,
or else is neutral. It looks as though Blake had at this point
decided to sharpen the contrasts in his symbolism. Perhaps he
had originally intended to make the American War of Independence a battle between two figures of energy. At all events, he
now endows the champions of England with all the characteristics of single vision—cold and darkness—as compared with the
heat and energy of Orc in America. Orc fights with flames,
Albion's angels with cold pestilence.

In the poem this symbolism is reinforced by Blake's reshaping
of the Exodus story. While Orc is identified with the Moses who
broke in pieces the tablets of stone, the forces of England are
divided between the pillar of cloud (single vision) by day and the
fire (twofold vision) by night. The first of these belong to the
'Angels' who govern England, the second to the ironically
named 'Guardian' of Albion: the energies of England mustered
in defence of the state and its interests.

The warlike energies of the latter reflect the Energy of the
true 'Guardian Prince', however; they rouse Washington and

his companions, who 'meet on the coast glowing with blood from Albion's fiery prince'. Washington denounces the tyranny which oppresses them, a bended bow lifted in heaven, a heavy iron chain descending link by link. (Los's chain of jealousy, in fact.) As he does so, Albion's Prince appears in dragon form, a fiery figure through the cloudy night. The words 'Albion is sick! America faints!' echo 'A Song of Liberty'. But as in that poem, a new figure rises to confront the tyranny:

> And in the red clouds rose a Wonder o'er the Atlantic sea;
> Intense! naked! a Human fire fierce glowing, as the wedge
> Of iron heated in the furnace . . .

With this apparition, recognizable as Orc, the scene is totally possessed by twofold vision—'heat but not light went thro' the murky atmosphere'. Albion's Angel sees this vision and is reminded of

> the planet red
> That once inclos'd the terrible wandering comets in its sphere.
> Then Mars thou wast our center, & the planets three flew round
> Thy crimson disk; so e'er the Sun was rent from thy red sphere . . .

This curious piece of lore suggests that Blake is again postulating, at some point in the past mythology of the heavens, a sudden isolation of energy (corresponding to the fall of Milton's Satan or the creation of the Tyger) the destructiveness of which was later followed by a more merciful dispensation (the creation of the sun, moon and stars). (See Appendix One, Section 4.) This state is reproduced in the affairs of humanity whenever men resort to war.

The illustration to this plate is particularly interesting. At the foot flames leap up, with a serpent spiralling from their centre. A figure leans down, looking into the spirals of its coils. This vividly suggests the confrontation of the serpent of twofold vision and the angel of single vision who, unable to deal with it in terms of its energy, simply leans down to analyse it, not recognizing that its coils move in spirals (like the observations of the five senses) monotonously returning upon the same pattern. Above these figures float others carrying scales and sword, symbols of war and conventional justice. Another carries a human being on his back: he represents the honest man rescuing innocence.[12] The illustration as a whole perfectly matches the confrontation of two levels of vision in the text.

On the next page the voice of Orc proclaims the gospel of liberty. The illustration here, which is also relevant to the text, shows a man raising himself upon the hillock above the grave where he has been lying. Orc, meanwhile, is singing of a dawn in which the Resurrection of man takes place ('The grave is burst, the spices shed, the linen wrapped up'). The victims of oppression are coming into the open, unable to believe their eyes at the beauty of the world, singing the song of the 'son of fire' from 'A Song of Liberty':

> . . . Empire is no more, and now the Lion & Wolf shall cease.

Albion's Angel, recognizing Orc, denounces him as 'Lover of wild rebellion, and transgressor of God's Law.' Orc replies in defiant Exodus-imagery:

> The fiery joy, that Urizen perverted to ten commands,
> What night he led the starry hosts thro' the wide wilderness:
> That stony law I stamp to dust . . .

Religion he will scatter to renew the life of earth, that the desert may blossom and human beings be recognized in their individuality ('For everything that lives is holy, life delights in life . . .'). He concludes with a fourfold vision of man conceived as walking through the fires and not consumed—

> Amidst the lustful fires he walks: his feet become like brass,
> His knees and thighs like silver, & his breast and head like gold.

On the previous page, the angel's accusation that Orc 'stands at the gate of Enitharmon to devour her children' is counter-pointed by an ironic illustration, showing children asleep against the fleece of a sleeping ram while a willow tree, symbol of innocence, bends over the grass. So far from 'devouring' Enitharmon's children, the energies of Orc would cleanse the world without consuming them, leaving them in the Paradisal sleep of threefold vision.

The Angel of Albion is deaf to the praise of liberty, however, hearing in it only the voice of destruction and terror. As he peers across the Atlantic he is aware of darkness and fear.

When he seems to be on the point of seeing what is really there,
his vision fails him:

> . . . terrible men stand on the shores, & in their robes I see
> Children take shelter from the lightnings, there stands Washing-
> ton
> And Paine and Warren with their foreheads reard toward the east
> But clouds obscure my aged sight. A vision from afar!

He sees Orc as the self-renewing of the 'rebel form that rent the
ancient Heavens', the Eternal Viper, and refers to the eternal
ambiguity of Orc—the fact that though expected to be an
incarnation of Love he is born as Energy:

> Ah terrible birth! a young one bursting! where is the weeping
> mouth?
> And where the mothers milk? instead those ever-hissing jaws
> And parched lips drop with fresh gore . . .

The Angel can think only in terms of war. The Colonies remain
silent, but activity is taking place within the silence.

> On those vast shady hills between America & Albions shore;
> Now barr'd out by the Atlantic sea: call'd Atlantean hills:
> Because from their bright summits you may pass to the Golden
> world
> An ancient palace, archetype of mighty Emperies,
> Rears its immortal pinnacles, built in the forest of God
> By Ariston the king of beauty for his stolen bride.

The mountains of Atlantis are several times used by Blake as a
symbol for the lost mountains of sublime visionary art and
reason, now swamped by the sea of Time and Space. Ariston,
on the other hand, only appears in one other place, where he
seems to represent sexual energy. If so, this palace might be
supposed to celebrate the liberation of energy and to stand,
symbolically, as an eternal place of meeting for all who value
liberty in any form. Politically, it has the status of an ideal
democratic Parliament: one may indeed trace a curious
correspondence with an account of the English parliament which
occurs in one of the cancelled plates:

> In a sweet vale shelter'd with cedars, that eternal stretch
> Their unmov'd branches, stood the hall; built when the moon shot
> forth,

In that dread night when Urizen call'd the stars around his feet;
Then burst the center from its orb, and found a place beneath;
And Earth conglob'd, in narrow room, roll'd round its sulphur
    Sun.

In both accounts there is a hint that the forms of political
democracy are a *pis aller*, established after the fall from a better
state. (See Appendix One, Section 4.) In the American council
the representatives of American liberty meet to proclaim the
virtues of honesty and generosity and to condemn the restraints
by which they are prohibited from exercising their energies.
They complain that pity becomes a trade and generosity a
science from which men can gain profit, while the strong are
banished to the sandy desert. This Rintrah-like utterance is followed by a declaration that they will no longer follow the
hypocritical forces which preach one thing and do another.

'Boston's Angel', their spokesman, can probably be identified
as Samuel Adams;[13] and Erdman may well be right in thinking
that this speech of his is related to Adams's thunderous appeal
for Independence. As usual, however, the Declaration is being
restated in Blakean terms. The background to the appeal is
expressed in two illustrations, both of which portray experience
organized by innocence—the one showing a youth riding
through the night on a swan (a symbol of fourfold vision which
combines winged beauty with a serpentine neck) and the other
(previously used at the end of *Thel*) children playing with a
bridled serpent.

The main lines of the symbolism have been drawn and the
poem now follows history more closely in its details. The forces
are assembled: America's Guardian Angels face England's
tyrannical 'Guardian' and rational 'Angels'. The naked,
flaming lineaments of the former are seen standing by Washington, Paine and Warren; the inept thirteen English governors,
who have failed to rule justly the states of which they are
ironically seen as the embodied spirits, 'convene in Bernards
house'. (Governor Bernard had been such a byword for mis-
rule that the English themselves had agreed to withdraw him.)
The British soldiers lose heart, and Albion's angel, by way of
revenge, opens his secret clouds and rains down diseases upon
the abyss. But when the Americans rush together and rage in

fire the plagues recoil upon Albion. The link with history is tenuous at this point, as David Erdman shows, relating not to American history but to British.[14] In the reign of Edward III (the subject of Blake's early historical drama) aggressive wars were followed by the spread of the Black Death, which the historian Barnes regarded as a judgment upon the country. One may recall, in addition, the well-known piece of popular lore by which the Great Fire of London, following closely upon the Great Plague, was said to have cleansed the City.

Blake's primary concern as usual has less to do with history than with 'mental causes'. His illumination to the plate shows an eagle devouring a human corpse on the mountain-side and fishes preying on a human corpse at the bottom of the sea. Such are Albion's plagues: the energies which ought to be assisting the life of man are turned upon him in destruction. When the Americans reply, rising in their own flaming humanity and turning away the devourers, all the hypocrites of England, including the priests, the warriors and the 'Bard of Albion' (a reference, perhaps, to the sycophancy of the contemporary Poet Laureate, William Whitehead)[15] hide beneath scales and reptile coverts while the fires of youth play around the golden roof 'leaving the females naked and glowing with the lusts of youth'. (The illustrations show first a young man looking up from his books at a priestess with her serpent, (Fig. 29) then a youth burning in flames of energy.) Urizen emerges from the holy shrine where he has been hiding, bringing all his resources of snow, ice and sea-foam to conceal the red demon and reinforce his power. But soon France receives 'the Demons light'. When this happens, the traditional tyrannies, France, Italy and Spain, look with horror at England where the ancient guardians, weakened by their own plagues, are at work on their last line of defence, the closing of the five senses.

> They slow advance to shut the five gates of their law-built heaven
> Filled with blasting fancies and with mildews of despair
> With fierce disease and lust, unable to stem the fires of Orc . . .

This final attempt at defence is doomed to failure, for the five gates are themselves consumed by the fierce fires of Orc which now burn round the heavens and round the abodes of men. So the words of the 'nameless female' are fulfilled: the energies of Orc burn against the snows of Urizen to consume them. The illustration to the final page shows the danger to humanity finally vanquished. The tree of moral law lies, destroyed, by the figure of Urizen, who is stretched forward in peaceful death, his hair and beard floating downwards, while over him walk unconcernedly the small figures of ordinary people, like Swift's Lilliputians, or Spenser's village folk.[16]

At the foot of the page, in the position occupied by a serpent two pages before, is a plant, its flower where the serpent's mouth had been. This repeats a *motif* from a previous page where women are shown consuming in flames which at the top of the plate, turn into fruit and foliage. Sexual energy, rescued from inhuman lust, is being consumed into the flower of human passion. The link with *Visions of the Daughters of Albion* is thus confirmed at the end, as well as at the beginning of the poem.

The poem *Europe* extends the picture presented in *America*. It is constructed to the same design, an opening Preludium setting the events of the poem within the appropriate section of the larger mythological pattern; the symbolism here, however, is more complicated, more directly relevant to the imagery of the poem.

In terms of illumination, the book opens finely. The first design, one of Blake's best, shows Urizen leaning out of the blank disk of his sun and extending a great pair of compasses to create his universe in the darkness beyond. The design was reproduced again by Blake on several occasions (see Fig. 24). In one place it carries a quotation from the well-known passage in *Paradise Lost*:

In his hand
He took the Golden Compassess, prepared
In God's eternal store, to circumscribe
This Universe, and all created things.
One foot he center'd, and the other turn'd
Round through the vast profundity obscure,
And said, thus far extend, thus far thy bounds
This be thy just circumference, O World![17]

It also appears in the Notebook, along with the designs from which *The Gates of Paradise* is taken, bearing the legend (which appears also in *Europe*) 'Who shall bind the infinite?'[18]

The title-page of *Europe* counterpoints its frontispiece. The words of the title, and other details, are all enwrapped within the heaving coils of a vast, colourful serpent. Against the visionless reason of Urizen is pitted the vast and visionless energy of Orc: originally intended for the service of visionary Reason, it will be shown in this work pitted against the tyranny of law.

The illustration to the Preludium carries the theme a stage further. Round a corner comes the honest traveller whom we have already met as a symbol of the plain good man. Behind a rock crouches a low-foreheaded villain, ready to strike with his dagger and rob him. The best commentary on the design is found in three lines of *Milton*:

> . . . the idiot Questioner who is always questioning,
> But never capable of answering; who sits with a sly grin
> Silent plotting when to question, like a thief in a cave;[19]

The result of his attack is seen at the foot of the page, in a parody of a well-known Egyptian design. Instead of the sun with a serpent and wings sprouting from it, we see a human head that is throttled by a serpent wound round it; from the central circle stretch the wings, not of beautiful infinity but of the Spectre. At the side appears the final stage of degeneration: a human body drawn down, inverted, by a weight fixed to its head. On the opposite page a figure who resembles the 'idiot questioner' is seen fighting with two others in clouds and darkness, strangling the one and attempting to strangle the other. The well-known design of Laocoön may well be relevant here.

The Preludium to the poem carries on naturally from that to *America*. The 'nameless shadowy female' who was there seen yielding to the fierce embrace of Orc now rises from his breast, 'her snaky hair brandishing in the winds of Enitharmon'. The snaky hair, like that of Hela in *Tiriel*, associates her with Death.[20] She complains to Enitharmon that she has been destroyed by the fierceness of Orc's embraces:

> O mother Enitharmon wilt thou bring forth other sons?
> To cause my name to vanish, that my place may not be found,

For I am faint with travel!
Like the dark cloud disburdend in the day of dismal thunder.

The metaphor is closely drawn. She has not the substantial
life of the earth, but the shadowy life of a cloud: even that life
has been taken away from her in the lightnings of Orc and the
low thunder of Urizen. She sees herself as an inverted being,
her roots waving vainly in the heavens above while her fruits
come to life in the earth beneath, soon born and soon consumed.[21] Her lot thus cast between the reason of Urizen and
the energies of Orc, she is unable to deal with either. If she
tries to hide herself in the world of Reason, clothing herself in
thick clouds and sheety water, the energies of desire wreak their
revenge: 'The red sun and moon, / And all the overflowing
stars rain down prolific pains.' If, on the other hand, she
rebels against the dictates of Reason, and reaches out into the
world of Desire, the result is the birth of destructive children:

Unwilling I look up to heaven! unwilling count the stars!
Sitting in fathomless abyss of my immortal shrine.
I sieze their burning power
And bring forth howling terrors, all devouring fiery kings.
Devouring & devoured roaming on dark and desolate mountains
In forests of eternal death, shrieking in hollow trees.
Ah mother Enitharmon!
Stamp not with solid form this vig'rous progeny of fires . . .

The sons which she brings forth by her association with the
fires of Orc are pure energies of twofold vision. Like the Tyger,
they roam in forests and on mountains, destroying and being
destroyed in their restless untamed power. Once given form
by Enitharmon in this way, they leave their mother 'void as
death', 'drown'd in shady woe, and visionary joy'. She is
aware of their existence only as it is separate from her—they
bring her none of the joy of energies existing within her, but
merely emphasize her loss.

Even while voicing her complaint, however, she has a dim
vision of something else which she cannot comprehend at all.
The mention of 'visionary joy' hints at some further potentiality
in the twofold energy of her sons, and for a moment she half
grasps what it might be. The twofold contains the essence of
the fourfold: the energies which rage unbridled could be the

inner fire of a true humanity, living in vision and desire. But how this contradiction could happen is inconceivable to her:

> And who shall bind the infinite with an eternal band?
> To compass it with swaddling bands? and who shall cherish it
> With milk and honey?
> I see it smile & I roll inward & my voice is past.

She has had the sudden image of an infant god who is not destructive. Krishna was fed on milk by his maidens; the infant Zeus was given honey and the milk of the goat Amaltheia; and Isaiah prophesied of the Messiah, 'Butter and honey shall he eat . . .'[22] The swaddling bands carry a clear reference to the swaddling-clothes in which the infant Christ was clothed. But how the infinite can also be human she does not know; and when she sees it *smile*, her existence is finally finished. No one smiles in the world of Orc ('Did he smile his work to see?'): this is the stamp of integrated, 'fourfold' human lineaments, not of the impersonal twofold. Like Tiriel at the end of his vision, she declares 'my voice is past'. For if the infinite could become human in this way, then the warring worlds of twofold and single vision between which she lives would automatically be banished and their functions taken up into the full personality of man in fourfold vision, his reason and energies fulfilled.

So the Preludium ends,

> She ceast & rolld her shady clouds
> Into the secret place.

The implication of the last line is taken up in the opening lines of the poem proper, which is immediately recognizable as a pastiche of Milton's 'Ode to the Nativity':

> The deep of winter came:
> What time the secret child,
> Descended thro' the orient gates of the eternal day:
> War ceas'd, & all the troops like shadows fled to their abodes.

The word 'secret', twice repeated, gives the clue to Blake's irony. The child is *not* the infinite made human. He is the Christ whom the Christians worship, a figure of secrecy and shame; and the rest of the poem is a satirical account of the Christian era, dominated by this church-Christ (who is not to be confused with Blake's own view of the Christ revealed in the Gospels). With such a Christ there can be no fourfold vision. The moment of his birth is rather a time of threefold vision, of peaceful harmony under a quiet moon, and of prophecies of peace on earth under the dominion of Urizen; but the scene has all the fragility of threefold vision: a fragility summed up in the 'crystal house' of Enitharmon.

> And Los, possessor of the moon, joy'd in the peaceful night:
> Thus speaking while his num'rous sons shook their bright fiery
>   wings
> Again the night is come
> That strong Urthona takes his rest,
> And Urizen unloos'd from chains
> Glows like a meteor in the distant north
> Stretch forth your hands and strike the elemental strings!

On the surface all seems to be well; it is only in the imagery and side-reference that cause for doubt appears. Los is 'possessor of the moon', holding fast to threefold vision but having nothing to do with fourfold. And this possessive note is reinforced when he calls all his sons to

> Sieze all the spirits of life and bind
> Their warbling joys to our loud strings . . .

It is a pleasant form of binding, but it is, nonetheless, a binding. The theme is reiterated as Los calls upon Orc to arise.

> Arise O Orc from thy deep den,
> First born of Enitharmon rise!
> And we will crown thy head with garlands of the ruddy vine;
>   For now thou art bound:
> And I may see thee in the hour of bliss, my eldest born.

Orc, too, has been bound by his father, to be honoured as a tamed god of wine: the lost Dionysus, source of energy in man, appears in propitious times as the genial Bacchus. But he may also appear as a god of madness, causing men to tear each other in frenzy. This other side of Orc's nature is revealed as he rises to Los's command:

> The horrent Demon rose, surrounded with red stars of fire,
> Whirling about in furious circles round the immortal fiend.

While Los and his sons set themselves to the enjoyment of their captive pleasure, heedless of the lurking danger, an illustration to the plate shows a woman drawing a cloak over the child of vision, who lies prone on the ground, his head surrounded by light. He is the true god, of whom Orc is only a partial caricature.

In the next plate the results of Los's limited vision begin to show themselves. The failure of the male to provide a full life for the female results in her setting up a feminine dominion of her own, which will establish power over men as well.

Enitharmon, lit by the red light of Orc, speaks:

Now comes the night of Enitharmons joy!
Who shall I call? Who shall I send?
That Woman, lovely Woman! may have dominion?

Her action is paralleled in the development of early Church doctrine in favour of abstinence, accompanied by a growing cult of the Virgin. Enitharmon gives instructions to her messengers, Rintrah and Palamabron, to establish beliefs among the human race that will banish joy to a future state and to maintain a cult of secrecy that will reinforce the domination of woman over the human race:

Go! tell the Human race that Womans love is Sin!
That an Eternal life awaits the worms of sixty winters
In an allegorical abode where existence hath never come:
Forbid all Joy, & from her childhood shall the little female
Spread nets in every secret path.

The imagery which she uses for Rintrah and Palamabron is revealing. Rintrah is a 'lion', who is ordered to 'raise thy fury from thy forests black'. He has therefore some of the qualities of Blake's tyger, but his energy is more controlled. He is a 'king of fire': his kinship to the fallen sun of energy is confirmed when Enitharmon calls him 'prince of the sun'.

The sun-imagery for Rintrah is matched by moon-imagery for Palamabron and Elynittria. Palamabron, the 'horned priest, skipping upon the mountains' is like a moon-priest, carrying a representation of the moon on his hat; he is also like a ram or goat, skipping on the mountains. There is something ridiculous about him. His counterpart, 'silent Elynittria, the silver bowed queen' is a chaste Diana, quiet and defensive.

While the fallen sun and fallen moon give Rintrah and
Palamabron their permanent status as limited protagonists of
a ranging twofold vision and a fragile, timorous threefold
vision, the illustrations at this point suggest their contemporary
relevance. Rintrah is seen, a crowned mailed figure, seizing his
sword while angels look on in wonder and fear; Palamabron is
an aged priest-figure, taking no notice of the woman who clings
to him for protection but fearfully thrusting away some invisible danger. Blake thus embodies his charges against
contemporary statecraft and priestcraft. Rintrah is the state
which uses energy for the purpose of enforcing authority,
Palamabron the church which ignores the claims of charity at
home while busily repelling some ghostly enemy. The figures of
King and priest, repressive energy and impotent charity, are as
significant in the eighteenth century as in the time of Herod and
Caiaphas.

Having set these two in their positions of authority, Enitharmon falls asleep and man is left as a 'female dream' for eighteen
hundred years—the length of the Christian era. The result is a
decline in the joy of human existence:

> Shadows of men in fleeting bands upon the winds:
> Divide the heavens of Europe:
> Till Albions Angel smitten with his own plagues fled with his
> bands.

The 'smiting with his own plagues', a feature also of *America*,
seems here to refer to the decline of vision in the seventeenth
century. The picture is partly reminiscent of the plight of the
revolting angels in *Paradise Lost*: the smitten Angels gather in
council, but the council house falls upon them.

> One hour they lay buried beneath the ruins of that hall;
> But as the stars rise from the salt lake they arise in pain,
> In troubled mists o'erclouded by the terrors of strugling times.

An illustration shows two figures with horns blowing diseases
into a corn harvest (Fig. 47).

The Angels manage to rise from the 'bright ruins' of their
council house, but since they have lost their abode, they now
look for solid stability, like Burgundy in *The French Revolution*.[23]
They follow the fiery King,

> who sought his ancient temple serpent-formd
> That stretches out its shady length along the Island white.
> Round him roll'd his clouds of war; silent the Angel went,
> Along the infinite shores of Thames to golden Verulam.

The mention of a serpent-formed temple shows us what is happening. Robbed of their palace of vision, the angels are falling back on Druid solidity, based on law and lack of vision. And the mention of 'Verulam' gives historic detail to the picture. The 'Druid solidity' will now be established upon the basis of the empirical philosophy of Francis Bacon, Lord Verulam, which will enable the rule of law to be extended to the physical world as well as to the race of men. A further passage describes the pillars of stone, surrounded by oaks, which they find there, reflecting the order of the stars. These were placed there when man ceased to see the world 'through' his eyes and began to make his own analytic mind the centre of all things, producing a static world of laws instead of a universe which everywhere revealed the infinite. This was the mental 'deluge', when man was overwhelmed by his own five senses:

> then turn'd the fluxile eyes
> Into two stationary orbs, concentrating all things.
> The ever-varying spiral ascents to the heavens of heavens
> Were bended downward; and the nostrils golden gates shut
> Turn'd outward, barr'd and petrify'd against the infinite.

The result of this fall was to change the nature of the universe. Fourfold vision was turned into twofold, losing in the process that threefold vision which had tempered its energy: the spirit armed in gold became the tiger, the sun-god of love was turned into Orc.

> Thought chang'd the infinite to a serpent; that which pitieth:
> To a devouring flame; and man fled from its face and hid
> In forests of night . . .

Against this menace of infinite energy man set up an image of infinity under rational control—the serpent formed into neat coils, the world a machine obeying strict laws, the tyrant imposing his will:

> Then was the serpent temple form'd, image of infinite
> Shut up in finite revolutions, and man became an Angel;
> Heaven a mighty circle turning; God a tyrant crown'd.

So was established the basis of the seventeenth-century world-picture, with its exaltation of the absolute monarch and the mathematical astronomer, each reflecting the ideas of the other. Law was triumphant. The King now leads his followers to

> the southern porch,
> That planted thick with trees of blackest leaf, & in a vale
> Obscure, inclos'd the Stone of Night . . .

This stone (related, probably, to the Stone on which Jacob rested his head when he saw his vision of heaven and earth with angels ascending and descending[24]) is all that remains of the Divine Vision. Man has shut up his faculties until they are no longer translucent. The Stone stands, a substitute for the human head in its true glory:

> . . . oblique it stood, o'erhung
> With purple flowers and berries red; image of that sweet south,
> Once open to the heavens and elevated on the human neck,
> Now overgrown with hair and coverd with a stony roof.
> Downward 'tis sunk beneath th'attractive north, that round the feet
> A raging whirlpool draws the dizzy enquirer to his grave.

The imagery thus swings back towards a familiar pattern—that of the lost Spirit in the Garden. The literary references here range from Shakespeare's 'sweet south,/That breathes upon a bank of violets,/Stealing, and giving odour' to the Song of Solomon: 'Awake, O north wind; and come, thou south; blow upon my garden, that the spices thereof may flow out . . .'[25] The 'attractive north' has an ideal polar magnetism without the polar coldness and remoteness. But the once-open south has hardened to a rock, while the once-present spirit has fled away to become a distant star in the sky, around which other stars move in circles. These circles are studied by the astronomer until they become a whirlpool in which he loses his true vision of the universe. He becomes the figure looking down into the receding coils of the serpent, a man of single vision. Between Scylla, the rock of hardened vision, and Charybdis, the whirlpool of analytical reasoning, Man is lost. The page (Europe 13) is illustrated, economically and tellingly, by the figure of a serpent, spiralling down from top to bottom of the page and crowned by a fierce head from which the tongue flames forth. The danger that threatens when Reason and Energy are isolated is thus kept before the reader.

The next plate in Blake's book has a very short and simple text, recounting the establishment of the Law:

> Albions Angel rose upon the Stone of Night.
> He saw Urizen on the Atlantic;
> And his brazen Book,
> That Kings & Priests had copied on Earth
> Expanded from North to South.

At the foot of the page stand two angels who bend down their wands to touch and form a single star, all that remains of Vision. Above, obscured by clouds, sits Albion's Angel in the form of a fat canting priest, his book open upon his knees, the triple-crown of the Pope upon his head, spectre-wings sprouting from his shoulders, a church-window behind.

The rock of hardened vision is now positively established as the massive Rock of the Law. The next plate in Blake's text shows life in a world dominated by Urizen and his laws. A figure lies on the ground surrounded by netting; above it spiders and insects stretch their webs everywhere. The text describes a London in which all are captives. Parents take their children to the vast rock where 'aged ignorance preaches, canting'. They see the whole island overshadowed by the serpent temple. But they are also aware of flames licking round the feet of Albion's Angel. The fires of Orc are beginning to attack him: and in his pain he will look for the trumpet of the Last Judgment.

In this apocalyptic atmosphere strange visions are seen. The guardian of the secret codes is driven out by the flames of Orc:

> . . . his furr'd robes & false locks
> Adhered and grew one with his flesh, and nerves & veins shot
> thro' them . . .

This grotesque 'unhappy hypocrite' is terrifying even to the soldiers, who flee as he drags himself off to the wilderness. Palamabron and Rintrah continue their work remorselessly, their lightning and thunder springing from the clouds of Urizen and establishing the dominion of Enitharmon and Woman.

Every house is a den, every man bound; prohibitions are inscribed everywhere.

At the same time, however, the flames are gaining upon the
limbs of Albion's guardian, until in his horror and torment he
seizes the trumpet of the Last Judgment. Unexpectedly, the
scene changes to high comedy.

> The red limb'd Angel siez'd, in horror and torment:
> The Trump of the last doom; but he could not blow the iron tube!
> Thrice he assay'd presumptuous to awake the dead to Judgment.

A mighty spirit comes to his rescue. What he could not perform
is done by Newton, who blows the blast which sends myriads of
Angelic hosts, like leaves of Autumn, falling through the skies.
The symbolic implication is clear. The discoveries of Newton,
by their exaltation of Law, have offered no challenge to the
existing systems of tyranny. But they are not indissolubly
bound to such systems: on the contrary, their exaltation of
Reason has also encouraged revolutionary ideals of the brotherhood of man which work against tyranny. The process which
began in confirming the tyrants is also assisting their future
overthrow. A design at the foot of the page (Fig. 49) shows a
chained figure, recognizably Blake's Newton, sitting in prison
and looking with alarm at a plague-spotted figure who is disappearing up the stairs from his cell. The religious Newton
could not foresee the extent to which his deification of Law
would first establish doubt and despair and then, by the natural
course of events, stimulate rebellion.

At this moment of judgment, when the Western clerical
tradition is relinquishing its dominance, Enitharmon wakes
again, not knowing that she has been asleep, and calls all her
sons and daughters around her to the sports of night. (There
may be a side-reference here to the demands by women for
advanced status which accompanied the movements for freedom.) As always, her main preoccupation is that Woman shall
have power: her song to her children shows, as she names each
one in turn, that each represents some different form of female
dominion over the male.

> Arise Ethinthus! tho' the earth-worm call;
> Let him call in vain;

Till the night of holy shadows
And human solitude is past!

Ethinthus queen of waters, how thou shinest in the sky:
My daughter how do I rejoice! for thy children flock around
Like the gay fishes on the wave, when the cold moon drinks the
 dew.
Ethinthus! thou art sweet as comforts to my fainting soul:
For now thy waters warble round the feet of Enitharmon.

Ethinthus is like Blake's Thel, who hesitated to enter the earth. Her symbol is the moon shining apart: virtuous but cold. From her detachment she showers pity and kindliness upon her children and receives nourishment from their response; but the 'earth-worm' calls in vain. She remains aloof from the energies of physical desire.

Her song continues,

Manathu-Varcyon! I behold thee flaming in my halls,
Light of thy mothers soul! I see thy lovely eagles round:
Thy golden wings are my delight, & thy flames of soft delusion.

Manathu-Varcyon seems to be the male counterpart to Ethinthus. While she remains in the moonlight of threefold vision, he has the male splendour of the eagle, the golden, flamy beauty of fourfold vision. But since he remains apart, a 'soft delusion', Ethinthus' dominion is not challenged.

Where is my lureing bird of Eden! Leutha silent love!
Leutha, the many coloured bow delights upon thy wings:
Soft soul of flowers   Leutha!
Sweet smiling pestilence! I see thy blushing light:
Thy daughters many changing,
Revolve like sweet perfumes ascending   O Leutha silken queen!

Where is the youthful Antamon, prince of the pearly dew,
O Antamon, why wilt thou leave thy mother Enitharmon?
Alone I see thee crystal form,
Floting upon the bosomd air:
With lineaments of gratified desire.
My Antamon the seven churches of Leutha seek thy love.

Leutha stands in direct contrast to Ethinthus, representing strong sexual attraction—the beauty of the rainbow or of coloured plumage, the sensual appeal of perfumes and silk. But

she too is an instrument of feminine dominion and so Enitharmon calls her a 'sweet smiling pestilence'. She can attract and
satisfy the senses of man, but uses this means to establish her
supremacy over him. Her lover, Antamon, is at present floating
upon the 'bosom'd air' with 'lineaments of gratified desire'
(Blake's imagery is particularly well wrought at this point).
Enitharmon, seeing the danger that he will escape altogether
from female domination, recalls him to further sexual activity.
Her call, 'the seven churches of Leutha seek thy love', with its
implied reference to the 'seven churches of Asia' in Revelation,[26] may carry a satirical side-glance at the theory that where
Occidental peoples suffer commonly from sexual shame,
Oriental peoples are more liable to be enervated by sexual
over-activity.[27]

> I hear the soft Oothoon in Enitharmons tents:
> Why wilt thou give up womans secrecy my melancholy child?
> Between two moments bliss is ripe:
> O Theotormon robb'd of joy, I see thy salt tears flow
> Down the steps of my crystal house.

Oothoon, as in *Visions of the Daughters of Albion*, is the innocent
virgin who longs for sexual liberty but finds herself under the
dominion of Urizen's law. It is in the language of Urizen that
Enitharmon appeals to her not to give up secrecy. With prudence and reason she argues that sexual bliss only comes to
ripeness 'between two moments' and is therefore not worth
possessing in a world of time. Blake's irony is evident: it is an
essential part of his beliefs that eternity is revealed 'between
two moments'—and in that revelation judges and illuminates
the whole of time. But Theotormon, refusing to accept the experience which might give him that brief revelation, remains
'robb'd of joy', a slave to the world of reason and calculation.

> Sotha & Thiralatha, secret dwellers of dreamful caves,
> Arise and please the horrent fiend with your melodious songs.
> Still all your thunders golden hoofd, & bind your horses black.
> Orc! smile upon my children!
> Smile son of my afflictions.
> Arise O Orc and give our mountains joy of thy red light.

With these two we reach the final sexual states induced by the
moral law. The male, left with dreamful images in place of

gratified desires, turns his energies towards violence and death. And by a familiar psychological process, war and violence themselves come to exercise a dangerous, quasi-erotic attraction over the dwellers in such a civilization.

As she calls Sotha and Thiralatha, Enitharmon seems dimly to grasp the flaw in her basic assumptions. The afflictions of her children necessarily suggest that something is unfulfilled in woman's condition. In each of these relationships there is lacking a visionary power that would restore it to its true status. Her moonlit landscape and crystal house need to be replaced by the dayspring and splendid sun-palace which would mark the presence of true love in man. And Enitharmon betrays an awareness of the insufficiency of her world: she calls upon Orc, the only manifestation of sun-like energy available to her, to give his red light to the scene.

But the ambiguity of Dionysus shows itself again. Orc's red light is the light not of dawn but of fury. Nor can he be contained as a genial Bacchus:

> But terrible Orc, when he beheld the morning in the east,
> Shot from the heights of Enitharmon;
> And in the vineyards of red France appear'd the light of his fury.

Orc, no simple tempering god of Love but a destructive fire, shows himself in unrestrained power. As the French Revolution breaks forth, the sun that shines is a sun of twofold vision, giving out heat alone; the energies released are those of wrathful lions and tigers. Enitharmon is aghast at the results of her summons, while Los can see no way of establishing the order which he wants except by taking up similar weapons:

> Then Los arose his head he reard in snaky thunders clad:
> And with a cry that shook all nature to the utmost pole,
> Call'd all his sons to the strife of blood.

Like *America*, *Europe* ends with violence: the honest man is forced to it as a last resort. But this use of his energies is a poor substitute for the vigorous, free pursuit of peaceful industry which is his natural right.

During the writing of these books the character of Los emerged more and more powerfully in Blake's imagination.

From being a toiler in the furnace, the strong man left to deal with the consequences of Urizen's rule, the Samson blinded but slowly renewing his strength, he was coming to be the hero of the myth.

The movement in Blake's mind is well shown by the fact that instead of rounding off his present series of political interpretations by writing two more books entitled *Africa* and *Asia*, he wrote one more short book, entitled *The Song of Los*, in which the names of the two latter continents appear above the two sections. Where *America* and *Europe* contained sizeable segments of human history, this further book, though brief in compass, comes nearer to an account of human history as a whole. Los, as the singer of the *Song*, is now of higher importance. He becomes, and is described as, 'the Eternal Prophet'.

The mythology of this book is extremely compressed, but a patient look at the contents is of assistance in seeing the development of Blake's symbolism. As always, a dialectic is involved, but now it has more intimate associations with the human body. The figure of Urizen is firmly established as a symbol of fallen vision, but Blake is finding greater difficulty in establishing a suitable adversary for him. In this poem he attempts to achieve his end by bringing in the figure of Ariston, hardly used elsewhere, to represent the genitals. (The Greek word ἄριστον means 'best'.) Thus it becomes possible to represent the fall of man as a separation between head and genitals, and to argue that it was the failure of the human heart which resulted in the break.

This symbolism could be extended in biblical terms. Noah, guiding his ark over the waters of the Deluge, was for Blake a symbol of the guardianship of the Divine Vision. Similarly, Adam's failure in the garden could be seen as a fall from love to lust (—as Jacob Boehme had conceived it).[28] The mountains of vision are clouded or covered with snow, the garden of love is burnt into a desert. So a new paradigm emerges, to express the tragic separation; the ideal harmony could be expressed thus:

Man	head	mountains of light
	heart	water and fire (sun-fountain)
	genitals	garden of Eden

This ideal interlocking harmony separates, through the 'flood of the senses' and conflagration of the destructive heart, to

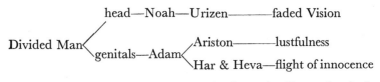

head—Noah—Urizen————faded Vision

Divided Man

genitals—Adam

Ariston————lustfulness

Har & Heva—flight of innocence

while the lost energy of Luvah in the heart is glimpsed only in the rise of Orc.

Once this paradigm is grasped, *The Song of Los* gives little difficulty. Africa, itself shaped like a heart, becomes representative of the disaster that has overtaken man. (It was in Ethiopia that the Angels were supposed to have fallen).

> I will sing you a song of Los. the Eternal Prophet:
> He sung it to four harps at the tables of Eternity.
>   In heart-formed Africa.
> Urizen faded! Ariston shudderd!
> And thus the Song began . . .

The fading of Urizen, prince of light, and the shuddering of Ariston, prince of love, is repeated in the next section in the persons of Noah and Adam respectively.

> Adam stood in the garden of Eden:
> And Noah on the mountains of Ararat;
> They saw Urizen give his Laws to the Nations
> By the hands of the children of Los.

> Adam shudderd! Noah faded! black grew the sunny African
> When Rintrah gave Abstract Philosophy to Brama in the East . . .

As Rintrah and Palamabron continue to spread various forms of abstract philosophy, men become steadily less able to cope with the forms of energy. The African is forced to become black in protection against the heat (in one of the *Songs of Innocence* the little black boy promises to shield the white boy until he can 'learn to bear the beams of love').[29] Meanwhile, the Deluge of the senses forces Noah to escape, while Adam turns into the Abraham who fled from the city of destruction (a form of the story of Har and Heva). With light extinguished and love feared, only the forms of Law are left to guide man:

Noah shrunk beneath the waters;
Abram fled in fires from Chaldea;
Moses beheld upon Mount Sinai forms of dark delusion . . .

The growth of abstract philosophy, already established in the
East, now spreads to the west:

To Trismegistus, Palamabron gave an abstract Law:
To Pythagoras Socrates & Plato.

This reference to Greek thought reminds us that the tradition of
divine 'jealousy' exists not only in the ambiguity of the literal
text of the Ten Commandments ('I the Lord thy God am a
jealous God') but specifically in the myth of Prometheus. And
the occasional awakening of a voice in favour of freedom in love
is unanswered: the gospel of Christ, for all its charity and insight, is lacking in encouragement for physical love. So Orc is
left to howl in his bonds and Oothoon receives no fulfilment
from Theotormon.

Times rolled on o'er all the sons of Har, time after time
Orc on Mount Atlas howld, chain'd down with the Chain of
   Jealousy
Then Oothoon hoverd over Judah & Jerusalem
And Jesus heard her voice (a man of sorrows) he recievd
A Gospel from wretched Theotormon.

The negative note in Christianity is reinforced by the establishment of ecclesiastical organizations and a growing cult of
virginity. Where any attempt is made to provide a place for
sexual energy, moreover, the form of expression becomes perverted. In Mohammedan countries, an exaggerated cult of
eroticism (encouraged by certain passages in the Koran) leads
to enervation and lack of spiritual awareness. In the north, on
the other hand, rigid abstinence leads to a side-tracking of
energy into the ways of death, resulting in a cult of violence and
war:

The human race began to wither, for the healthy built
Secluded places, fearing the joys of Love
And the disease'd only propagated:
So Antamon call'd up Leutha from her valleys of delight:
And to Mahomet a loose Bible gave.
But in the North, to Odin, Sotha gave a Code of War,
Because of Diralada thinking to reclaim his joy.

As in *The Mental Traveller*, the circumscribing of vision and desire leads men to try to perpetuate these goods in some tangible form—but without the sustaining spirit which would make them truly valuable and ensure their survival.

> These were the Churches: Hospitals: Castles: Palaces:
> Like nets & gins & traps to catch the joys of Eternity
>   And all the rest a desart;
> Till like a dream Eternity was obliterated & erased.

In order to explain how War and Lust result in the loss of vision, the story of Har and Heva is told. These two innocents, fleeing from such terrifying phenomena, enact the myth of Cadmus and Harmonia: they automatically cut themselves off from the energies of twofold vision, lapsing into the impotence of single vision.

> Since that dread day when Har and Heva fled.
> Because their brethren & sisters liv'd in War & Lust;
> And as they fled they shrunk
> Into two narrow doleful forms:
> Creeping in reptile flesh upon
> The bosom of the ground:
> And all the vast of Nature shrunk
> Before their shrunken eyes.

So the sons of Har become enslaved to the law until the logical conclusion of legalism is brought about in the evolution of a philosophy of the five senses by Newton and Locke. When this happens, the intellectual life of Europe and Asia alike is finally blighted, while in Africa the fallen Angels witness to the loss of desire in its glory, leaving only the creativity of the 'Guardian Prince', burning in its prophetic fires.

> Clouds roll heavy upon the Alps round Rousseau & Voltaire:
> And on the mountains of Lebanon round the deceased Gods
> Of Asia; & on the desarts of Africa round the Fallen Angels
> The Guardian Prince of Albion burns in his nightly tent

The last line is probably the subject of the full-page illustration on the next page, which shows a bearded man sitting with a reclining woman in the petals of a giant flower, keeping watch in the starry night.

The second section, 'Asia', takes place after the revolt of Orc

against the situation at the end of the previous one. As the fires
of Orc race across Europe, their light is seen in Asia, and the
ancient kings of the continent respond to the threat in the same
way as the English rulers: their solution is to impose their restraints and controls more heavily and ingeniously than before.
The King and Priest will call for Famine and Pestilence respectively 'to restrain! to dismay! to thin!' The Chancellor will
find ways and means to curb prosperity—'To fix the price of
labour;/To invent allegoric riches . . . ', sinister fires will be
started in the city in the 'night of prosperity & wantonness'—
all to ensure that men may lose life and have it less abundantly.

> To turn man from his path,
> To restrain the child from the womb,
> To cut off the bread from the city,
> That the remnant may learn to obey,
>
> That the pride of the heart may fail;
> That the lust of the eyes, may be quench'd;
> That the delicate ear in its infancy
> May be dull'd; and the nostrils clos'd up;
> To teach mortal worms the path
> That leads from the gates of the Grave.

But the result of their policy is that the laws of Eternity begin to
take their inexorable course. Those who seek to save their lives
will lose them; those who turn from the gates of the grave will
find themselves flung there by a more violent way.

Urizen, hearing the voice of the Kings of Asia, begins to
despair and flies through the heavens, his books melting as he
does so. He stretches his clouds over Jerusalem, the holy city
from which revelation ought to come, but which is lifeless—

> For Adam, a mouldering skeleton
> Lay bleach'd on the garden of Eden;
> And Noah as white as snow
> Upon the mountains of Ararat.

Over this dead world bellow the thunders of Urizen. His cloud
is answered, as in Blake's version of the Exodus story,[30] by a
pillar of fire. The fire, however, is the raging energy of Orc,
pitted against the darkness of Urizen 'like a serpent of fiery
flame'. As with Har and Heva, the response of the Earth is a

peevish withdrawal towards single vision—'The sullen Earth/ Shrunk!'

But there comes an apocalyptic moment in which the fires of Orc reveal all life in its true holiness:

> Forth from the dead dust rattling bones to bones
> Join: shaking convuls'd the shivring clay breathes
> And all flesh naked stands: Fathers and Friends;
> Mothers and Infants; Kings & Warriors:

The revolution produces vision merely because it brings about a premature consummation of human life, however. Instead of coming to the grave each in his due time, men are forced there in droves in the prime of life. The usual sexual double-play is present. What might have been a renewed marriage between Spirit and Earth is represented instead as a great orgy between the Nameless Shadowy Female (here personifying the Grave), and Orc, the destructive energy unleashed in the revolution. The Grave no longer receives men when their bodies are ripe for death (an analogue of normal intercourse) but participates in a great orgy of lust, as revolution brings a release of destructive cosmic energy:

> The Grave shrieks with delight, & shakes
> Her hollow womb, & clasps the solid stem:
> Her bosom swells with wild desire:
> And milk & blood & glandous wine
> In rivers rush & shout & dance,
> On mountain, dale and plain.

The poem ends with this great worldwide orgy, created by the revolutionary fires. Los, who lives in the world of energy, can delight in the events to the end, for he knows no other vision:

> The SONG of LOS is Ended.

But for Urizen, who, despite his laws and restraints, retains vestigially the original vision and knows that this is not what was intended for man in Eternity, there is in the scene only a great sorrow:

> Urizen Wept.

6 The Descending Vision

The 'short-circuiting' effect which is a feature of *The Song of Los* corresponds to a change in Blake's main field of interest. The over-compression of symbolism in that work is a sign that symbolic thinking was becoming his major concern. He wished to take mythological incidents such as those which had formed the Preludia to *America* and *Europe* and weave them into the longer narrative of an epic poem.

The results of this long endeavour are to be found in the long manuscript poem known as *Vala, or The Four Zoas*. A full account of the interrelated successes and failures of that work belongs to the story of Blake's more extended myth-making, culminating in *Jerusalem*, and cannot be given here. It is enough to say that for the purposes of the poem Blake took the figures of Urizen and Luvah and added two others, Tharmas and Urthona, to create a cycle of four Zoas (or human faculties) which had originally formed a cyclical whole in the body of Eternal Man but which by a cosmic dislocation (referred to as 'the sleep of the Eternal Man') had become separated and at war with one another. The story of the poem is that of their struggles and final reconciliation when the Eternal Man rises again to his proper stature.

The poem is a heroic attempt to write the first psychological epic. For various reasons it was not completed, and the failure was accompanied by symptoms of stress in Blake's health. His removal to Felpham in Sussex in 1800 was the occasion of a letter to John Flaxman in which he spoke of 'Nervous Fear'[1] and of others in which he spoke of his hope that Felpham would be propitious to the arts and that he would be able to work there with greater pleasure than ever.

The success and failure of *Vala* marked a crucial stage of Blake's development in several ways. In the poem Los, the representative of Urthona and the one surviving positive force among the fallen Zoas, finally emerged as a great heroic figure.

This evolution was matched by a change in Blake's own attitude. He began to suspect his own tendency to passivity and to assert his own individuality more vehemently. His preoccupation with the dislocation within an Eternal Man gave place to a new assertion of the importance of the artistic Genius as the true redeemer of mankind. At Felpham this urge to self-assertion was encouraged by a growing suspicion of Hayley, his patron there. Hayley's condescension to Blake, couched as it was in a winning amiability, proved a considerable irritant. Although at first referred to in a poem as 'the bless'd Hermit',[2] he became the object of some of his bitterest personal epigrams. Blake came to feel that Hayley's combination of an effeminate nature with a failure to grasp the nature of true artistic genius deserved an extension of his mythology to itself. He would, once and for all, denounce this type of 'humaneness' and assert his own humanism, which was rooted in the assertion by each man of his own masculine genius and his recognition of the genius in other men.

Blake's bitterness grew with the years, as he found himself isolated even in London and subject to the prevarications of his friends. One of his constant themes during these years was the assertion that Corporeal Friends were Spiritual Enemies. And when such duplicity threatened his whole livelihood his exasperation grew. About 1810 he wrote a Public Address in defence of his art which included the words, ' . . . & the manner in which I have routed out the nest of villains will be seen in a Poem concerning my Three years Herculean Labours at Felpham which I will soon Publish. Secret Calumny & open Professions of Friendship are common enough all the world over but have never been so good an occasion of Poetic Imagery.'[3] It has been supposed that the poem *Milton* is here referred to. It may be: but if so, it would be foolish to mistake Blake's enthusiasm for a detailed account of his poem. The theme of secret calumny and open friendship is certainly there, and one or two passages echo the Hayley epigrams. In one of the latter he writes:

Thy Friendship oft has made my heart to ake
Do be my Enemy for Friendships sake[4]

In *Milton* we read,

And in the midst of the Great Assembly Palamabron pray'd:
O God, protect me from my friends, that they have not power
   over me
Thou hast giv'n me power to protect myself from my bitterest
   enemies.[5]

Yet it is as unprofitable to look for a series of specific personal
events in *Milton* as it is to look for specific historical happenings
in the earlier prophetic books. It is always Blake's way to
generalize from the particular, and what he has to say about the
relationship between friendship and enmity in *Milton* is intended
to stand as a universal commentary on what happened to him at
Felpham, not as a detailed record of it.

The main effect of these events, so far as his poetry is concerned, is that Blake becomes less interested than before in
communication. He becomes more the 'pig-headed' Blake of
the Epigrams and the Public Address, confident of his own
rightness and no longer concerned whether he is understood or
not. There is even an indication that he composes sometimes in
a trance-like state, allowing his poetry to come to him as it will
and exercising less control over what part of it he puts into the
published version.[6]

Yet, paradoxically, a greater consistency of style begins to
show itself. Whatever the level of communication, however
irritating the obscurities, there is an intangible homogeneity of
style which is readily grasped by those who become familiar
with Blake's way of writing. It is as though the 'visionary' style
is now an organism in its own right, failing to communicate
precise meaning at some points, but true to itself and to its own
imaginative organization. If appreciation of the later books is
sometimes a nebulous experience, it also has a subterranean
intensity.

This is not to say that *Milton* has no plot. It has a general
story running through it, of which the construction is an improvement upon the overloaded organization of *The Four Zoas*.
There the three main elements in the poem were the Fall of
the Zoas, the struggle between Urizen and Orc, and the Reawakening of Man. In more general terms, these could be
identified with The Fall, Revolution and Redemption. It will
be observed that the second of these themes has no necessary

relationship with the other two. Only under the shadow of the French Revolution and in the apocalyptic atmosphere of the 1790s did it seem natural to link all three together. When the revolutionaries had proclaimed their atheism and crowned a whore, the pious of the age had seen in the event that union of the Beast and the Scarlet Woman which was the biblical signal of the Apocalypse. But as the century turned, with no sign from heaven, apocalyptic fervour died. Those for whom faith in the Revolution and hope of freedom had been replaced by the dull certainty of continuing restraint began to look for some principle which would enable them to reassert their belief in liberty during the years that lay ahead,

The three major poets of the day all found their thoughts turning in the same direction. Was not the seventeenth century in England the period which had seen the greatest flowering of liberty so far known to man? Coleridge thought so, and turned more and more to the authors of that century for his inspiration. And did not one particular figure of that century stand out as offering the union of liberty, godliness and poetic inspiration by which England might still regain her true stature in the world? Wordsworth thought so, and wrote a sonnet beginning, 'Milton, thou shouldst be living at this hour!'

Blake was drawn to Milton even more strongly. His early poetry, culminating in *Vala*, had betrayed a minor obsession with *Paradise Lost* and a desire to recast the symbolic elements of that poem into a new pattern. Now he took a further step. Re-enacting a familiar argument, he had come to the conclusion that the hero of the poem was not Adam, or Satan, or the Son of God, or even God the Father, but Milton himself. An epic poem devoted to the Fall can have no hero: the only possible hero is the poet who creates the Fall and shows it to the world. He is humanity's hero, the inspired Bard who tames Chaos.

This conclusion once established, other changes in the Miltonic pattern followed naturally. The incidents which had long fascinated Blake, the eruption of Satan from Hell and his journey through Chaos, coupled with the parallel offer of the Son in Heaven to redeem man, were now brought together into a single decision by Milton, among the Eternals, to journey to Man and once again proclaim the Truth. Blake's poem would be the story of that heroic journey, followed by the resurgence of Milton into the world, after the lapse of a century, in the person of Blake himself.

For the purposes of this poem, therefore, the story of the Fall was put into the background. The Zoas are heard of only fitfully; instead, Blake ascribed the precipitating error to two figures whom he had always used to express the specific eighteenth-century situation, Rintrah and Palamabron. Their nature, of course, reflects a more important lapse in the Eternal Man, but that is referred to only occasionally. It is their particular error which is in question and which must be dealt with by this reincarnated Milton, William Blake.

The story of the Fall of the Zoas is still present in the background, but Blake's new poem suggests that he is moving away from apocalyptic fervour. The Fall remains a fact, together with the potentiality of the Apocalypse, but it is no longer to be assumed that judgment is imminent. It is more important to perceive the right thing to do in the present situation.

Seen in this light, Blake's identification of himself with Milton is not presumptuous. It actually marks a retreat from the position of absolute prophet to a recognition that in each age there exists a specific task for the inspired bard in the unending battle of truth against error. Blake's new position corresponds with that of those early Christians who were forced to recognize that the return of Christ would probably not, after all, take place in their lifetime, and that since, in one sense, the Judgment had already happened, the pressing need was for a body of men to reiterate that judgment constantly within the life of the world. Where the early Christians put their faith in the Church, Blake puts his in Art.

His interest in the nature of true art is growing throughout this period, as can be seen by examining some of the plates which were inserted into the final versions of *Milton*, and by looking at polemical works such as the *Descriptive Catalogue*, the *Public Address* and *A Vision of the Last Judgment*. At the point of departure, Blake's interest lay mainly in the relation between Vision and Poetic Inspiration. It was one of his main reasons for admiring Milton that he had recognized clearly that Inspiration, not Memory, was the source of art. In one of his own annotations to Reynolds's *Discourses*, he quoted with approval Milton's central statement on the subject:

> A work of Genius is a Work 'Not to be obtaind by the Invocation of Memory & her Syren Daughters. but by Devout prayer to that Eternal Spirit. who can enrich with all utterance & knowledge & sends out his Seraphim with the hallowed fire of his Altar to touch & purify the lips of whom he pleases.' Milton[7]

At the climax of Blake's poem, similarly, Milton announces it as one of his tasks

> To cast off the rotten rags of Memory by Inspiration . . .

The theme goes back a long way. It was already there in an early prophetic book when Tiriel re-entered the garden to find Har and Heva under the guardianship of Mnetha, goddess of memory. Now it assumes new prominence as Blake begins his poem with an exhortatory preface to the young men of his age.

> The Stolen and Perverted Writings of Homer & Ovid: of Plato & Cicero. which all Men ought to contemn: are set up by artifice against the Sublime of the Bible. but when the New Age is at leisure to Pronounce: all will be set right: & those Grand Works of the more ancient & consciously & professedly Inspired Men, will hold their proper rank, & the Daughters of Memory shall become the Daughters of Inspiration. Shakespeare & Milton were both curbd by the general malady & infection from the silly Greek & Latin slaves of the Sword.

The Preface reiterates the lesson of *The Four Zoas*: men spend their time in 'Corporeal War' when they should be devoting themselves to 'Mental War'. It is summed up in Blake's most famous lyric, where the Sublime and the Pathos of true England are compared with the analytic darkness of contemporary society. The England of Vision was a place where Man walked in a fourfold vision of sublime love upon his mountains and a threefold vision of tender love in his valleys; the sun-god of fourfold vision on the hills had not yet been hidden by clouds, nor the building of the holy city of open friendship and creativity stifled by the setting up of analytic mills (—the mills which provide a pattern for the dark mills of the Industrial Revolution and without which humanity would not allow the latter to exist). Man was not set against man, nor vision shredded into

meaningless fragments. Against this nightmare, Blake invokes
the energies of twofold vision, possessing the assurance that they
will be crowned by the intervention of full fourfold vision—the
chariot of fire which descends to the prophet and translates him
into eternity. Only so will Jerusalem be built—and then only if
all men enter into the prophetic vision.

> And did those feet in ancient time.
> Walk upon Englands mountains green:
> And was the holy Lamb of God,
> On Englands pleasant pastures seen!
>
> And did the Countenance Divine
> Shine forth upon our clouded hills?
> And was Jerusalem builded here,
> Among these dark Satanic Mills?
>
> Bring me my Bow of burning gold:
> Bring me my Arrows of desire:
> Bring me my Spear: O clouds unfold!
> Bring me my Chariot of fire!
>
> I will not cease from Mental Fight,
> Nor shall my Sword sleep in my hand:
> Till we have built Jerusalem,
> In Englands green & pleasant Land.
>
> Would to God that all the Lords people were prophets.
>   Numbers XI.Ch 29 v.

The poem itself begins with an invocation to the sources of
Blake's inspiration—the 'daughters of Beulah':

> Daughters of Beulah! Muses who inspire the Poets Song
> Record the Journey of immortal Milton thro' your Realms
> Of terror & mild moony lustre, in soft sexual delusions
> Of varied beauty, to delight the wanderer and repose
> His burning thirst & freezing hunger!

This invocation of figures associated with threefold vision is
associated with Blake's criticisms of Milton. He evidently felt
that Milton had not taken enough account of threefold vision.
For Blake, sexual experience contained, in temporary and
muted form, the total visionary experience. It was like a moonlight which indicates, without fully revealing, the landscape on

which it shines. The sublime was embodied in it, even though its glory and colour might be reduced to 'terror and mild moony lustre' respectively. Milton's limited treatment had given little hint of this.

Blake announces that his theme is the False Tongue, an object of worship and sacrifice that increases in power until Jesus himself becomes its victim. He goes on to enquire into Milton's purposes in undertaking his journey:

Say first! what mov'd Milton, who walkd about in Eternity
One hundred years, pondring the intricate mazes of Providence
Unhappy tho in heav'n, he obey'd, he murmur'd not. he was silent
Viewing his Sixfold Emanation scatter'd thro' the deep
In torment! To go into the deep her to redeem & himself perish?

Milton is described in terms which echo his own descriptions of the devils—he is 'unhappy tho in heaven' as Beelzebub was 'Majestic though in Ruin', 'pond'ring the intricate mazes of Providence' as the devils reasoned 'Of Providence, Foreknowledge, Will, and Fate/ . . . And found no end, in wandring mazes lost.'[8]

The reference to Milton's 'sixfold emanation', evidently his three wives and three daughters, may well be a further indication of his supposed neglect of Beulah: there is even a hint that if Milton had given more attention to the women with whom he lived, he would have had less domestic strife to endure.

For the opening structure of his poem Blake reverts to the method which he used in *America* and *Europe*, inserting a piece of general mythological interpretation before the poem proper. The interpretation does not appear as a separate 'Preludium', however, but stands in loose connection with the plot as a 'Bard's Song' which Milton hears sung in Eternity. The events which are described by the Bard are subsequent to those immediately preceding the Apocalypse in *The Four Zoas*. (In examining the Song, we may pass directly from plate 2 to plate 7 in Blake's text, since the intervening plates were all inserted later to amplify the poem's meaning.)

It begins with a division of men into three classes: the Elect, the Redeemed and the Reprobate. These classes can be interpreted in terms of the familiar 'levels of vision'. The Elect, the class to which Satan belongs, consists of those whose fourfold vision has fallen into single vision—light into darkness, transparency into opacity, illumination into analysis. Above this fallen realm exist two intermediate states: the world of generation and wrath in twofold vision which is inhabited by Rintrah, and the threefold world of Beulah and pity inhabited by Palamabron. The reappearance of these last two figures encourages an interpretation of the myth more specifically in terms of the eighteenth century. In an Age of Reason, the two great remaining positives are honest indignation and honest pity.

The myth proceeds by describing a cosmic disruption. Satan, as Miller of Eternity, was constantly asking Los that he might for once take Palamabron's station, and use his harrow. Since Palamabron was constantly wearied by his work, Los consented and Satan took his place for one day (consisting of a thousand years). When Palamabron took his place again, he found that his horses had been maddened and his gnomes oppressed. He called Los and Satan, whereupon Satan in his mild manner accused Palamabron of crimes which he himself had committed and suggested that Palamabron was Los's enemy. Los, arbitrating, advises that in future all shall keep their proper station. Satan, returning to his mills, finds that there, too, all is in disorder. He complains again to Los, who blames himself for having allowed the interchange:

> Mine is the fault! I should have remember'd that pity divides the soul
> And man, unmans . . .
>
> (8. 19–20)

The point of the incident seems to lie in Blake's belief that reason and pity ought both to be rooted in true humanity, and not to invade each other's province. The failure of the male (as in Hayley) produces these subsidiary dislocations. His description of the aftermath also displays his hatred for double-dealing—a double-dealing which he had lately seen, in the case of Hayley, appearing as 'benevolence' and as a self-deception so complete that it could not even be called deliberate falsification. Against Satan's dissimulation there arises the wrath of Rintrah,

and in the subsequent disorders, Palamabron calls down a
solemn assembly in order that the truth may be revealed—

> That he who will not defend Truth, may be compelled to
> Defend a Lie, that he may be snared & caught & taken . . .

Rintrah, in being invoked, is actually given power, so that
Satan, instead of indulging in mild accusations, finds himself
raging, Rintrah-like, against Palamabron. But the power of
Rintrah also automatically involves Los, who gives it creative
expression by displacing the continents and oceans of the world
and altering the pole. In Satan, on the other hand, the wrath
burns inwardly, causing him to create the seven deadly sins, to
draw up moral laws and cruel punishments and to proclaim
himself God alone. In a fine piece of fantasy, Blake pictures the
burning within him which, instead of shining splendidly as a
part of his fourfold glory, is combined with lightlessness, an
opacity against the divine vision:

> Thus Satan rag'd amidst the Assembly! and his bosom grew
> Opake against the Divine Vision: the paved terraces of
> His bosom inwardly shone with fires, but the stones becoming
>   opake!
> Hid him from sight, in an extreme blackness and darkness . . .
>
> (9. 30–33)

While Satan rages, the Assembly stand astonished. But Rintrah
creates rivers, moats and columns of fire between him and
Palamabron to guard the latter: Satan, 'not having the Science
of Wrath, but only of Pity', rends the two qualities asunder and
sinks down in 'a dreadful Death'. Thus Palamabron's object is
achieved: Error is revealed by means of the energies of indignation. Los and Enitharmon now recognize the true nature
of Satan: he 'is Urizen / Drawn down by Orc & the Shadowy
Female into Generation'. We are back in the situation immediately following the French Revolution. When any out-
burst of energy has taken place, as in a revolution, there is an
immediate rallying of the forces of reason to contain the new
force, and the tyranny thus established involves a further
hardening against Vision. It is now Enitharmon's task to
'create' what has been established, and this she does by creating
a space named Canaan for Satan. This space, of its very nature,

seems infinite to those who are within it, while they themselves seem finite. This reverses the order of Eternity, where men see the universe as finite but are aware that within themselves they contain infinity.

Los finds himself shut away from Eternity. But he refuses to have anything to do with the new order, seeing that Light is extinguished in favour of Law, Jealousy reigns supreme where generosity ought to shine between man and man, and even the lights of the physical universe are analysed according to laws instead of being gazed at in wonder and love. He protests against the rule of priest and tyrant which is secured by such an order:

> Satan! Ah me! is gone in his own place, said Los! their God
> I will not worship in their Churches, nor King in their Theatres
> Elynittria! whence is this Jealousy running along the mountains
> British Women were not Jealous when Greek & Roman were
>   Jealous
> Every thing in Eternity shines by its own Internal light: but thou
> Darkenest every Internal light with the arrows of thy quiver,
> Bound up in the horns of Jealousy to a deadly fading Moon
> And Ocalythron binds the Sun into a Jealous Globe
> That every thing is fixd Opake without Internal light . . .
>   (10. 12–20)

Elynittria is the emanation of Palamabron: her jealousy reflects the isolation which he now suffers. Unmoved by Los's complaint, however, Satan goes on in triumph to divide the nations and sets his face against Jerusalem (who is the ultimate emanation) in order to destroy her too.

Los hides Enitharmon from these events 'Upon the Thames whose lulling harmony repos'd her soul'. So she is kept from 'Tyburn's awful brook', the emblem of human execution and the cruelty of human justice. And this separation between the light of Beulah and the darkness of Satan's world means that a 'moony space' is preserved around the whole cruelty of the law.

Meanwhile the question is raised in the Assembly why the innocent should suffer for the guilty, Rintrah for Satan. The reply suggests that by the Fall all are inter-involved, Palamabron, Rintrah and Satan. If Palamabron is to be redeemed from Satan's law, then Satan must first be created: this can only happen if Rintrah enters him and creates him as rage. But even then it is Rintrah that suffers, not Satan. It is the constant law of Eternity that one die for another.

At this point, however, Leutha, the Eternal who represents sexual desire, intervenes.

> And Leutha stood glowing with varying colours immortal, heart-
> piercing
> And lovely; & her moth-like elegance shone over the Assembly
> (11. 32–33)

She tells the Assembly that Satan's transgression was really her fault. Loving Palamabron and being repelled by the jealous Elynittria, she found a dragon form issuing from her limbs to seize Elynittria's new-born son. In order to prevent this happening she entered Satan's brain, stupefying his masculine perceptions while keeping his feminine awake, and so created the 'soft delusory love' which he bore to Palamabron. When Satan drove Palamabron's horses, it was she who unloosed them, taking Elynittria's place, and maddened them. It was at this point that

> The Harrow cast thick flames & orb'd us round in concave fires
> A Hell of our own making . . .
> (12. 22–3)

This echo of the Hell of *Paradise Lost*[9] is followed by a still more distinct parallel as she recalls that she then hid in Satan's brain and coming forth from his head was named as Sin.[10] Then Elynittria met Satan and gave him 'wine of wildest power' so that he became a prophet of the new doctrine, 'in selfish holiness demanding purity / Being most impure . . .' Now therefore she is Sin and Satan is Death.

These obscure incidents can best be approached by a return to first principles. In Blake's universe, such activities take place within one Man. Here, he is trying to explain the splitting of Man into deprived male and jealous female. Deprived of the full Love which issues in generosity and selflessness, his Selfhood or Satan begins to be active, while at the same time the failure to satisfy sexual desire damps down his masculinity: instead of being energetic in opposition, it settles into a delusory pretence of living by emasculated 'love'. The Satan who can be dealt

with when he rises up in the state Rintrah against the mildness
of Palamabron, is less easy to cope with when he exists in this
state of hypocritical benevolence.

At the same time, Leutha recognizes that her faults are only
reflections of some deeper cosmic tragedy;

> The Sin was begun in Eternity, and will not rest to Eternity
> Till two Eternitys meet together, Ah! lost! lost! lost! for ever!
> (13. 10–11)

After Leutha has spoken, the Assembly takes the space where
Satan lies protected and gives to it a Time, six thousand years
(the traditional time-span of the world). Various guardians of
the space are set up and fail in different ways until the final
guardian, Jehovah, leprous in his laws, causes the 'Body of
Death' to be 'perfected in hypocritic holiness' around the Lamb.
And when the Lamb dies as a reprobate, the Elect and the
Redeemed are reconciled, for they see that this Reprobate
figure is indeed the Saviour:

> And the Elect shall say to the Redeemd. We behold it is of
> Divine
> Mercy alone! of Free Gift and Election that we live.
> Our Virtues & Cruel Goodnesses, have deserv'd Eternal Death.
> (13. 32–4)

At the same time, Elynittria and Leutha are also reconciled:
Elynittria throws aside her bow and her arrows and brings
Leutha to Palamabron's tent. But this is no final solution to the
real disjunction in Eternity, it is simply an intellectual victory:
Leutha in dreams bears Rahab, the mother of Tirzah, and her
sisters, 'In Lambeth's vales, in Cambridge and in Oxford,
places of Thought'.

With this cryptic reference to contemporary intellectual life,
the Bard ceases his Song. The Eternals who have listened dis-
cuss it, some holding that Pity and Love (the attributes assumed
by Satan) are too venerable for the imputation of guilt. When
challenged as to the source of his song, the Bard replies by
asserting his own, self-justifying authority:

> I am Inspired! I know it is Truth! for I Sing
> According to the inspiration of the Poetic Genius

Who is the eternal all-protecting Divine Humanity
To whom be Glory & Power & Dominion Evermore Amen
(13. 51–14. 3)

There arises a murmuring concerning generation and the vegetative power (the imperfect states of twofold and single vision do not exist in Eternity) and Albion shudders in a convulsion of doubt which is communicated to the other nations. The Bard, in terror, rushes into the bosom of Milton.

The Bard's song has already established certain differences from the narrative in *Paradise Lost*. Sin and Death, for example have been created as a result of delusions of holiness. Now Milton arises to take upon himself the journey to Eternal Death. He recognizes in his own Selfhood the Satan who has been described, and sees that only by subduing this Satan can he be restored to his own lost emanation:

What do I here before the Judgment? without my Emanation?
With the daughters of memory, & not with the daughters of
   inspiration?
I in my Selfhood am that Satan: I am that Evil One!
He is my Spectre! in my obedience to loose him from my Hells
To claim the Hells, my Furnaces, I go to Eternal Death.
(14. 28–32)

With these words, Milton goes forth into the world of human experience. He perceives the body which is prepared for him like a shadow, twenty-seven fold and extending into all the twenty-seven states of experience which exist between the depths of direst Hell and the land of Albion where Blake is writing.

A full-plate illustration at this point shows him stepping forth in his full glory and in the sunrise of imagination, thrusting aside the robes of eternity, as described in the text.

The text of the next plate contains some of Blake's most interesting, if elusive, writing. As Milton departs into his Shadow, he becomes a double figure. On the one hand his eternal body still walks in eternity with the Seven Angels of the Presence

    as an Eighth
Image Divine tho' darken'd; and tho walking as one walks
In sleep . . .
(15. 5–7)

On the other his human existence is entering the Shadow, which
appears from Eternity like a great Polypus, vegetating beneath
the sea of Time and Space. The dwellers in Eternity see him as
one asleep; they 'give him their emanations' and feed him with
the food of Eden as before. To himself, he is a wanderer lost in
dreary night. Yet his journey is so swift and brilliant that he
appears to the shades of Hell like a comet travelling into Chaos
and so is protected from their malice.

Blake, in lines which recall his favourite concept of 'the
mental traveller', describes the nature of journeying through
infinity.

> The nature of infinity is this: That every thing has its
> Own Vortex; and when once a traveller thro' Eternity
> Has passd that Vortex, he percieves it roll backward behind
> His path, into a globe itself infolding; like a sun:
> Or like a moon, or like a universe of starry majesty . . .
>
> (15. 21–5)

This passage contains the key to a good deal of his specula-
tion. The imagery of light is central. We are invited to imagine
that the whole physical universe, as perceived by the reason,
is, by that token, an experience already passed; in Eternity, on
the other hand, light exists everywhere. Travellers through
physical space would discover that the planet which was at one
moment immediate to them, unorganized, became, once left,
a perfectly contained sphere, giving light to their path. So it is
with experience, also. But it is the moment of unorganized
immediacy, not the later illuminated path through darkness,
which is the fuller revelation of Eternity. In the same way, a
true man thinks of the physical world not as the world of dead
planets known to the astronomers, but as the acres immediately
surrounding his dwelling, on which he sees the sun and moon
rise and set. He is right: he perceives the true infinity, which
does not consist in the endless dimensions of space but exists at
the heart of present experience:

> Thus is the earth one infinite plane, and not as apparent
> To the weak traveller confin'd beneath the moony shade.
> Thus is the heaven a vortex passd already, and the earth
> A vortex not yet pass'd by the traveller thro' Eternity.
>
> (15. 32–5)

While they are still on earth, human beings are naturally caught within the vortex of earth, unable to grasp its pattern or its meaning. To Milton, poised for a moment between heaven and earth, the patterns of both are visible, and he sees the impending vortex of earth as the body of Albion, outstretched upon the rock of ages while the sea of time and space beats around it. Then his shadow falls thundering into that sea.

Simultaneously, the viewpoint is shifted. Milton enters Blake's left foot, the symbol of his creative power, the Los within him. The entry creates an automatic division in Blake, for as the new light shines Blake sees the rest of earthly experience darkened.

Milton is pictured entering the world of experience, as represented by the six females who ministered to the historical John Milton. As he perceives the cruelties of Ulro, he causes them to write them down at his dictation—an activity which, while recalling Milton's dictation of his poetry, corresponds also to Jehovah's dictation of the law upon Mount Sinai. His journey brings him to the Mundane Shell,

> a vast Concave Earth: an immense
> Hardend shadow of all things upon our Vegetated Earth
> Enlarg'd into dimension & deform'd into indefinite space. . . .
> (17. 21–3)

which apparently corresponds to the world as seen by the darkened eye of analysis and has its heart in the rocky fastness of absolute opacity which is called 'Satan's seat'. Conscious of his approach, Enitharmon rejoices in the belief that she is about to be released from her bond of jealousy, while Los, terrified that he will lose her, responds by shooting forth his limbs like roots of trees against Milton's progress. An illustration to the text shows him doing just this: within the roots Urizen looks out at the approaching Milton. The text goes on,

> Urizen beheld the immortal Man,
> And Tharmas Demon of the Waters, & Orc, who is Luvah . . .
> (17. 36–18. 1)

Urizen's vision of Milton here (as representing those energies from which he himself is now cut off) is followed by the voices of Orc and the Shadowy Female. The Female declares that she will lament over Milton, and that her lamentation will consist of all the afflictions of mankind—the poor, the starving and the prisoners. Blake felt that Milton was ultimately a supporter of the *status quo*: *Paradise Lost*, for all its seventeenth-century splendours, was still devoted to that worship of the law which is the seedbed of cruel tyranny. The forms which she declares herself about to take correspond therefore to Milton's ambiguous nature:

> For I will put on the Human Form & take the Image of God
> Even Pity & Humanity but my Clothing shall be Cruelty
> And I will put on Holiness as a breastplate & as a helmet,
> And all my ornaments shall be of the gold of broken hearts. . . .
> (18. 19–22)

These things she sees as defences against the terrors of Orc. Orc replies by urging her not to take this 'Human Form' (the phrase has the irony of the poem beginning 'Cruelty has a Human Heart . . . '[11]) and suggests that so far from acting as a defence against his terrors, it is this very putting on of Holiness which brings out his wrath and causes him to rend her asunder.

> When wilt thou put on the Female Form as in times of old
> With a Garment of Pity & Compassion like the Garment of God
> His Garments are long sufferings for the Children of Men
> Jerusalem is his Garment & not thy Covering Cherub O lovely
> Shadow of my delight who wanderest seeking for the prey.
> (18. 34–7)

Such is Blake's answer to those prophets who call on Jerusalem or London to 'put on holiness'. But Orc's prophetic vision, which is stimulated by Oothoon and Leutha, the figures respectively of frustrated sexuality and over-indulged sexuality, receives no reply from the Shadowy Female, the one figure who might give him true and natural sexual love. As he stretches out his hands to woo, he is met only by accusations of sin until, as he warned, he begins to destroy the female.

Simultaneously, Urizen emerges from his Rocky Form and begins to struggle with the approaching Milton. Milton finds that the clay on which he treads is turned to marble and then meets with Urizen by the waters of Arnon. The scene which follows is reminiscent of the baptism of Jesus in the Jordan—particularly as that incident is recounted in *Paradise Regained*.

But it is typical of Blake that the incident becomes a struggle
between the two powers involved—this Jesus resists the attempt
to baptise him with the waters of Holiness and endeavours instead to convert John the Baptist to his own vision. As Urizen
pours his cold water upon Milton's brain, Milton tries to mould
Urizen into a human form:

> with cold hand Urizen stoop'd down
> And took up water from the River Jordan: pouring on
> To Miltons brain the icy fluid from his cold broad palm.
> But Milton took of the red clay of Succoth, moulding it with care
> Between his palms; and filling up the furrows of many years
> Beginning at the feet of Urizen, and on the bones
> Creating new flesh on the Demon cold, and building him,
> As with new clay a Human form in the Valley of Beth Peor.
>
> (19. 7–14)

The struggle continues for a long time: it is the major task
which Milton faces in his new incarnation, for it is the correction
of the errors of his former work. Blake turns aside to set the
struggle in its full context by recapitulating his doctrine of the
Zoas, who are pictured in the form of four Universes, chaotic
round the Mundane Egg (the residual body which Los keeps in
existence so that Form may be preserved, vestigially, in the
midst of Chaos). These geographical locations are to be understood in relation to the original landscape of Eden, with its
mountains of sublime glory in the south, its earth of desire in the
north and, in between, the garden of human love enclosing in
innocence the fountain of human energy. When passion and
vision changed places, light was replaced by fire in the south,
the garden and fountain turned into a desert and a raging sea,
and in the north the earth of human desire was hardened to
rock and metal:

> But when Luvah assum'd the world of Urizen to the South:
> And Albion was slain upon his mountains, & in his tent;
> All fell towards the Center in dire ruin, sinking down.
> And in the South remains a burning fire; in the East a void,
> In the West, a world of raging waters; in the North a solid,
> Unfathomable! without end. But in the midst of these,
> Is built eternally the Universe of Los and Enitharmon:
> Towards which Milton went, but Urizen oppos'd his path.
>
> (19. 19–26)

The struggle between the two continues, with Rahab and Tirzah endeavouring to seduce Milton away from it. These two figures, whom we know from the Bard's Song to have been engendered after the rapprochement between Leutha and Elynittria (sexual desire and chastity each conceived as ends in themselves), are another version of the Sin and Death in *Paradise Lost*: Rahab the 'great Whore', the monstrous figure of Female Love who is created by treating love as a sin, and Tirzah the deathly cult of analysis which springs from the loss of innocence. (In the Bible Tirzah was the wife of Abel.) Between them, these two watch over the analytic science of modern universities and the tyranny of law—'The banks of Cam, cold learning's streams, London's dark frowning towers'. As Tirzah numbers every fibre, and Ahania, Vala and Enion remain cut off from their respective Zoas, these last become three separate entities: the knot of nervous fibres is turned into a white brain (which becomes a rock), the knot of bloody veins is turned into a red-hot heart (so that fallen passion stands in armour before the gate of Reuben or fallen nature), and the knot of milky seed is turned into two lovely Heavens which are one. These separated human faculties are the Heavens offered by Rahab and Tirzah. If united they would create the land of Beulah or three-fold vision; in isolation they exist only beneath its shades.

While these 'daughters of Memory' are singing their siren song, Milton does not reply; he simply continues with his task of creating Urizen—standing before him and then walking round, like a sculptor at work. Against the three 'heavens' offered by Rahab and Tirzah Blake sets the true glory of the fourfold man. This is to be attained by opening the gates of each of the three faculties, so that instead of standing as separate entities, each becomes opened within to the fourfold vision. So the response of the Fourfold Man to 'the electric flame of Miltons awful precipitate descent' is compared to the simple existence of a fly which, despite its insignificance, does respond to the forces of eternity:

Seest thou the little winged fly, smaller than a grain of sand?
It has a heart like thee; a brain open to heaven & hell,
Withinside wondrous & expansive; its gates are not clos'd,

> I hope thine art not: hence it clothes itself in rich array;
> Hence thou art cloth'd with human beauty O thou mortal man.
> (20. 27–31)

It is no use to seek the Father beyond the skies, which are the realms of Chaos and ancient Night: it is *within* that eternity must be sought—

> for in brain and heart and loins
> Gates open behind Satans Seat to the City of Golgonooza
> Which is the spiritual fourfold London, in the loins of Albion.
> (20. 38–40)

Yet against such an opening of the 'gates' stand Og and Anak, grim figures representing respectively the moral and the natural laws which shut off man from Vision.

So by Albion's response to Milton's descent, Milton, even while travelling through the realms of Ulro, is paradoxically enabled to fall through Albion's heart. Simultaneously the Eternals, enraged at the prospect of Death which is opened up by Milton's actions, cut him off from them and fling him down, together with his Watchers, as a fiery circle into the deeps of Ulro.

This is the nadir of the poem. Poetic inspiration seems finally cut off from the earth. Even Los begins to despair, afraid that his two sons Rintrah and Palamabron, the only energies left in eighteenth-century England, will also depart. But now he recalls an ancient prophecy

> That Milton of the Land of Albion should up ascend
> Forwards from Ulro from the Vale of Felpham: and set free
> Orc from his Chain of Jealousy, he started at the thought . . .
> (20. 59–61)

A new point to the poem is emerging. Just as Coleridge's buried dissertation upon the nature of genius in *Kubla Khan* turns finally into the first person as he imagines what it would be like to be a genius,[12] so Blake now sees himself as a reincarnation of Milton, set to perform anew the task which had been only partly carried out in the writing of *Paradise Lost*. Milton had been occupied with three separate realms of vision, Heaven, Hell and Paradise, corresponding roughly to the separate

realms of head, heart and genitals offered by Rahab and Tirzah
to the man who lives within their laws. Blake will take these
three regions and open each one inwardly to show the fourfold
vision that lies beneath, bringing them into human harmony
instead of warring chaos. Where Satan flew to tempt man in
Paradise, Blake's Milton will fly to redeem man in Beulah. So
will be created Golgonooza: the city which is implicit in
Milton's creative energy, but not in the poetic universe which he
presented to his seventeenth-century readers.

When Los remembers the prophecy concerning Milton he
descends into Udan-Adan, where Satan's shadow is awake.
Simultaneously, Blake begins to record his own vision as Milton
enters his foot. He is not completely aware of what has happened, of course: he is, however, conscious of a new vision of the
world:

> And all this Vegetable World appeard on my left Foot,
> As a bright sandal formd immortal of precious stones & gold . . .
>   (21. 12–13)

Meanwhile in Eden there is a weeping from those who drove
Milton down into Ulro, heard as a lamentation from the banks
and plants and mountains by the river Ololon. It is at dawn
that this lamentation is heard: at the time when the Prince of
Light ought to arise, but when there appears instead the dark
sun of power. The light of true Humanity is recalled only to be
swallowed up in burning heat.

> When Luvahs bulls each morning drag the sulphur Sun out of the
>   Deep
> Harnessd with starry harness black & shining kept by black slaves
> That work all night at the starry harness, Strong and vigorous
> They drag the unwilling Orb: at this time all the Family
> Of Eden heard the lamentation, and Providence began.
>   (21. 20–4)

This lament is heard by Los and Enitharmon, who are imprisoned within the Mundane Shell, the only Form known to
them, and who now lament that they failed to recognize Milton
and so drove him into Ulro.

Ololon is first described as 'a sweet River, of milk and liquid
pearl'. She is not to be identified with any particular object,

however; she is a state. She represents the phase in which communication is established between this world and Eternity: she is Vala in her transfigured state of revelation. So Ololon is represented variously as a river of Eden, a descending dove and a maiden of inspiration. Always, some descending revelation is implied. Her very presence before the Divine Family in Eternity reveals to them the absence of Milton and his descent to Eternal Death. Ololon proposes that she also should descend and give herself to eternal death, but Divine Family give her the task of watching over the world of sorrow in pity, renewing it to eternal life with her brooding wings. (The image of the dove may be sensed here). At the same time, they draw together as one Man, Jesus, and when they are united with Ololon they appear as 'Jesus the Saviour, . . . coming in the Clouds of Ololon'.

Los, in his state of twofold vision, hears these things only indistinctly and so they are something of a terror to him. He descends to Blake and stands behind him as 'a terrible flaming Sun'. When Blake turns round to see him, he finds himself possessed by this flaming power (Fig. 25), which stoops down to bind on his sandals of vision, and causes him to rise in fury and strength. Los reveals himself to Blake as the shadowy prophet who fell from his station in the eternal bosom six thousand years ago (in other words, at the creation of the world as we know it) and whose task it has been to create those six thousand years as Time and Space, in order that men may not fall utterly into the satanic power of anti-vision but have a created fabric through which they can pass and find some correspondence with their eternal form.

> The generations of men run on in the tide of Time
> But leave their destind lineaments permanent for ever & ever.
>
> (22. 24–5)

As Los and Blake walk along, they are met by Rintrah and Palamabron, who advise Los to cast his companion into the furnaces, in view of the prophecy that Milton will unchain Orc and free Satan, Og, Sihon and Anak. They tell him that the Shadowy Female is shuddering and the daughters of Los are creating a new religion through 'new Jealousy of Theotormon'. 'Miltons Religion is the cause.' (The meaning of this seems to

be that the failure to accept sexual experience which is sym-
bolized by Theotormon has become still more abysmal as a
result of Milton's poetry, with its note of abstinence and its
strong emphasis upon Necessity and Law.) They go on to say
that because of the total failure of the churches, Voltaire and
Rousseau were created to set up a new religion of self-righteousness—which would at least offer some hope against the
despair created by a doctrine of necessitarian law. Yet this new
religion mocks the confessors and martyrs of the old religion and
perpetuates the cult of war and military glory: Jerusalem is
destroyed as a harlot, while in her place is raised up 'Mystery
the Virgin Harlot Mother of War'. Swedenborg's vision of
Heaven and Hell has been perverted by the churches to a
heaven which is a place of warriors and a hell which contains
transgressors—the punishers and the punished respectively.
Plato and the Greeks have been invoked simply in order to set
up the warlike gods of Priam against the promise of forgiveness
in Christianity. In face of such a situation, Methodism was at
least a lonely hope (prophetic Rintrah raised up the vehement
Whitefield, priestly Palamabron the milder Wesley) for it
preached the gospel of a God who took upon himself the likeness
of Man and became obedient even to death. Now, even these
witnesses lie dead in the great city (another of the biblical signs
of the Apocalypse).[13] Yet if miracles are demanded by a
sceptical age, the lives of Whitefield and Wesley ought to be
miracles enough, lives devoted to scorn, injury and death. Indeed the trumpet of judgment is sounding at this moment, but
Albion remains asleep. Orc has risen on the Atlantic in the
American Revolution, but even that has failed to stir him. They
therefore plead with Los to let them bind this Milton, whose
alliance with the Covering Cherub has resulted in so much ill.

Los's reaction is vivid. As a storm will appear and cover the
sky, driving the sun 'into Chaos' and the stars 'into the Desarts',
his face darkens. Yet just as the storm is full of richness for the
earth beneath, so pity and love are present even in his terrible
frowns. He points out that he has already united himself with
the figure of Death at his side and that it is proper for him and
his sons to live not by wrath but by mercy. He recalls to them
the prophecy that Milton will rise up from the vale of Felpham

and break the Chain of Jealousy. They are to remember the
women of Beulah who patiently form a sweet night in silence
and obscurity in order to protect the loves and graces from the
analytic gaze of 'Satan's watch-fiends'. Their true moment will
come with the harvest of wine and wheat in heaven: they are
not to follow the erroneous examples of Luther and Calvin, who
simply stirred up war and violence between Papists and Pro-
testants. It is their task to set limits to the death that is abroad
and to wait patiently for the final redemption which will consist of the Last Vintage and the quenching of the Sun of Salah in
the Lake of Udan-Adan (or the reappearance of the Eternal
Man in his full, generous form and the consequent putting
down of the false Selfhood which has arisen to take his vacant
place).

Los pleads with his sons not to leave him, as twelve of his sons
have already done, for they are the only forces now at his
disposal:

> Still my four mighty ones are left to me in Golgonooza
> Still Rintrah fierce, and Palamabron mild & piteous
> Theotormon filld with care, Bromion loving Science . . .
>
> (24. 10–12)

If they leave him, they will simply pass into Ulro and be
vegetated. He offers them his own interpretation of the world
around them, based upon an idiosyncratic reading of the story
of the raising of Lazarus. When Jesus said of the dead Lazarus,
'our friend Lazarus sleepeth'[14] he was referring not to his body
but to the Eternal Man within every man. And so, when he
raised Lazarus he was still only raising the spectre of the
Eternal Man (as his name might suggest). This interpretation
is now applied to the death of Jesus. When Jesus died, the
Eternal Man in him remained sleeping: what arose was a
spectre Religion which resolved itself into the militaristic
religions of Paul, Constantine, Charlemaine and Luther. From
such a dispensation, governed not by the vision of Jesus but by
the covering cherub of the Church, Los calls his sons away. The
thought and vision which Jesus possessed are not present there;
in their stead remain Law and Commerce. And yet these
forces (given the names of Bowlahoola and Allamanda) still
contain a residual humanity, for 'justice' still has a regulative

value (however much it may feed upon the energies of its slaves) just as the stomach serves a purpose in the human body; and Commerce still keeps alive some creative forces. Both are contributing something towards the building of Golgonooza, Los's city of art and manufacture. And the return of this Elected Figure (Milton) shows that the Last Vintage cannot be far away.

Los's sons are not finally convinced by his arguments, for, lacking the full power of fourfold vision, he can express himself only in alternations of wrath and pity, which are likely to continue in unceasing succession. They go down to Bowlahoola, which is described, in one of Blake's more witty passages, as the interior of a vast body, lungs, heart and stomach, served by many forces which give forth a music to ameliorate the sorrows of slavery and drown the howls and groans of the suffering, reducing the whole process to apparent harmony—like military music drowning the noises of a fierce battle:[15]

> The double drum drowns howls & groans, the shrill fife, shrieks & cries:
> The crooked horn mellows the hoarse raving serpent, terrible, but harmonious
> Bowlahoola is the Stomach in every individual man.
>
> (24. 65–7)

While this minor operation of Los's is in progress, he is still at his major work of creating Time. Time is one of the mercies of Eternity, for without the potentiality of dealing with experience serially, life would be an eternal torment, incessant exposure to the energies of infinity—the noonday sun experienced by Coleridge's Ancient Mariner.[16] And this dynamic view of Time leads Blake to refute the picture of 'Father Time' which appears in popular art:

> Los is by mortals nam'd Time Enitharmon is nam'd Space
> But they depict him bald & aged who is in eternal youth
> All powerful and his locks flourish like the brows of morning
> He is the Spirit of Prophecy the ever apparent Elias
> Time is the mercy of Eternity; without Times swiftness
> Which is the swiftest of all things: all were eternal torment . . .
>
> (24. 68–73)

BH — M

This statement leads Blake into a long description of the work of Los and his sons, in which one point is made again and again. The universe which is regarded by the analytic scientist as a well-ordered machine, running according to strictly organized Laws, is nothing of the sort. It is a piece of continuous creation, raised against the forces of chaos and disintegration. The fourth of the Zoas and his emanation must preside over the dynamism of the space-time continuum, creating in every moment, in order that the fabric may be kept in being at all.

Before this point is developed, however, there is a further glimpse of the impending apocalypse, as Rintrah and Palamabron, accompanied by Los, descend to the Wine-presses, where the sons of Luvah are at work. The Wine-presses, we learn, are most intensely at work in the major cities of the nations, 'Where Human Thought is crush'd beneath the iron hand of Power.' As the labourers sing that this is the last vintage the souls howl, begging to be given either to the heavens or to the earth, in order that they may preach righteousness and punish the sinner, but Los refuses, waiting for the whole vintage to be gathered. He explains in a long speech that the Vintage and Harvest is now due, for the whole globe has been explored and every atom of intellect is being subjected to investigation. The new awakening of intellect has also brought about a generation of men who 'mock at Faith and deny Providence'. The harvest will therefore consist of separating men not by nations and families but according to whether they belong to the Elect, the Redeemed or the Reprobate: the Elect who cannot believe in Eternal Life except by miracles and a New Birth and who have subdued everything, under pretence of benevolence; the Reprobate who never cease to believe; and the Redeemed who are perpetually the victims of doubts and fears raised by the Elect. The Elect are to be protected from Eternal Death, which would destroy the whole earth, by being formed into the Churches of Beulah (which sound like a type of scientific humanism). The other two classes are to be prepared for the consummation. Meanwhile the reapers are to be patient, waiting for the consummation, which will be followed by a new and better form of 'vegetation'—the supper of the Lamb and his bride.

The Sons of Los obey: their activity is described by imagery

drawn from vivid natural phenomena. They are like the con-
stellations—not the isolated stars of single vision, but the
visionary groupings of stars which move 'with harp & heavenly
song/With flute & clarion, & cups and measures filled with
foaming wine.' In their intricate harmony they are like flies
that dance and interweave in summer:

>   every one the dance
> Know in its intricate mazes of delight artful to weave:
> Each one to sound his instruments of music in the dance,
> To touch each other & recede; to cross & change & return . . .
>   (26. 3–6)

In their thunders of prophecy they are like trees on mountains
when the wind is roaring. Yet such forms of nature only faintly
suggest the power of their spiritual counterparts:

> . . . we see only as it were the hem of their garments
> When with our vegetable eyes we view these wond'rous Visions
>   (26. 11–12)

The beautiful poetry of this passage is followed by a few lines
of obscure geographical detail, in which the North and South
gates of Porphyry's Cave of the Nymphs[17] are translated into
northern and southern coasts of the British Isles. Except to give
a sense of immediacy of reference, the lines have little apparent
purpose; the main theme is picked up again as Blake goes on to
describe how the sons of Los work, giving lineament and form
to the 'piteous Passions & Desires' of mankind which would
otherwise exist only like watery clouds, or dreams. When they
are generated, on the other hand, the bodies of men acquire
magnificence.

> And every Generated Body in its inward form,
> Is a garden of delight & a building of magnificence,
> Built by the Sons of Los in Bowlahoola & Allamanda
> And the herbs & flowers & furniture & beds & chambers
> Continually woven in the Looms of Enitharmons Daughters
> In bright Cathedrons golden Dome with care & love & tears.
>   (26. 31–6)

Yet the spiritual remains always the true reality; the natural
power of itself 'seeks & tends to Destruction'. The same principle is true of all things:

> And every Natural Effect has a Spiritual Cause, and Not
> A Natural: for a Natural Cause only seems, it is a Delusion
> Of Ulro: & a ratio of the perishing Vegetable Memory.
>
> (26. 44–6)

In the next plate, Blake describes the 'Wine-press of Los', drawing many of his lines directly from the text of the earlier poem *Vala*, but developing the significance of the image. The wine-press was founded by Luvah and finished by Urizen. It is called war on Earth and is the Printing-press of Los. From these hints, we may deduce that he is using one and the same image for three related ideas. The fierce intercrush of energies in the wine-press can represent both the cruel consummation of love-making in Luvah's fallen threefold world and the destructive consummation of war in the world of Urizen's single vision. The same process, between the two extremes, can exist, less cruelly, as the mode of 'twofold' artistic creation, by which prophecy is delivered to the world. In each case, insects still sport around the wine-press, uninvolved with what is going on, wise within the limits of their creation. The wine-press, at each of the three levels, is only a substitute for the humanized energy of fourfold vision.

The Sons of Los also labour mightily in Allamanda, the field of commerce, in order that man may not fall into eternal death, and even in the Mills of Theotormon—those processes of intellectual analysis which bring man perilously close to abysses of doubt ('the starry voids of night & the depths and caverns of earth').

Having glanced at war, commerce and scientific investigation, the main channels into which the energies of his contemporaries are directed, Blake turns away to examine the fourfold activity of man in Eternity.

> But in Eternity the Four Arts: Poetry, Painting, Music,
> And Architecture which is Science: are the Four Faces of Man.
>
> (27. 55–6)

In Time and Space, on the other hand, only Science remains, the mainspring of War and Commerce.

Blake now develops an earlier idea, to show the sons of Los actually giving form to the passions. A Shakespearean phrase enforces his point:

Some Sons of Los surround the Passions with porches of iron &
    silver
Creating form & beauty around the dark regions of sorrow,
Giving to airy nothing a name and a habitation
Delightful! with bounds to the Infinite putting off the Indefinite
Into most holy forms of Thought: (such is the power of inspira-
    tion) . . .

                                                    (28. 1–5)

In the remainder of this plate there is a persistent under-
current of sexual reference as the various sons of Los are shown
devoted to their work of giving form to human doubts and fears.
Antamon, elsewhere described as possessing the 'lineaments of
gratified desire', moulds the little spectres like a lover:

Antamon takes them into his beautiful flexible hands,
As the Sower takes the seed, or as the Artist his clay
Or fine wax, to mould artful a model for golden ornaments.
The soft hands of Antamon draw the indelible line:
Form immortal with golden pen; such as the Spectre admiring
Puts on the sweet form; then smiles Antamon bright thro his
    windows
The Daughters of beauty look up from their Loom & prepare.
The integument soft for its clothing with joy & delight.

                                                    (28. 13–20)

Theotormon and Sotha, on the other hand, the two sons of
Los who refuse sexual pleasure, exercise a different guardianship. According to Blake's interpretation of human psychology,
sexual abstinence may result in the cultivation of cruelty and
violence. Therefore, Theotormon and Sotha are made to
create images of cruelty—the crested cock and then the lion and
tiger—in order that the spectre may be terrified and take refuge
in human linaments.

The sons of Ozoth, finally, stand in the optic nerve, hardening
it into an opaque bone so as to shut out all external sights
while, like a diamond in the mine, it preserves at the heart of
its rugged covering a jewel heart of inward beauty. This is the
guardianship of the 'inward eye': Blake employs what may be a
phallic image to express further the theme of a rough exterior which

        is open all within
And in his hallowd centre holds the heavens of bright eternity . . .
                                                    (28. 37–8)

This interpretation is reinforced in the last phrase by the apparent reminiscence of Marvell's 'To his Coy Mistress' and its 'deserts of vast eternity'.

The plate concludes with a long description of the sons of Los creating a Time seen through the eyes of eternity:

And every Moment has a Couch of gold for soft repose,
(A moment equals a pulsation of the artery),
And between every two Moments stands a Daughter of Beulah
To feed the Sleepers on their Couches with maternal care.

(28. 46-9)

At the end, the concept of Time is rounded by equating the eternal moment, between two pulses, with the whole of time (popularly supposed in Blake's day to have lasted nearly six thousand years) and showing that each is, paradoxically, the 'time' of inspiration in a way that no period in historical time could be.

Every Time less than a pulsation of the artery
Is equal in its period & value to Six Thousand Years.
For in this Period the Poets Work is Done: and all the Great
Events of Time start forth & are concieved in such a Period
Within a Moment: a Pulsation of the Artery.

(28. 62-29. 3)

To such a view of Time, in which the greatest moments of joy and creation occur 'between two moments', the Newtonian universe with its carefully constructed time-scales can be of secondary relevance only. The same is true of space. The vastness of the universe, the speed of spinning planets and the distance of far galaxies, is less important than the quality of living which each man brings to his own situation. For just as Space is created by Los and Enitharmon, so each man creates his own universe, beginning at the point where he is now.

The Sky is an immortal Tent built by the Sons of Los
And every Space that a Man views around his dwelling-place:
Standing on his own roof, or in his garden on a mount
Of twenty-five cubits in height, such space is his Universe;
And on its verge the Sun rises & sets, the Clouds bow
To meet the flat Earth & the Sea in such an orderd Space:
The Starry heavens reach no further but here bend and set
On all sides & the two Poles turn on their valves of gold:

And if he move his dwelling-place, his heavens also move.
Wher'eer he goes & all his neighbourhood bewail his loss . . .
                                                (29. 4–13)

The Los within each man responds thus to the Los who
creates the form of the universe at large;

As to that false appearance which appears to the reasoner,
As of a Globe rolling thro Voidness, it is a delusion of Ulro
The Microscope knows not of this nor the Telescope. they alter
The ratio of the Spectators Organs but leave Objects untouchd.
For every Space larger than a red Globule of Mans blood.
Is visionary: and is created by the Hammer of Los
And every Space smaller than a Globule of Mans blood opens
Into Eternity of which this vegetable Earth is but a shadow:
The red Globule is the unwearied Sun by Los created
To measure Time and Space to mortal Men. every morning.
                                                (29. 15–24)

Blake's humanized universe exists between two poles: the atom
of blood beating within an individual man and the vast
pulsation of energy by which the sun gives light to the earth
each day. At the heart of each pole is eternity.

After this powerful climax, Blake turns towards the limitations of man. All men are joined by their common flesh into
one vast 'polypus', within the bonds of which the fires of Orc
howl in eternal youth. A further statement of the Fall follows.
By the Spectre of Orc, or Satan, sleep is transformed into death,
desire into sin. A further loss of Vision brings man into the
'cruelties of Demonstration', but he is saved from a total lapse
into the indefinite by the activity of the Saviour, who creates the
solid and the opaque, calling them respectively Adam and
Satan. Los, whose creative power has been present here, also
creates the sun and moon to help by their splendour, while
Rintrah and Palamabron assist by encouraging activity and so
guiding souls clear of the Rock of Death. Finally, Los conducts
them still further by freeing them from those negative virtues
which are the pillars of single vision (temperance, prudence,
justice and fortitude) in favour of the more generous and self-
giving qualities of Golgonooza.

Meanwhile it is the task of Enitharmon and her daughters to
provide 'heavens' for these souls, opening for them the way

from twofold to fourfold vision: but since Rahab and Tirzah are in control this purpose is thwarted. Men, made to believe that their bodies are sinful, become conscious of their mortality: instead of heaven the 'black woof of death' is woven before them. Nevertheless as the work of Los continues Nature is seen for what it is: 'a Vision of the Science of the Elohim.' Its identity is validated, but also limited, by the Judaeo-Christian civilization which called it forth.

Book One ends with the conclusion of this long analysis of the nature of artistic inspiration. Book Two is concerned mainly with the theme of redemption through sublimity. Its opening page carries a design showing the rising and falling of humanity and inscribed with the words 'How wide the gulf and Unpassable! between Simplicity and Insipidity' and

> Contraries are positives
> A Negation is not a contrary

These lines both refer us back to the earlier themes of the three classes of men (for wrath and pity are contraries, Satan no more than a negative) and remind us of Blake's dialectic in such works as *The Marriage of Heaven and Hell*. Contraries need to be 'married'—to rise to the state of threefold vision.

It is not surprising, therefore, that the opening of the second book should be set in the country of Beulah, 'a place where Contrarieties are equally True'. But Beulah is here seen also from a different angle. Viewed from Eternity, it is a place of resting after the exercise of fourfold vision. When Milton descends from Eternity, the sons and daughters of Ololon, deprived of his inspiring presence, go down into Beulah as their natural refuge.

The description of their descent and their mourning for Milton is followed by lines describing Beulah more fully. Its nature differs according to whether it is seen from Eternity or from earth. Beulah is always a land of threefold vision, of Pathos, but whereas in Eternity, pathos is a resting-place from the sublime, in earth it becomes an ideal in itself: love, pity and compassion are so important in a visionless world that the dangers of depending upon them exclusively are not apparent.

Beulah is evermore Created around Eternity; appearing
To the Inhabitants of Eden, around them on all sides.
But Beulah to its Inhabitants appears within each district
As the beloved infant in his mothers bosom round incircled
With arms of love & pity & sweet compassion. But to
The Sons of Eden the moony habitations of Beulah,
Are from Great Eternity a mild & pleasant Rest.

                                                            (30. 8–14)

Blake pictures this region as having been created for the
Emanations who could not endure the 'wars', the mental fight
of Eternity.

As the breath of the Almighty. such are the words of man to man
In the great Wars of Eternity, in fury of Poetic Inspiration,
To build the Universe stupendous: Mental forms Creating

                                                            (30. 18–20)

Beulah provides not only a shield from the heat of this fight but
a shadow into which the sons of Eternity can pass, when there is
danger of their falling into error, and repose before returning to
the fight.

When the children of Ololon, deprived of the defining power
of Milton that would enable them to survive the heat of fourfold vision, descend into Beulah, Beulah weeps, for this irruption
from fourfold vision is an emblem of the Last Judgment which
they fear, when the divine power will finally break through the
clouds in fourfold glory. Just as Christ wept over the hard-
hearted Jerusalem, declaring that not one stone should be left
upon another, so Beulah weeps over 'rocky Albion' (which
contains the lost Jerusalem). The weeping spreads to the rest of
the earth: to the nations, from America and India, where the
coming of the Lord 'in the clouds of Ololon' is also foreseen; and
to the fairies, nymphs, gnomes and genii of the four elements
which know only of generation, not of regeneration—of
destructive war, and the furnaces of creative energy, not of the
mental wars of inspiration in Eternity. These apocalyptic
rumours of destruction cause Orc to howl, Enitharmon to
tremble and Beulah to weep.

But the weeping of Beulah is gradually transmuted into an
unearthly music. For the lament of Beulah over Ololon reflects not only a terrified foresight of destruction but a dim

recognition that the same event would be desirable if it took place in fourfold power: it represents the yearning of the temporal for the eternal.

So Blake expresses its effects by two of his finest symbols of the relation between time and eternity: the lark, rising at daybreak, and the flower, opening to the sun. Both represent a response to the light of glory, but in opposite forms. The soaring lark expresses the reaching of the human spirit beyond the confines of the finite universe, while the opening flower expresses the presence of Eternity within the smallest measurable space, its response of beauty imaging the opening of the human heart to a world from which the Og and Anak of moral and natural law would keep it. An erotic reference is evident throughout. The accomplishment of Blake's genius is so sustained in the two visions that they deserve quotation in full:

> Thou hearest the Nightingale begin the Song of Spring;
> The Lark sitting upon his earthy bed: just as the morn
> Appears: listens silent: then springing from the waving Cornfield!
>   loud
> He leads the Choir of Day! trill, trill, trill, trill,
> Mounting upon the wings of light into the Great Expanse:
> Reechoing against the lovely blue & shining heavenly Shell:
> His little throat labours with inspiration; every feather
> On throat & breast & wings vibrates with the effluence Divine
> All Nature listens silent to him & the awful Sun
> Stands still upon the Mountain looking on this little Bird
> With eyes of soft humility, & wonder love & awe.
> Then loud from their green covert all the Birds begin their Song
> The Thrush, the Linnet & the Goldfinch, Robin & the Wren
> Awake the Sun from his sweet reverie upon the Mountain:
> The Nightingale again assays his song, & thro the day,
> And thro the night warbles luxuriant; every Bird of Song
> Attending his loud harmony with admiration & love.
> This is a Vision of the lamentation of Beulah over Ololon:

> Thou percievest the Flowers put forth their precious Odours!
> And none can tell how from so small a center comes such sweets
> Forgetting that within that Center Eternity expands
> Its ever during doors, that Og & Anak fiercely guard.
> First eer the morning breaks joy opens in the flowery bosoms
> Joy even to tears, which the Sun rising dries; first the Wild Thyme
> And Meadow-sweet downy & soft waving among the reeds.
> Light springing on the air lead the sweet Dance: they wake

The Honeysuckle sleeping on the Oak: the flaunting beauty
Revels along upon the wind; the White-thorn lovely May
Opens her many lovely eyes: listening the Rose still sleeps
None dare to wake her. soon she bursts her crimson curtaind bed
And comes forth in the majesty of beauty; every Flower:
The Pink, the Jessamine, the Wall-Flower, the Carnation
The Jonquil, the mild Lilly opes her heavens! every Tree,
And Flower & Herb soon fill the air with an innumerable Dance
Yet all in order sweet & lovely, Men are sick with Love!
Such is a Vision of the lamentation of Beulah over Ololon.
                                          (31. 28–63)

The next plate, a later interpolation, may be left on one side
for the moment. There follows a 'Song of Beulah in the Lamentations of Ololon': the Divine Voice is heard singing a reproach
to his bride. Whereas she was lovely, mild and gentle when he
first married her, she has become 'terrible in jealousy & un-
lovely'—and this jealousy, in cutting her off from the love of her
husband, has robbed her of her own pleasures. Milton, however,
has descended to redeem her by his death and misery. When the
Sixfold Female perceives that he has cut himself off completely
from female loves and is thus annihilating himself, she will
relent and give her maidens to her husband. Babylon will no
longer turn away Jerusalem as a harlot, but will bring her in her
arms.

   This plate is doubly significant. The mention of Jerusalem
and Babylon indicates the germ of the next poem, *Jerusalem*,
where the theme of jealousy and forgiveness rises to full
prominence. And that theme suggests a comment on the historical John Milton—a hint that the failure of love on the part of
Milton's daughters and successive wives helped to produce a
slight neglect of sensitivity and grace which is noticeable in
Milton's later poetry in spite of its grandeur and energy.

   A full-page plate at this point shows Robert, Blake's favourite
brother, his right foot about to be penetrated by the falling star
of inspiration. This design, which is symmetrical with an earlier
design showing the less favoured brother William with the star
about to enter his left foot, helps to stress the inward symmetry
of the poem's structure: as Milton descends anew to death, so
Blake rises to redeem the human race from the bonds of
jealousy. The lamentation of Ololon in the songs of Beulah are

followed by Beulah's songs of comfort over her, for it is now recognized that Ololon, formerly glimpsed as a 'fiery circle' expelling Milton and the other seven Immortal Starry-Ones from Heaven, is filled with lamentations of pity and forgiveness. (There is a long throwback here, by way of Milton's God, who expels Satan yet afterwards looks down from heaven in pity, to the replacement of Old Testament vengeance by New Testament forgiveness.)

As the inhabitants of Ololon descend further, they see the four states of humanity in its repose: the head, the heart, the loins and seminal vessels and finally the stomach and intestines —which symbolizes, yet again, the fourth gate, behind the other three, where inspiration is finally lost. This last state, Or-Ulro, is the object of their search. To find it, they must pass down in the track of Milton's course. Just as Satan in his journeying passed the spot where the elements warred in the realms of Chaos and Old Night, so they pass a spot where the Contraries of Beulah, instead of striving in friendly contention, war in mutual destruction 'beneath Negations Banner'. From now on they see the whole of Ulro as a vast polypus of living fibres growing down into the Sea of Time and Space. Here, too, the ever-present danger of Beulah is revealed. To linger within the pleasures of Beulah is to vegetate within the bounds of family and parental love (in Greek, 'storge') and so eventually to die, enslaved by the five senses and the Nameless Shadowy Female their mother, the creators of human death,

> Spinning it from their bowels with songs of amorous delight
> And melting cadences that lure the Sleepers of Beulah down
> The River Storge (which is Arnon) into the Dead Sea . . .
>
> (34. 28–30)

In this universe of vegetation the regions of the Zoas exist, chaotic since their fall: the only defence lies in the universe which Los creates, the Mundane Egg containing Adam and Satan, the two limits of the human condition, and giving them form within the prevailing chaos. A diagram on a previous plate presents this idea in schematic form, showing Adam and Satan as states within an egg-shaped figure at the heart of four interlocked circles, bearing the names of the Four Zoas, which are in turn surrounded by the fiery tentacles of a flower-like figure (probably the Polypus). A line marked 'Milton's track' passes to the top part of the egg by way of the regions Luvah and Urizen, and is no doubt intended to suggest that Milton's previous work was mainly concerned with the struggle between God the Father's law and Satan's energy (Urizen and Luvah); whereas his new struggle will be truly central to the human condition by taking up the struggle of Adam (in the region of Urthona) against Satan (in the region of Urizen). This struggle for final integration between Los and Urizen is the struggle with which the artist must now be concerned: the battle of inspiration to reclaim reason underlies and interprets all other contentions in the world.

The sons of Ololon, following Milton's descent, take up their station at the same point of intersection between Urizen and Luvah, the point of the breach caused by Milton's entry. We know from the previous lines, which recount the story of *Vala*, that this was the point, between head and heart, where the fall of the Zoas was set in motion as Luvah assumed the world of Urizen. But this event was dependent upon a more profound disorder within the Eternal Man. To restore head and heart to their proper functions may be an adequate preparation for the redemption of man, but the redemption itself demands something more: the moment of inspiration which will break into the cycle and reintegrate its various functions. The sons of Ololon, who wish to awaken Urizen, can at present do no more than stand in his dark world of death, surveying the dismal state of a world governed by abstract reason.

As they look, they see how the world of Eternity is deformed and corrupted in the world of Vegetation; how the beasts, birds, fishes, plants and minerals which preserve their separate identities in Eternity are here huddled into a single shapeless mass; and how War and Hunting, which in their original forms of mental conflict and mental search are the 'Two Fountains of the River of Life' become in their worldly forms murderous and destructive. Brotherhood is finally corrupted, for even ideas, which ought to be the 'Divine Members' by which mental war is waged, are slain in offerings of sin. The Woof of Death covers the whole earth.

So enwrapped are they by this world of death that they cannot see the one great fact of life that does exist there—the world of Golgonooza constructed by Los. In fact Immortals cannot see it: only mortals can see it, because only they can die and so pass the Polypus. In their death they will be granted this image of eternity, just as in their sexual 'death' they may be granted a similar vision at the very moment when they are most in peril of vegetating.

> For Golgonooza cannot be seen till having passd the Polypus
> It is viewed on all sides round by a Four-fold Vision
> Or till you become Mortal & Vegetable in Sexuality
> Then you behold its mighty Spires & Domes of ivory & gold.
>
> (35. 22–5)

Ololon, likewise, can explore the world of death, not enter it. But in the course of this examination, the sons of Ololon come to the couch where Milton and the seven Starry Ones lie. Immediately they prostrate themselves before them, asking their forgiveness. And as they do so, a way is opened between Ulro and Eternity, the counterpart of that great causeway between Earth and Hell which was created by Satan's victory in Milton's Eden.[18] In the moment of seeking forgiveness, Ololon has descended to Los and Enitharmon: the forces of creativity have been linked once more with eternity.

So important is this moment that Blake goes on to describe its significance in further images. It is 'the Moment in each Day that Satan cannot find / Nor can his Watch Fiends find it'— that moment of inspiration, exempt from the searchings of destructive analysis, which can fructify in the other moments of the day and renovate them. Because it unites Ulro with Eternity, it can be described in terms of that moment of dawn in our world which daily images a restoration of eternal light. The imagery of lost paradise can also be used for it. As in Milton's Eden,[19] the fountain's two streams eventually reunite: there is a direct stream through Golgonooza and Beulah to Eden (a direct ascent through the levels of vision); there is also a stream which 'flows thro' the Aerial Void & all the Churches' to rejoin the other in Golgonooza. The two streams evidently reiterate the idea that inspiration, an immediate, self-contained experience, yet exerts its influence over all the uninspired moments of the day and all the uninspired days of the centuries, redeeming their negativeness.

The image of the fountain is accompanied by that of the wild thyme (inspiration expanding from an inward centre) and that of the lark (inspiration ascending to the infinite). Both are now seen as Los's messengers to Eden. The thyme is an unsightly root, appearing poisonous in Ulro; yet it marks the spot where Luvah slept in death: his empty tomb is fragrant with its scent, the spices speak of the Eternity to which he is gone. The lark, likewise, arises at dawn, irrupting into the endless, fruitless cycle of twenty-seven heavens with a twenty-eighth that renovates all the others. As he ascends to his highest point he meets another lark in the height—an image, perhaps, of the meeting together of all forms of inspiration at their purest:

> When on the highest lift of his light pinions he arrives
> At that bright Gate, another Lark meets him & back to back
> They touch their pinions tip tip: and each descend
> To their respective Earths & there all night consult with Angels
> Of Providence & with the Eyes of God all night in slumbers
> Inspired: & at the dawn of day send out another Lark
> Into another Heaven to carry news upon his wings
>
> (36. 1–7)

When the Lark ascends to the gate of heaven it meets Ololon descending. The lark in Eternity is no longer a small bird but a mighty angel; Ololon, descending, endures the reverse process: she is no longer a host of immortals but a single female, 'a virgin of twelve years'. In this form, which enables her to be received by mortals, she descends into the garden of Blake's cottage at Felpham (shown in his accompanying illustration). He greets her and asks her for her message, promising that he will undergo further afflictions if she wishes, but asking her to spare the fatigue of his wife. The virgin Ololon tells him that she is looking for Milton, terrified by her act in Eternity which set in motion all these events.

As she does so, Blake has a sudden vision of Milton's full nature. Despite his 'strength impregnable of majesty & beauty infinite' he has not resolved the inward struggles of his own self. The God of *Paradise Lost* is 'the Covering Cherub & within him Satan / And Rahab'—in other words, he retains that ultimate devotion to moral and natural law which is a protection for the selfhood. The God who will not completely forgive Adam and Eve when they kneel in penitence, but insists that the law must take its course, is himself a worshipper of Necessity and exists 'beyond the outline of Identity, in the Selfhood deadly'. To express the twofold nature of the Law to which Milton's God conforms, Blake runs together two ideas—that of the 'wicker man', in which 'vegetated' image the Druids used to sacrifice their victims to the moral law (Fig. 51)[20] and that of the dehumanization of the stars, by which they are turned from revelations of light and glory into the components of mathematically worked out patterns, and sacrificed to the cult of natural law.

> And he appeard the Wicker Man of Scandinavia in whom
> Jerusalems children consume in flames among the Stars
> (37. 11–12)

By his approval of such a God, Milton has shown that he contained within himself the horrors which he described in his own poem. The false gods whom he mentioned—Baal and Ashtaroth; Molech; Thammuz; Osiris, Isis and Orus[21]—had all been *created* by the cult of law and secrecy. The Egyptian religion, for example, expresses perfectly the contrast between a religion of secrecy and shame, in the nightly rites of Osiris, Isis and Orus, and a human religion, in the rising of the true lost Osiris, the sun-god of light.

> Osiris: Isis: Orus: in Egypt: dark their Tabernacles on Nile
> Floating with solemn songs, & on the lakes of Egypt nightly
> With pomp, even till morning break & Osiris appear in the
> sky. . . .
> (37. 27–9)

All such dark deities are the 'Spectre sons of the Druid Albion'. So the twenty-seven Heavens and their churches, involving within them the unholy marriage of Sin and Death, the Scarlet Woman and the Beast, Laws of Chastity and Rites of War, still exist unsubdued within Milton's original achievement. They exist because Milton's Shadow (to be distinguished from the inspired Milton) is still identified with the law-dominated world of the seventeenth and eighteenth centuries. In such a visionless universe, the Orc of Energy lies perpetually as a potential destroyer:

> The Spectre of Albion in which the Spectre of Luvah inhabits
> In the Newtonian Voids between the Substances of Creation
> (37. 45-6)

These voids are the darknesses of time and space into which scientific analysis marshals the existence of the stars. As elsewhere, Blake reverses the normal picture of the universe: where the average observer sees a world of darkness flecked with random points of light, he sees a world of light, broken by the darkness between the stars—

> . . . Caverns whose remotest bottoms meet again beyond
> The Mundane Shell in Golgonooza, but the Fires of Los, rage
> In the remotest bottoms of the Caves, that none can pass
> Into Eternity that way . . .   (37. 55-8)

The process of scientific analysis does not in itself lead to non-existence, but it does lead back to the world of Los; it can reach further only by passing through his fires into the world of twofold vision.

In fulfilment of this vision Milton, that being of 'impregnable strength' who created a whole epic of inspiration, yet based his heavens upon the Law, hardens into a single figure, the familiar, strong-faced puritan of the portraits.

> And Milton collecting all his fibres into impregnable strength
> Descended down a Paved work of all kinds of precious stones
> Out from the eastern sky: descending down into my Cottage
> Garden: clothed in black, severe & silent he descended.
> (38. 5-8)

Now the conflict is made vaster as this spectrous selfhood of Milton is expanded into the Spectre of Satan, a mighty Demon which roars upon the sea, rolling his formless thunders against 'Milton within his sleeping Humanity'—the Blake who still guards his Vision. By yet another twist of *Paradise Lost* and its imagery[22] Milton's selfhood is described in terms of Milton's Hell,

> A ruind Man: a ruind building of God not made with hands;
> Its plains of burning sand, its mountains of marble terrible:
> Its pits & declivities flowing with molten ore & fountains
> Of pitch & nitre: its ruind palaces & cities & mighty works . . .
> (38. 16-19)

BH — N

But in the midst of this ruined world, at its eastern point of inspiration, Milton himself stands and declares his intention. He knows that he has the power to destroy this Satan (just as the God of *Paradise Lost* had destroyed *his* Satan or as the Greek gods overcame each other in a succession of celestial dynasties). But this would be in effect to bow down to the laws of Satan's universe. The laws of Eternity are otherwise: they demand not destruction but 'Self Annihilation'. This self-annihilation is not a matter of abject humility. It is the Priests and Churches who inculcate such humility by impressing on men the fear of death. Milton, by contrast, will advance in fearless majesty, laughing to scorn the 'Laws and terrors' of Satan and continually exposing self-righteousness and hypocrisy wherever they are to be found.

In response to this supreme challenge, Satan comes in a cloud with trumpets and burning fire, imitating the figure of the Divine Judge and commanding Milton to fall and worship him. He bears the scales of justice and the sword. He alone is God. He demands obedience until all become 'One Great Satan', a single formless mass drawing all things into itself in a holiness which excludes Mercy and 'the Divine Delusion, Jesus' for ever.

Milton/Blake, in reply, burns with the fires of his own inspiration, while the Seven who descended with him sound their own trumpets and stand in a column of fire, entirely free from the cloud that lurks over Satan. Their call to Milton is a universal call to Albion (and so to all mankind) to awake and subdue his reasoning spectre to the divine mercy, casting him into the burning lake of Los. In reply, Satan sets up a howl against Milton. He can only hover expectantly by him, however, for if he ever touches a vital part he will be plunged into unendurable torment. He is allowed to imitate the form of the 'Eternal Great Humanity Divine', possessing his own paved-work of precious stones and surrounded by his own cherubim. But his Cherubim are not the glorious beings of 'happy Eternity', they are inhabitants of the world through which Milton's Satan passed on his way from Hell: Sin and Death to right and left, Chaos beneath and Ancient Night spreading out his laws above.

Albion tries to respond to the summons, but rears himself

only to fall back in weakness. Nevertheless, there are signs that
the struggle is going in favour of Milton's inspiration. In a
return to the former 'baptismal' image, Urizen begins to faint
before the power of Milton's spirit in their struggle among the
Brooks of Arnon. Ololon, watching the conflict, comments in
amazement on one feature of it: the supporters of Urizen are
also the supporters of religion. She asks herself whether this
'Natural Religion'—an impossible self-contradiction which is
yet possessed of deadly power by virtue of the resources on
which it draws—can be in some way due to her.

> . . . how is this thing? this Newtonian Phantasm
> This Voltaire & Rousseau: this Hume & Gibbon & Bolingbroke
> This Natural Religion! this impossible absurdity
> Is Ololon the cause of this? O where shall I hide my face
> These tears fall for the little-ones: the Children of Jerusalem
> Lest they be annihilated in thy annihilation.
>
> (40. 11–16)

The earlier part of her speech makes it clear that she sees the
feminine gestures towards religion which accompany the
masculine acceptance of scientific analysis as a possible consequence of Leutha's having awakened the feminine perceptions of Satan (as described in the Bard's Song). As soon as she
has spoken against this effeminate religion of sensibility, there
appears against her the figure of Rahab Babylon, Religion
hidden in War, the hidden Harlot associated with the Beast in
Revelation, who is the cruel Moral Virtue of single vision. There
is a danger that Ololon, like the reactionaries of Blake's time,
will encourage the cult of dogmatic Religion as a defence
against Natural Religion, to protect the Children of Jerusalem
from the annihilation which she sees threatening Milton.
Milton, however, turns to Ololon and points out that annihilation, provided that it is annihilation of the Selfhood, is the very
thing that is needed if the Children of Jerusalem are to be
rescued from slavery. 'The Negation must be destroyed to
redeem the Contraries.' The annihilation of the spectral
reasoning power in man will result in a cleansing of his Immortal Spirit. The poem is reaching its climax: this plate,
with a design showing the selfhood Urizen striving against the
serpent Orc, is followed by a design at the head of the following

page showing a row of spirits linked in love and joy as Milton
further describes his self-annihilation:

> To bathe in the Waters of Life; to wash off the Not Human
> I come in Self-annihilation & the grandeur of Inspiration
> To cast off Rational Demonstration by Faith in the Saviour
> To cast off the rotten rags of Memory by Inspiration
> To cast off Bacon, Locke & Newton from Albions covering,
> To take off his filthy garments, & clothe him with Imagination
> To cast aside from Poetry, all that is not Inspiration
> That it no longer shall dare to mock with the aspersion of Madness
> Cast on the Inspired, by the tame high finisher of paltry Blots,
> Indefinite, or paltry Rhymes; or paltry Harmonies.
> Who creeps into State Government like a catterpiller to destroy
> To cast off the idiot Questioner who is always questioning,
> But never capable of answering: who sits with a sly grin
> Silent plotting when to question, like a thief in a cave:
> Who publishes doubt & calls it knowledge; whose Science is
> Despair,
> Whose pretence to knowledge is envy: whose whole Science is
> To destroy the wisdom of ages to gratify ravenous Envy;
> That rages around him like a Wolf day & night without rest
> He smiles with condescension; he talks of Benevolence & Virtue
> And those who act with Benevolence & Virtue, they murder time
> on time
> These are the destroyers of Jerusalem, these are the murderers
> Of Jesus, who deny the Faith and mock at Eternal Life!
> Who pretend to Poetry that they may destroy Imagination;
> By imitation of Natures Images drawn from Remembrance
>
> (41. 1–24)

Milton concludes his great speech by declaring that his act will
involve casting off the Sexual Garments in order to reveal the
Human Lineaments, the swallowing up of Generation in
Regeneration. At this final assertion of the superiority of
fourfold vision over threefold and twofold, Ololon trembles.
Like Enitharmon at the rise of Orc, the virgin female in her, the
part which is aligned with Milton's feminine emanation, feels
her very existence threatened by his masculine power:

> Altho' our Human Power can sustain the severe contentions
> Of Friendship, our Sexual cannot: but flies into the Ulro.
> Hence arose all our terrors in Eternity! . . .
>
> (41. 32–4)

Yet even as she pronounces her sexual fears, the fears which
originally produced the Female Will in opposition to the
Male, she recognizes that another truth is working behind
her terror. Milton and she are contraries only in the sexual
world: once restore the Human Vision and the Void outside
Existence will become a Womb; death will turn into fructifying
life.

As she recognizes this, the virgin element in her divides sixfold and passes into the depths of Milton's Shadow, where it
broods like a dove upon the stormy sea. And this negative
symbol of inspiration is accompanied by a positive one as
Ololon herself descends 'as a moony Ark' to Felpham's Vale.
This is the essential female, the Miltonic Eve ('He for God only,
she for God in him') who reflects the light of the male and acts
as a moon to his sun, reflecting his light back to him and sustaining his inspiration. As Ololon takes upon herself this eternal
function, the Seven surrounding Milton fuse with him, eight
into one Man, Jesus the Saviour, who walks forth into Albion's
bosom of death while the angels put their trumpets to their lips
and sound them to the four winds.

In this final action, Blake expresses the eternal act of the
inspired man. It is his task to enter into the very body of death
in his age in order that a revelation of selflessness may be
granted to it at its heart. But inspiration at its most intense is
also apocalyptic: by the light which it brings, it reveals that all
creation is judged continually and in each moment. So Blake
pictures his own inspiration as a moment of terrible revelation,
followed by a restoration to the mortal condition. Simultaneously the symbols of inspiration, the Lark and the Wild Thyme,
appear again, bringing with them a vision of the whole human
condition, a vast vegetation dominated by the figures of Los and
Enitharmon. The latter are now pictured as clouds over
London, and the image is presently broken down into that of
Oothoon, weeping like rain over the harvest, and Los, like a
heavy storm-cloud, louring over the scene, dark with anger at
the injustices suffered by the poor. These milder and ever-
present images are in turn replaced by images of thunder and
lightning, in the shape of Rintrah and Palamabron, which
bring the theme to a climax by predicting an apocalyptic

storm of revolution which will be at once the moment of harvest
and of total judgment.

In this final image of humanity as 'vegetated', Blake has
produced a symbol for the state of man which allows him to
express both continuing judgment, through Los and Enitharmon and their message to man, and a 'final' judgment, through
the imagery of the imminent harvest. Instead of trying (as he
had done in *Vala*) to describe the Last Judgment, with the
implication that it is about to happen, he can exploit this
subtler myth—continually valid whether the Last Judgment
happens tomorrow or is deferred indefinitely. Man is always
under judgment in his 'vegetable body': the fruit of his actions
is constantly being harvested. And this is true on a world-wide
scale as well as in the individual. As Rintrah and Palamabron
stand ready to go forth to the Harvest, the animals which sport
and play in readiness express the eternal ambiguity of the
human situation. They are lions and tygers, symbols of twofold vision. According to the situation that arises, so will be
their role in the harvest: either the wheat-crop of Wisdom and
the vintage of Love will be brought to the barns and the wine-
presses, in which case their sport and play will continue, or, if
thought and sexual energy continue to be inhibited by natural
and moral laws, respectively, the resultant coupling of the
Beast and the Whore in a riot of war and violence will release
the animal energies in destruction.

Posing this everlasting alternative before his readers, Blake
concludes his poem. His final design shows a man and woman,
rooted in the ground like ears of corn, looking in ambiguous
wonder at a female figure, casting aside her veil: she is the
Nature who can either be worshipped for her own sake as Vala,
or reverenced as Ololon, the revelation of eternity within the
natural order. According to the alternative followed, the
actions, and ultimately the harvest which follows those actions,
will be determined.

> Terror struck in the Vale I stood at that immortal sound.
> My bones trembled. I fell outstrctchd upon the path
> A moment, & my Soul returnd into its mortal state
> To Resurrection & Judgment in the Vegetable Body
> And my sweet Shadow of Delight stood trembling by my side

Immediately the Lark mounted with a loud trill from Felphams
    Vale
And the Wild Thyme from Wimbletons green & impurpled Hills
And Los & Enitharmon rose over the Hills of Surrey
Their clouds roll over London with a south wind, soft Oothoon
Pants in the Vales of Lambeth weeping oer her Human Harvest
Los listens to the Cry of the Poor Man: his Cloud
Over London in volume terrific, low bended in anger.

Rintrah & Palamabron view the Human Harvest beneath
Their Wine-presses & Barns stand open; the Ovens are prepar'd
The Waggons ready: terrific Lions & Tygers sport & play
All Animals upon the Earth, are prepard in all their strength

To go forth to the Great Harvest & Vintage of the Nations.
                                        (42. 24–31. 1)

In spite of some obscurities, *Milton* is a surprisingly coherent
poem. In it, Blake managed to purge away many of the gothic
turgidities which rose in the pages of his earlier prophetic
books, achieving at last a myth of the apocalyptic which could
include all the relations between Time and Eternity, from the
continuous judgments which are enacted in everyday life to the
Last Judgment itself.

But the main theme of the poem is inspiration. The designs
in the poem give a strong clue: they are nearly all concerned
with the Inspired Man and his struggles against the forces of
Reason and Law. And this preoccupation, it will be noticed,
has gradually led Blake away from the field of political events to
a consideration of art and its nature. His prose writings during
this decade show the same trend. Constantly, as he defends
his mode of painting, he asserts the cause of Inspiration against
Tradition in the visual arts. The statement in *Milton* that the
Inspired Man is mocked with 'the aspersion of Madness' by
'the tame high finisher of paltry Blots / Indefinite, or paltry
Rhymes, or paltry Harmonies', can be matched by this piece of
detailed criticism in the *Public Address*:

The unorganized Blots & Blurs of Rubens & Titian are not Art
nor can their Method ever express Ideas or Imaginations any
more than Popes metaphysical Jargon of Rhyming.[23]

The direction of Blake's interests can also be seen from some
plates inserted into two copies of *Milton* which he issued after

the earliest version. Of these plates, two were simply intended to introduce passages from the earlier prophetic books, one consisting of the description of the binding of Urizen and the other of the closing up and imprisoning of the senses. These plates, probably the last to be engraved, would thus bring more of Blake's essential beliefs into the early pages of *Milton*. Of the others, three contain references to Druidism as the enemy of true art. Plate 6 (in Blake's text), an early interpolation, seems to have been intended originally for *Jerusalem* (where it would in fact fit well after Plate 69) and was probably transferred for the sake not of the text, which is more related to the themes of the later book, but of the design, a large druid trilithon and rocking stone, both completely overshadowing a man on horse-back who is passing beneath. Plate 4, which also carries designs showing druid temples, ends by describing creative men

> Mocking Druidical Mathematical Proportion of Length, Bredth Highth
> Displaying Naked Beauty! with Flute & Harp & Song. . . .

while Plate 32 consists of a discussion between Milton and his Seven Angels, who tell him that they are still combined into Human Form because they were combined in freedom and brotherhood at the time when Satan turned those who were completely in his power into shapeless rocks, 'Retaining only Satans Mathematical Holiness, Length: Bredth & Highth.' These remarks are matched in the prose works by such comments as the one prompted by Reynolds's remark that certain qualities in art were 'as true as mathematical demonstration'. Blake writes, 'God forbid that Truth should be Confined to Mathematical Demonstration.'[24]

The Seven Angels go on to point out that they are not Individuals but States. States, like Time and Space, are mercies which are granted in order that mankind may pass through them. The Imagination is not a State, it is the Human Existence itself. On the other hand,

> The Memory is a State always, & the Reason is a State
> Created to be Annihilated & a new Ratio Created
> Whatever can be Created can be Annihilated Forms cannot
> The Oak is cut down by the Ax, the Lamb falls by the Knife
> But their Forms Eternal Exist, For-ever. Amen Hallelujah

The preoccupation with Form which may have been stimulated by the passage from Dryden that serves as a background to
The Gates of Paradise (see Appendix Two) is paralleled and
glossed by the description of 'the Nature of Visionary Fancy'
in 'A Vision of the Last Judgment':

> ... the Oak dies as well as the Lettuce but Its Eternal Image & In-
> dividuality never dies. but renews by its seed. just so the Imagina-
> tive Image returns by the seed of Contemplative Thought. . . .[25]

The latter work is full of statements which echo the references
to artistic experience in *Milton*. Its apocalyptic note, for
example, is summed up in the simple statement, 'Whenever any
Individual Rejects Error & Embraces Truth a Last Judgment
passes upon that Individual.'[26] And the contrast between
'vegetative' humanity and man in the vision of Eternity is
expressed to the height of Blake's powers in the famous passage
which concludes the work.

> What it will be Questiond When the Sun rises do you not see
> a round Disk of fire somewhat like a Guinea O no no I see an
> Innumerable company of the Heavenly host crying Holy Holy
> Holy is the Lord God Almighty I question not my Corporeal or
> Vegetative Eye any more than I would Question a Window con-
> cerning a Sight I look thro it & not with it.[27]

An examination of the illustrations to *Milton* shows one unexpected feature. The bard is not a figure burning in the fires of
his own energy. Instead, a soft moon-like halo surrounds him.
Milton's gesture of self-giving is made in the mild light of
threefold vision. His final, fourfold triumph is not depicted
visually.

This advance corresponds to a change in the organization of
Blake's attitudes which is described briefly in the poem 'William
Bond'.[1] William Bond goes to church on a May morning and
returns home sick with love for a girl whom he has seen. He
tells his wife

> . . . thou art Melancholy Pale
> And on thy Head is the cold Moons shine
> But she is ruddy & bright as day
> And the sun beams dazzle from her eyne

His wife's reaction is selfless: she says that she is willing to be
the servant to the other girl if she becomes his wife. Her feelings
are too much for her, however, and she falls down in a swoon.

When she recovers, William Bond declares that he has discovered the true nature of love:

> I thought Love livd in the hot sun shine
> But O he lives in the Moony light
> I thought to find Love in the heat of day
> But sweet Love is the Comforter of Night

The sun and moon imagery here is linked to the states of twofold vision in energy and threefold vision in love. Despite the
attractions of both, William Bond is forced to recognize the
superiority of threefold.

Whether or not the poem refers to an actual incident in
Blake's personal life, William Bond's final conclusion corresponds to a change of attitude in Blake himself. During the

composition of the shorter prophetic books he was constantly toying with the idea that since the energy of twofold vision was the key to fourfold an exploration of the world of desire might prove to be the true way of inspiration. That idea is potent in *The Marriage of Heaven and Hell, Visions of the Daughters of Albion* and *America*. Here Blake achieves a verse which glows with sexual life: his mood may be compared with that in which D. H. Lawrence wrote *The Rainbow*. Further evidences of Blake's sexual preoccupations may be found in the phallic illustrations to the manuscript of *Vala* and in his pencil drawings to illustrate the Ethiopic Book of Enoch;[2] it is probable that other drawings of the type were destroyed after his death.

Blake, if he had wished, could have mined this vein further. He could have made it a major resource of his later vision, as Lawrence did. He refused this possibility, however, and held fast to the hierarchy of his fourfold vision—a hierarchy which had been invoked before. At the end of his long poem *Vala*, for example, one of the Zoas enunciates the doctrine that man is greater than his desires and individual faculties,[3] while Milton's great victory is won neither in the fulfilment nor in the abnegation of physical desire, but by self-giving in the light of vision. In Blake's final long poem, *Jerusalem*, the dominant theme is not liberty but forgiveness. Desire is always accepted; it is acknowledged that 'Jerusalem is named Liberty among the sons of Albion';[4] but light, not energy, love, not desire, are the final keys to the fourfold vision in which Albion rises again.

This change in the economy of Blake's beliefs had also been influenced by the changing pattern of events in Europe. The self-contradiction involved in the suppression of liberties in Switzerland and the advent of Napoleon shook the loyalties of staunch supporters of the French Revolution who had been able to explain the earlier violence as necessary in the cause of liberty. Blake, who had always been aware of the dangers inherent in revolutionary energy, was evidently moved also: an unexpected swing towards patriotism may be traced in his work at this time. We find, for example, a pair of paintings entitled 'The Spiritual form of Nelson guiding Leviathan . . .' and 'The Spiritual form of Pitt guiding Behemoth . . .'[5] which he offers to reproduce, if commissioned, as frescoes for the nation.[6] This can hardly be cynical opportunism; it springs rather from a new recognition of the intractability of certain forces in human affairs and of the need for visionary leaders to tame and guide them in every sphere. Men such as Pitt and Nelson have a potential rôle—which they may or may not fulfil adequately.

At the time that Orc, spirit of revolutionary energy, ceased to play an important part in Blake's poetry his sexual doctrines, as has been suggested, underwent a shift of emphasis. The important piece of evidence is a letter of October, 1804, which recounts a change in his artistic fortunes:

> For now! O Glory! and O Delight! I have entirely reducd that spectrous Fiend to his station, whose annoyance has been the ruin of my labours for the last passed twenty years of my life. He is the enemy of conjugal love and is the Jupiter of the Greeks, an iron-hearted tyrant, the ruiner of ancient Greece. I speak with perfect confidence and certainty of the fact which has passed upon me. Nebuchadnezzar had seven times passed over him; I have had twenty; thank God I was not altogether a beast as he was; but I was a slave bound in a mill among beasts and devils; these beasts and these devils are now, together with myself, become children of light and liberty, and my feet and my wife's feet are free from fetters . . . Suddenly, on the day after visiting the Truchsessian Gallery of pictures, I was again enlightened with the light I enjoyed in my youth, and which has for exactly twenty years been closed from me as by a door and by window-shutters . . . O the distress I have undergone, and my poor wife with me: incessantly labouring and incessantly spoiling what I had done well . . .
> . . . Dear Sir, excuse my enthusiasm or rather madness, for I am really drunk with intellectual vision whenever I take a pencil or graver into my hand, even as I used to be in my youth, and as I have not been for twenty dark, but very profitable years . . .[7]

There is not such a complete renaissance of his art in 1804 as this letter might suggest. What does happen is that he becomes steadily more and more reliant upon inward vision for his inspiration, less concerned to stress the need for any particular form of behaviour or to yearn for an all-embracing mythology. Simultaneously, he becomes less concerned to press his own ideas at the expense of other people's, more ready to let them exist side by side.

One further event may be mentioned. In the summer of 1803, Blake found a soldier in his garden and expelled him. As

a result the soldier, named Schofield, falsely accused Blake of
using seditious language and caused him to be committed for
trial.[8] In the account of the affair which he sent to Butts, Blake
included a brief reference to his own character.

> Perhaps the simplicity of myself is the origin of all offences com-
> mitted against me. If I have found this I shall have learned a most
> valuable thing well worth three years perseverance. I have found
> it! It is certain! that a too passive manner, inconsistent with my
> active physiognomy had done me much mischief I must now
> express to you my conviction that all is come from the spiritual
> World for Good & not for Evil.[9]

The Schofield affair seems to have had the good effect of
rousing him towards fresh positiveness and activity—an
activity of which the reillumination just described may well
have been a result. Paradoxically, the new activity involved
making an end to the long obsession with energy. For a time
this obsession had helped to produce some of his finest works—
not only in poetry but in visual art. The illustrations to
America are made particularly effective by the concentration
on line-drawing.

Blake's total paradigm had always, however, involved seeing
the world of energy as a subordinate world. His return to the
primacy of 'vision' was a renewal of his devotion to the structure of his original visionary universe. Even while he was
flirting with the idea of the primacy of energy he did not lose
sight of that structure, as we have seen; the same is true of his
visual art. Round about 1795 he produced several paintings
which show clearly the structuring of his ideas. Two enlarged
versions (Fig. 30) of a design from *The Marriage of Heaven and
Hell* show a man, blinded, possessed by the lineaments of
energy, reaching through the flames of twofold vision while a
woman and child shrink from him.[10] The fatal effects of a
division between the energies of twofold vision and the light of
threefold, the blind heat of the one, the anxious restriction of
the other, are thus emblematized. Other paintings of the period
complete the fourfold paradigm: one (Fig. 48), shows Newton, a
beautiful figure seated at the bottom of the ocean, bending his
gaze on the limited mathematical diagrams of single vision,[11]
another Elisha standing by Elijah (who is exactly like him,

but sits in the chariot of fire) ready to be translated into the fourfold prophetic vision.[12]

Other designs display Blake's preoccupations in reading *Paradise Lost*. The first and most famous is the design 'The Ancient of Days', (Fig 24) which shows Urizen leaning from his fading sun-disk with a pair of compasses and which, as we have seen, is accompanied in one version by the quotation from Book Seven of Milton's poem,

> He took the golden Compasses, prepared
> In God's Eternal store, to circumscribe
> This Universe, and all created things.[13]

Another design complements this by showing the Lazar House in Book Eleven.[14] Here, the briefest of hints from Milton is the cue for a full-scale reproduction of life in Urizen's world. Over a set of suffering men, a tyrannical god brandishes the dart (in one version, the phallus)[15] of his moral law. The simple 'circumscribing' of Book Seven has gradually turned the whole universe into a gloomy, disease-ridden prison.

Two designs reflect another major preoccupation of Blake's at this time. The first, 'The Elohim creating Adam' (Fig. 34), shows an aging but virile God stretching himself over a man who is being created in his image except for the lower part of his body, where the presence of serpent coils betrays the dangerously autonomous activity of his energies.[16] In the second design, 'Satan exulting over Eve' (Fig. 35), it is Eve who is lying on the ground, while over her hovers a male figure. The coiled serpent which has taken possession of him now rears its head above his own.[17] Thus Blake illustrates the fall of Man by the rearing of his energy, isolated from vision, into an autonomous Selfhood which governs all his actions.

A critique of liberalism was always implicit in the existence of Blake's various levels of vision, but at first this hardly touched his view that mankind could and would awaken to liberty after the French Revolution, and that free indulgence of desire could lead to nothing but good. As time went by, however, he saw that absolute liberty was an impossibility in this world except in a state of shared vision; and since the indulgence of the energies in any lesser state led automatically to corruption, it was Vision, not Liberty, which must come first. This movement of his thought harmonized with the experience recorded earlier, when he found himself flooded again by the vision which had possessed him in youth.

The change of attitude affects his approach to other writers. He becomes more willing to accept their own view and then to use it as a vehicle for his own vision. In the case of Chaucer's *Canterbury Tales*, indeed, he seems to go further than his author in tolerance. When we remember his vituperations against the hypocrites and rogues of his own day, we might expect that he would speak out more strongly than Chaucer himself against such characters as the pardoner or the friar. Instead, however, he dwells upon the good rather than the bad in each. Even when he comes to the pardoner, he finds something to be said in favour of the man:

> But I have omitted to speak of a very prominent character, the Pardoner, the Age's Knave, who always commands and domineers over the high and low vulgar. This man is sent in every age for a rod and scourge, and for a blight, for a trial of men, to divide the classes of men, he is in the most holy sanctuary, and he is suffered by Providence for wise ends, and has also his great use, and his grand leading destiny.[18]

The reason for Blake's tolerance is that he is at this time possessed by his view that there are eternal 'states' which contain the living and moving form of all things. This he makes clear in his earlier description of Chaucer's work:

> The characters of Chaucer's Pilgrims are the characters which compose all ages and nations: as one age falls, another rises, different to mortal sight, but to immortals only the same; for we see the same characters repeated again and again, in animals, vegetables, minerals, and in men; nothing new occurs in identical existence; Accident ever varies, Substance can never suffer change nor decay.
>
> Of Chaucer's characters, as described in his Canterbury Tales, some of the names or titles are altered by time, but the characters themselves for ever remain unaltered, and consequently they are the physiognomies or lineaments of universal human life, beyond which Nature never steps. Names alter, things never alter. I have known multitudes of those who would have been monks in the age of monkery, who in this deistical age are deists. As Newton

numbered the stars, and as Linneus numbered the plants, so Chaucer numbered the classes of men.[19]

Some of Blake's best art is produced when he is working in the light of this idea. Instead of painting pictures in which the various energies of a single man are divided against each other (a conception which requires some habituation in the mind of the spectator) he can portray varying types of men, with a corresponding variety of lineaments. Even so, however, his basic attitude remains the same: the illustration *The Canterbury Pilgrims*[20] does not make sense until one has grasped the point that basically every character *has the same face.* Looking at the Wife of Bath, the Reeve and the Miller, we discover that in spite of widely varying features, there is a common pattern underlying each, the lineaments of the 'human face Divine'. And within this pattern each has its own identity.

Blake's interpretation of Chaucer is also at work in his engraving of the gateway from which the pilgrims are issuing, which is gothic in design, yet which, in one of the versions, is inscribed, 'The Tabarde Inne by Henry Bailly. The Lodgynge House for Pilgrims who Journey to Saint Thomas's Shrine at Canterbury'. The idea of giving the Tabard Inn a gothic architecture springs from a familiar theme of Blake's: in the true state of Vision, men would combine the imaginative beauty of religious worship at its best with the cheerfulness and humanity of the alehouse. The staff of the inn, who have come out to minister to the pilgrims as they set off, are also created into visionary figures, like the inhabitants of Jerusalem: as they stand watching the human pageant pass away from them, their faces shine with innocence.

The illustration *The Canterbury Pilgrims* is one of Blake's major successes in the fusion of his own vision with another man's. For if he is kinder to the unpleasant pilgrims than Chaucer, his tolerance extends the humanitarianism of the latter's work.

The shift in Blake's attitude is to be seen very clearly when he comes to execute a set of designs for Milton's poem. In his revolutionary days, he was most attracted by the figure of Satan and repelled by the Urizenic necessitarianism of God the Father. He does not now abandon his view that when Satan is thrown out of heaven both he and the inhabitants of heaven are deprived, but he shows a greater sympathy for the Father and the angels. If Satan remains the protagonist of human energy, God is now more clearly the protagonist of Vision. So the Fall of the Angels is depicted with God the Son in the midst of the sun-disk, wielding a bow at its circumference and plunging Satan and his followers downward in anguish, their faces expressing their perverted energy, while the loyal angels look on with mingled fear and admiration.[21] The use of the serpent as an emblem of energy rising into selfhood, already used in Blake's earlier illustrations to Milton, reappears in these designs. When Adam is depicted making love to Eve (Fig. 38) Satan is nearby, the coiled serpent rearing around him.[22] When Raphael descends from heaven, the serpent is reared above Satan's head.[23] In both cases, Satan expresses the dangerously active state of Adam's selfhood. While Raphael is talking to Adam and Eve (Fig. 3) Paradise is seen in its true state, wild animals wandering innocently and the serpent coiled round the Tree.[24] At the Fall, on the other hand (Fig. 39) Eve is seen accepting the apple from the jaws of the serpent, while Adam, unaware, stands away from her, wondering at the anger of the elements.[25] Finally, as Adam and Eve leave Paradise (Fig. 40) they both glance down at the serpent crawling at their feet.[26] This is the Selfhood of debased energy with which they must both henceforward live.

The nature of Satan, on the other hand, is little changed in this later work of Blake's. When, in a separate drawing (Fig. 44), he depicts 'Satan in his original glory',[27] the face, like those sometimes possessed by adolescent boys, has a feminine quality: the lineaments bear a notable resemblance to those of Eve. Satan, before the fall, combined the virtues of both sexes. (Nevertheless, his slight effeminacy must be compared with the masculinity of the Great Sun, in the illustrations to 'L'Allegro' (Fig. 45).) In the *Paradise Lost* sequence he is shown first summoning up his fellow angels, then encountering Sin and Death at the gates of Hell.[28] These two figures, who bear a distinct resemblance to the Beast and Whore of the Bible and Prophetic Books, are seen again when Adam and Eve receive the judgment after their Fall: Death, a kingly tyrant, throws down his darts at one side, while at the other Sin pours down a vial of poison.[29] But when Michael shows to Adam the figure of Christ on the Cross (Fig. 41), the serpent is seen with his eye pierced by the nail that holds Christ's foot and beneath the cross Sin and Death lie stretched in dreamlike death: before them Earth stirs and wakens as a young girl (the Lyca of *Songs of Experience*).[30] Blake's main themes, the rising of energy as selfhood, the subsequent creation of Sin and Death and the ultimate entrancement of energy by visionary power are deployed fully in this series and his use of symbolism—by contrast with the bewildering detail in some of the Prophetic Books— is both economical and deft.

In the designs for *Comus* and *Paradise Regained*, Blake once again focuses on the struggle between Vision and fallen Energy. He grasps the very evident relationship between Comus's temptation of the Lady by means of a banquet and the preparation of a miraculous feast for Christ by Satan (a detail invented by Milton).[31] In both cases he shows the visionary human being refusing delights offered by figures in whom an apparent attractiveness barely covers the lineaments of distorted energy. In the designs for 'L'Allegro' and 'Il Penseroso', finally, Blake is able to give free rein to a gift for light fantasy which he indulged all too rarely. One of the most striking designs is the one in which (to quote his own description) 'Mountains Clouds Rivers Trees appear Humanized on the Sunshine Holiday' (Fig. 53). The gaiety of the scene concentres in two mighty figures whose general forms correspond to the kingly Death and the whorish Sin of *Paradise Lost*, but who are shown in the peace of fulfilment and the lineaments of gratified desire; in the lap of the Woman is a large and peaceful city.[32] The last design to the same poem (Fig. 54) carries Blake's humanism to its heights. His own description of it runs as follows:

6. The youthful Poet sleeping on a bank by the Haunted Stream by Sun Set sees in his Dream the more bright Sun of Imagination under the auspices of Shakespeare & Johnson. in which is Hymen at a Marriage & the Antique Pageantry attending it[33]

In the imagination of the young visionary, at least, the human universe is articulated into a fourfold vision.

8 Unwanted Prospero

Blake lived through all the main stages of the Romantic Revival. As a young man, he had welcomed the 'Gothic' fashion and given it a more coherent intellectual basis than most of its supporters; he had lived to see that fashion give way to an Age of Taste, in which the extravagances of horrific writing were lightly mocked by Jane Austen and the ideal of Liberty subsumed into the easy exuberance of Lord Byron's writing. Although the new age brought a revival in the arts, Blake could hardly feel at home in it. Elegance, ease and sensibility were not qualities that he had ever cultivated for their own sakes. The new civilization was too closely associated with the rising upper middle-class to appear to a man who had avoided identifying himself with any particular stratum in society: Bath, in *Jerusalem*, is the ambiguous city, source both of healing waters and of social poisons. In consequence, he did not succeed in solving the problem which had dogged his early efforts. His need to communicate with contemporary society and his desire to create an art that was true to his own vision remained at variance.

The conflict appears, in an unusually simple form, in 'Auguries of Innocence',[1] a poem which is one of his best-known and which contains some of his most quoted lines:

A Robin Red breast in a Cage
Puts all heaven in a Rage.

A Horse misusd upon the Road
Calls to Heaven for Human blood.

The tone of these firm couplets might suggest that they represent the controlling attitude of the whole poem—a vivid indignation. Read under this expectation, however, other sections of the poem would appear to consist of little more than colourful exaggeration: and the reader might be puzzled by an apparent veering into Christian pietism in lines such as the following:

> The Bat that flits at close of Eve
> Has left the Brain that wont Believe
> The Owl that calls upon the Night
> Speaks the Unbelievers fright

Taken by themselves, such couplets read like cautionary verses for the children of pious households. To those who are more familiar with Blake's use of ideas such as that of 'Belief', they are, if less straightforward, more relevant to the rest of the poem. Blake's central purpose is not to attack cruelty directly. It is to advance a positive view of life, under the spell of which cruelty would automatically cease to exist. 'Belief' does not consist of subscribing to a set of doctrinal articles, but of joining in the general affirmation by which the universe exists:

> If the Sun & Moon should doubt
> Theyd immediately Go out.

The true point of the poem can be discovered by setting the epigraph at the beginning against the conclusion.

> To see a World in a Grain of Sand
> And a Heaven in a Wild Flower
> Hold Infinity in the palm of your hand
> And Eternity in an hour

This opening stanza is more than a positivist recommendation of the delights of nature. The words 'world', 'heaven', 'infinity' and 'eternity' are not being used hyperbolically. Each is subtly modified by the precision of Blake's thought and the power of his imagination. He is describing a state in which a single object can literally become the focus of the universe, acting symbolically to reveal its coherence and form. A grain of sand, the least of things, is given, by its power to reflect light, a crystalline beauty that it shares with the furthest stars. In just the same way the universe can either be seen as a collection of opaque objects, or transformed by the imagination into a world of endless light.

The wild flower acts differently. It is completely self-sufficient, and yet its beauty is constantly opening out; it grows

again when it is plucked; its scent has the power to possess the
human senses totally for a brief time. In each of these ways, it
is a miniature revelation of the eternal world.

Neither the grain nor the flower acts of itself, however;
each demands the presence of an imagination which is willing
both to see and to receive.

The syntax of the quatrain is ambiguous. It is often taken
to be a series of co-ordinate statements, each presupposing the
initial 'to', and constituting a series of aims. But it can be
read with a break at the end of the second line, to be followed
by two instructions: *in order to* see these things, *do the following*
(Hold Infinity, etc.). Whichever way one reads the quatrain,
the real key is left to the end of the poem. For the holding of
infinity in the palm of your hand and eternity in an hour,
whether conceived as a means or an end, depends in turn on the
fuller vision which is hinted at throughout the poem and
emerges in simple statement at the end.

> God Appears & God is Light
> To those poor Souls who dwell in Night
> But does a Human Form Display
> To those who Dwell in Realms of day

As we have seen elsewhere, this is a statement less of naïve
assurance than of sophisticated awareness. It is not that God
will reveal himself in human form as a special favour; for Blake,
this is the *only* way in which he *can* be fully revealed. Orthodox
Christians often think that God is partly seen in every human
being but that the full revelation of his glory would be an unendurable light. Blake reverses the idea. To conceive of God as
light is unnecessarily limiting—it was the sin of Moses to worship an unbearable holiness. In the full revelation God is seen
as human, the perfection of humanity. And this in its turn
leads to the redemption of all other vision, so that this 'infinite
and eternal' humanity, inhabiting an individual, actually pre-
vents him from seeking God in a realm of light beyond the
stars or within the atom, revealing instead a World in a Grain of
Sand and a Heaven in a Wild Flower.

'Auguries of Innocence', although fragmentary in the original
version, has a loose organization which goes some way to com-
pensate for its lack of a total form. When the first and the last

quatrains are set together, a basic tension is exposed—a tension to which every intervening couplet is in some way related. The paradoxical relationship between the grain of sand and the infinite, between the individual flower and eternity, is superseded by the identification of the divine and the human, which at once resolves the paradox and illuminates the relationship, by annulling the hegemony of dazzling light in the physical universe and of holiness in the moral world. All the other statements of the poem stand in the shadow of this one.

In this respect the poem is a microcosm of Blake's work as a whole. It has, supremely, the immediate appeal of his best work; a note of true feeling accompanied by touches of elegance and sensibility which reminds one of, say, Keats's letters. Beyond this, however, the poet relies on an indirect communication, an identification of the reader with the poet behind the poem.

Both sorts of communication are found in a couplet such as

The Emmets inch & Eagles Mile
Make Lame Philosophy to smile

A direct meaning is available to the eye of common sense; and this is given depth if the reader remembers the 'Motto' to *Thel*, with its assertion that the Eagle and the Mole have different experiences of reality, the eagle being unable, for all his airy ranging, to know what the mole discovers in his laboured exploration of the earth. But knowledge of *Thel* also lays bare a symbolic meaning. Blake is using the eagle and the mole to represent imaginative and physical experience respectively, and to assert that neither can be a substitute for the other: each complements 'lame philosophy' in a different fashion.

I doubt whether the casual reader grasps immediately the meaning of 'the Emmet's inch', or whether, if he does, he appreciates the extreme concentration of meaning within the couplet. But even if he does, he is still making a different sort of response from that which is invited by

A Robin Red breast in a Cage
Puts all Heaven in a Rage

Here the attention is focused entirely upon the imprisonment of the bird: the fact that its situation is symbolic of all other forms of imprisonment does not detract from its immediate and dominating presence before us. With the eagle and the emmet, on the other hand, physical reality, though important, is inseparably yoked to symbolic meaning. To read the couplet at its face value, as an assertion that animals are more vivid than philosophers, would leave an unnecessary residuum of uneasiness in the mind.

The poem contains many such examples. The reader is required constantly to make an adjustment to the balance between reality and symbolism—often in successive couplets. If he is already fully conversant with Blake's thought, the shifts will be made, one by one, without difficulty; if he is not, he will skim the surface of the more symbolic couplets, pass impatiently over those which contain philosophical imagery, and rest at the end in insecure possession of a poorer poem, a succession of notable fragments.

This critical problem hangs over Blake's work as a whole. Failure to communicate is not in itself a reason for condemnation. We do not charge Langland with incomprehensibility; we do not blame Pope if a reader brought up on the Victorian poets finds him unreadable. In both cases, we recognize that a degree of education is required, whether to learn Middle English, or to learn those exact nuances of meaning which would have been immediately present to an eighteenth-century reader.

But where the medieval poet has the defence of a shared language, or Pope the defence of a shared culture, so that to communicate with them is also to make contact with other minds in that country or period, Blake has only the narrower plea of a private vision. And since that vision is consciously at war with the artistic tradition of his time, the failure of communication must sometimes seem deliberate. There are moments when Blake, in the strength of his obstinacy, has recourse to a purely arbitrary symbolism.

Happily, such moments are rare; they are the product of a mind which, in the interests of communication with humanity, has cut itself off from communication with the contemporary artistic tradition. We have in our turn to choose between applying the canons of our own critical tradition or going on to accept the inextricable intertwining of reality and symbolism which, held successfully in the couplets of 'Auguries of Innocence', shades off, in his poetical work as a whole, from passages of brilliantly achieved imagery at the one extreme to arid patches of obsessed versification at the other.

Blake's most important mistake was to juxtapose various levels of symbolism in the same work of art and to pretend that every level corresponded equivalently. It is tempting to believe that every universe of discourse has the same shape, structure and dynamism. Every time that we speak of the body politic or the kingdom of heaven or the sovereignty of reason, we betray our liking for such reconciliation between the spheres in which we live. Unfortunately, however, no attempt to find a common myth which can be applied equally to the various spheres of man's physical, social, political and religious activity has succeeded. At every level, normally, special circumstances obtrude, peculiar to the nature of that particular sphere. Organizing patterns like the myth which he developed for *Vala* irritate by their manifest failure to reconcile disparate forms of experience as often as they please by their felicities of identification.

Blake succeeded best in this sphere with works such as *America*, *Visions of the Daughters of Albion* and *The Marriage of Heaven and Hell*, where one particular idea dominated the work, holding other identifications in strict subjection. Once we leave such works behind, we can proceed only by isolating the spheres of his discourse and evaluating each in turn.

First the personal, including the sexual. Here Blake's impact is most immediate and successful. Since he is always at his best in portraying visionary states of mind, it is not surprising that he succeeds so well with children, eliciting that visionary power which can for them invest the world with spendour and make every object subsist within its own light and form. Such an experience, common to children, can also visit adults in states of exaltation.

There is no need to press the point: we can best illustrate it by quoting a passage from a seventeenth-century writer which has already been cited by Bernard Blackstone for its authentic 'Blakean' quality of vision,

The corn was Orient and Immortal Wheat, which never should be reaped, nor was ever sown. I thought it had stood from everlasting to everlasting. The Dust and Stones of the Street were as precious as GOLD. The Gates were at first the End of the World, The Green Trees when I saw them first through one of the Gates Transported and Ravished me; their Sweetnes and unusual Beauty made my Heart to leap, and almost mad with Extasie, they were such strange and Wonderfull Thing: The Men! O what Venerable and Reverend Creatures did the Aged seem! Immortal Cherubims! And yong Men Glittering and Sparkling Angels and Maids strange Seraphick Pieces of Life and Beauty! Boys and Girles Tumbling in the Street, and Playing, were moving Jewels. I knew not that they were Born or should Die. But all things abided Eternaly as they were in their Proper Places. Eternity was Manifest in the Light of the Day, and som thing infinit Behind evry thing appeared: which talked with my Expectation and moved my Desire. The Citie seemed to stand in Eden, or to be Built in Heaven. The Streets were mine, the Temple was mine, the People were mine, their Clothes and Gold and Silver was mine, as much as their Sparkling Eys Fair Skins and ruddy faces. The Skies were mine, and so were the Sun and Moon and Stars, and all the world was mine, and I the only Spectator and Enjoyer of it. I knew no Churlish Proprieties, nor Bounds nor Divisions: but all Proprieties and Divisions were mine: all Treasures and the Possessors of them. So that with much adoe I was corrupted; and made to learn the Dirty Devices of this World. Which now I unlearn, and becom, as it were, a little Child again, that I may enter into the kingdom of GOD.[2]

The Blakean note is so strong here that one would be forced to conclude that he had read the works of Traherne—were it not for the fact that they remained unpublished until the present century. The coincidences of imagery and style therefore reflect not an influence but a common vision. Both writers have glimpsed a world where the revelation of eternity and infinity, so far from reducing all things beneath a single law, brings out the varying identity of each individual creature. Blake would have moved away in disagreement only at the end, where Traherne sees the loss of vision as part of a greater, sinful corruption. For him, that loss was itself the cause of corruption: corruption was the state left after vision had faded.

Although, as Blake pointed out, moments of illumination such as that described by Traherne are sometimes the accompaniment

of sexual activity, they are in general less frequent in adult
life. Even to those who experience them, awareness of the
adult world is likely to intrude and limit their effect. In childhood, on the other hand, the visionary experience more readily
colours the whole of life. Blake insisted, however, that the
visionary power remained potentially active in all men and
that a greater readiness to cultivate their imaginations would
make them aware of the fact. Edwin Muir once made a
similar suggestion. He thought that the full visionary state, in
which external world and inner imagination were perfectly
harmonized, was to be sought in early childhood; later it was
inevitably broken and darkened:

> I have often fancied . . . that in a child's mind there is at moments
> a divination of a hidden tragedy taking place around him, that
> tragedy being the life which he will not live for some years still,
> though it is there, invisible to him, already. And a child also has
> a picture of human existence peculiar to himself, which he prob-
> ably never remembers after he has lost it: the original vision of the
> world. I think of this picture or vision as that of a state in which
> the earth, the houses on the earth, and the life of every human
> being are related to the sky overarching them; as if the sky fitted
> the earth and the earth the sky. Certain dreams convince me that
> a child has this vision, in which there is a completer harmony of
> all things with each other than he will ever know again.[3]

Such totality of vision is expressed perfectly in the lyric which
forms a prelude to the second chapter of *Jerusalem*:

> The fields from Islington to Marybone,
> To Primrose Hill and Saint Johns Wood:
> Were builded over with pillars of gold,
> And there Jerusalems pillars stood.
>
> Her Little-ones ran on the fields
> The Lamb of God among them seen
> And fair Jerusalem his Bride:
> Among the little meadows green.[4]

The vision which reaches intensity in passages like this is also
present throughout the whole of Blake's writing. It is part of
the total effect of every passage that he writes. The impossibility
of completely producing it in language was evidently one
reason for his resorting to 'illumination' of his pages. The in-

ward beauty which cannot be fully projected into the word-continuum is glimpsed in the borders of his printed poem. One also needs to bear in mind that Blake had a strong musical sense. He sang several of his early songs at evening gatherings, and may have intended some of his other lyrics for the same purpose. Some of the *Songs of Innocence and of Experience* and other lyrics possess a banal effect rhythmically, which disappears if one imagines them sung.

> But he who kisses the joy as it flies
> Lives in Eternitys sun rise.[5]

It is difficult to speak the last line without making it sound lame: sung, the last two words are both stressed, with impressive effect.

When we turn to the element of social criticism in Blake's writing, we find some of his most unequivocal successes. In attacking the evils of his age, he is automatically licensed to use the full resources of contemporary language. Indignation was justified, moreover. England was at the height of the movement towards economic individualism which led men to view with detachment the distresses of their neighbours, relying upon an occasional subscription to charitable organizations for the expression of their compassion. Even the mild inroad upon the autocracy of the individual manufacturer which was to come with the first Factory Acts had not yet taken place.[6]

Blake's indignation was not primarily intended to produce legal reforms, however. He was more stirred by the inhumanity of his contemporaries—the coldness which allowed charity to be administered through impersonal organizations, the individualism which could not see the essential interdependence of man and man. The sense of social solidarity which was to be aroused in England in a limited form by the cholera epidemics of 1831–1865[7] was already fully active in the man who wrote

> But most thro' midnight streets I hear
> How the youthful Harlots curse
> Blasts the new-born Infants tear
> And blights with plagues the Marriage hearse[8]

One looks in vain for a detailed social philosophy in Blake. At all points his statements on the subject refer back to individual

human beings. Nevertheless, it is a useful corrective to mis-
conceptions of him to recall the strength of his social protest.
In this respect he is directly aligned with the tradition of warm-
hearted generosity that runs through much eighteenth-century
writing and persists into the Victorian age. It is a little surprising, for instance, to find in *Joseph Andrews* views which might
have come straight out of Blake's writings. In one of his
'author's disquisitions', Fielding protests that if he pillories a
lawyer, he has in mind no particular lawyer but the characteristics of the profession as a whole:

> . . . when the first mean selfish Creature appeared on the human
> Stage, who made Self the Centre of the whole Creation, would
> give himself no Pain, incur no Danger, advance no Money, to
> assist or preserve his Fellow-Creatures; then was our Lawyer
> born . . .[9]

Again, when Blake projects, behind the struggles of the Zoas,
the Eternal Man from whom they are all fallen, the image dis-
cerned is that of a ruddy-faced, generous husbandman. The
same figure haunted Cobbett's imagination. When the latter
announced that it was the chief aim of his writings to restore to
country labourers the status that they had had when he was a
boy he was pursuing the ideal of a central class of men, close
to the soil and generous to their fellows.[10] The tradition
reaches its climax in the novels of Charles Dickens, where the
open heart of humanity and the imaginative innocence of
childhood are basic values.

Blake did not, however, think that the ills of mankind could
be cured simply by acts of physical benevolence between man
and man. More, even, than Dickens, he saw that men are made
unhappy not only by lack of bread but by lack of vision. He
was thus brought within the range of a different tradition.
Belief in the human imagination as an instrument of truth, a
constant theme in the mystical writings of the seventeenth
century, was currently being revived by English visionaries.
And Blake's writings reveal that he shared the contemporary
interest in the work of Jacob Boehme, Swedenborg and Thomas
Taylor.

He stood at an angle to such traditions. He had the Neoplatonists' love of eternity, but not their hatred of the physical

or their shame at being in the flesh. He might declare that men ought not to cling to the physical, nor to fear that return of the body to its clay which is called death, but his own love of life was stronger, not weaker, than other men's. His inheritance from the 'perennial philosophy' is therefore limited; he would have regarded Plotinus' 'flight from the alone to the alone' as Urizenism in one of its purest forms.

Although the traditions of benevolence and Platonism are important to Blake, they are tributary. A line more relevant to his career as a poet and artist is to be traced through the Elizabethan writers, where kindliness and vision are brought into the service of an artistic vitality that transcends them. Read Blake after reading the Elizabethans and a spark jumps from one to the other.

The Renaissance had also produced a new way of looking at evil. Once its roots had been displaced from a physical Hell, men were forced to seek them in the human soul itself. Marlowe's Mephistophilis cried, 'Why this is Hell, nor am I out of it'; Milton's Satan recognized, more grandly, 'Myself am Hell'. Blake now completed the process. He removed all the energy and grandeur from Satan and turned Milton's fire wholly into darkness. His state of Hell was not just Satan, but Satan in his final meanness—it was the contracted Selfhood of Urizen.

Blake handled the puritan tradition in a similar way. He paid allegiance only to puritanism in its positive affirmations. He could sympathize with the stubborn, individualistic Milton who defended personal liberty in *Areopagitica* and the sensuous Milton who wrote the early poems, but not with the ascetic Milton who thought certain pleasures sinful. He defined his attitude to puritanism with accuracy when he rewrote *Paradise Lost* with a hero who combined the vision of the Son with the energy of Satan and who subdued a Hell consisting of the darkness of abstinence and the torturing wheels of analytic reason.

Milton's attempt to find a psychological interpretation of human nature by means of an allegorical reading of the biblical narrative was also a part of the Renaissance movement towards interest in the inward life of man. Another writer in the same tradition was William Law, whose *Treatise on Prayer* contains the following passage:

> The greatest Part of Mankind, nay of Christians, may be said to be asleep; and that particular Way of Life which takes up each Man's Mind, Thoughts, and Actions, may be very well called his particular Dream. . . . But why so? It is because Man has an Eternity within him, is born into this World, not for the sake of living here, not for any Thing this World can give him, but only to have Time and Place, to become either an eternal Partaker of a divine Life with GOD, or to have an hellish Eternity among fallen Angels: And therefore, every Man who has not his Eye, his Heart, and his Hands, continually governed by this twofold Eternity, may be justly said to be fast asleep, to have no awakened Sensibility of Himself.[11]

Blake takes over the imagery and positive content of passages like this—especially the supposition that men are spiritually asleep, unaware of the Eternity within themselves—but quietly eliminates the pietism in favour of a philosophy which allows eternity to illuminate, not condemn human life. Similarly, he could find a powerful aid to his speculations on the Fall and Eternity in a passage such as the following from the same treatise, where God is telling Adam of the fall of the Angels, and how their belief that they contained an 'Infinity of Power' within themselves resulted in a precipitate descent into their own 'dark, fiery, working Power'. This headlong, self-induced fall was stopped only by a limiting act on the part of God:

> 'My creating *Fiat* stopped the Workings of these rebellious Spirits, by dividing the Ruins of their wasted Kingdom, into an Earth, a Sun, Stars, and separated Elements. Had not this Revolt of Angels brought forth that disordered *Chaos*, no such Materiality as this outward World is made of had ever been known. Gross compacted Earth, Stones, Rocks, wrathful Fire here, dead Water there, fighting Elements, with all their gross Vegetables and Animals, are Things not known in Eternity, and will be only seen in Time, till the great Designs are finished, for which Thou art brought forth in Paradise. And then, as a Fire awakened by the Rebel Creature, began all the Disorders of Nature and turned that glassy Sea into a Chaos, so a *last Fire*, kindled at my Word, shall thoroughly purge the Floor of this World. In those purifying Flames the Sun, the Stars, the Air, the Earth and Water, shall part with all their Dross, Deadness and Division, and all become

again that first heavenly Materiality, a *glassy Sea* of everlasting
Light and Glory, in which Thou and thy Offspring shall sing
Hallelujahs to all Eternity . . .'[12]

The contrast between disorders in Time and Designs in
Eternity is fully Blakean: he would differ only in seeing
Eternity in the present as well as the future. Similarly, when
Law speaks of the 'Pearl of Eternity' hidden in each man[13] he is
thinking mainly of a future revelation—whereas Blake would
think of the 'grain of sand' which can be transformed at every
moment by the vision of men. He would have agreed with
Law's affirmation that the kingdom of Satan is within the
'self' ('The Works of the Devil are all wrought in *Self*, it is his
peculiar *Workhouse* . . . '). But he would have parted company
when Law went on to call for 'Humility, Self-dejection, and
Self-abhorrence' as proper means of combating the Devil.
Blake would prefer self-fulfilment to self-abhorrence.

Historically, Law's work had marked a stage in the movement
towards reading the Bible as psychological allegory. Blake
carried the process still further. When he errs, it is because he
stresses the obscurer details of the Bible instead of devoting himself to the interpretation of human nature. His exegetic in-
genuity is likely to exasperate the modern reader—particularly
when it is exercised at the expense of developing further his own
psychological insights.

The only answer to the charge of obscurity would be that the
Bible is itself totally sound as mythology. In some criticism of
Blake there is a suggestion that the Bible is composed entirely of
archetypal symbols, and that Blake's reading of it is therefore
justifiable. The argument hardly stands up to investigation,
however. At one point in his symbolism, for example, Blake
identifies the two Rahabs of the Old Testament—Rahab the
harlot and Rahab the 'great beast'.[14] There is no linguistic
authority for such a step. The two names come from different
Hebrew roots and are unlikely ever to have been associated,
even in the primitive mind. Any suggestion that Blake was
always putting himself in touch with an archetypal truth by his
reading of the Bible falls to the gound.[15]

Nevertheless, in spite of his use of obscure Biblical detail,
Blake's method gave him certain advantages. The greatest

hindrance to modern allegorists is their lack of a firm frame of reference outside their work of art. Blake's adherence to the Bible gave him a point of permanence and assurance from which he could build.

In the long run, one concludes, there is no halfway house. Blake's poetry must either be taken in small fragments or treated as a whole, so closely are its imperfections woven into the full texture. But so far in this chapter, we have dwelt mainly upon the imperfections, the failures to communicate, and ignored the mitigating factors, including the indirect communication. The style, for example, makes a constant appeal by its energy and vivacity: to the reader who has once responded to Blake, his words spring into idiosyncratic life, and gleam with a running thread of imaginative light. The symbolism, too, a formidable jungle at first sight, gains in clarity as it is seen to be organized by simple, massive ideas. The loss of vision and the failure of desire are regarded as the chief failure of modern society, and mourned by a man of such imaginative power that he casts a harmonizing light over the commonplaces of Hebrew and English history. The reader who yields to his spell finds that even Biblical and Druidical names acquire a music and colouring from the common vision.

Moreover the style and symbolism may at first seem to exist in separation from each other, but closer acquaintance draws them together. The style, always energetic by comparison with contemporary modes, has a versatility which corresponds to the range of Blake's themes. At times it stands in the cold, dark, craggy desolation of single vision; at times it runs with the energy of twofold; at times it softens to moonlit pathos or to the sensuous attraction of rising lark and opening thyme. The one element which it cannot fully express is that of the fourfold vision which contains all the others. This is best transmitted by a few isolated images, such as that of the ruby tear falling from the eye of the lion; to present it in sustained form was perhaps beyond the reach of art.

The same inner relationship is evident in the subject-matter. The curious labyrinths of the Prophetic Books spring to life as they are seen to be not merely accounts of loss, but 'negatives' in which the lost vision is obliquely cast. The wastes and

horrors become more comprehensible as one grasps that the
features of their desolation are features also of the lost paradise
garden; the agonized struggles of the Zoas fall into place as the
dislocations of functions which ought to act in generous, overflowing harmony. One understands Blake as one comes to
sense the imprisoned music that lies in him, his art being the
medium through which he tries to release that music.

His imprisoned music is a part of Blake's total reality, the
reality which he tries to present to a civilization which he sees
as basing itself on a single, inadequate 'realism'. But we must
still ask ourselves how well Blake deals with that realism, the
'realism' of his age and ours. A great deal has been said in
these pages about landscapes of the mind, for example, but
what of the landscapes of fact? Did Blake, indeed, ever come to
terms with 'nature' as the eighteenth-century poets understood
the word?

Comparison with Wordsworth is invited at this point. Nor is
there any need to resort to conjecture: for Blake's own comments on his contemporary have come down to us, recorded in
marginalia to copies of *The Excursion* and the *Poems* of 1815.
Even without such aid the contrast between the two poets
would be self-evident—at times, indeed, almost incredibly
pointed. For the very rocks which are the enemies of Blake's
vision are the guarantee of Wordsworth's; the thorn which
stands like an old man in the way of Blake is for Wordsworth an
emblem of enduring humanity;[16] the decline of faculties in old
age which is in Blake the signal for growing tyranny can move
Wordsworth to tears. Wordsworth distrusts the imagination,
for he has watched it fade within himself: in consequence he
finds it desperately important that nature and affection should
endure, the anchors of his being in an unstable world. Blake,
by contrast, distrusts nature as soon as it ceases to be informed
by vision: desire and imagination are the very root and flower
of his being.

Blake's attitude to Wordsworth follows logically. When
Wordsworth begins his catalogue of the powers requisite to
the poet with 'those of observation and description', Blake
comments, 'One Power alone makes a Poet—Imagination
The Divine Vision'. Against the title 'Influence of Natural

Objects / In calling forth and strengthening the Imagination / In Boyhood and early Youth', Blake writes, 'Natural Objects always did & now do Weaken, deaden & obliterate Imagination in Me . . .' And to Wordsworth's famous aspiration, voiced in the preface to the Excursion, to show 'How exquisitely the individual Mind . . . to the external World / Is fitted:—and how exquisitely too, / . . . The external World is fitted to the Mind,' Blake replies, 'You shall not bring me down to believe such fitting & fitted / I know better & Please your Lordship.'[17]

Blake's assertion that imagination is actually weakened in the presence of natural objects can be matched elsewhere in romantic literature. A similar belief is voiced, for example, by Proust.[18] And when Blake writes in another note, 'I do not know who wrote these Prefaces they are very mischievous & direct contrary to Wordsworths own Practise',[19] we are reminded that Wordsworth too, for all his praise of natural objects, found it difficult to produce poetry in immediate response to them. His emotion is recollected and recreated when he *returns* to a scene; it is only then that the creative powers are released. Evidently, then, something in Wordsworth, too, is weakened in the presence of natural objects.

The difference between the two poets is brought out at this point, however. Blake cut to the heart of it when he wrote simply at the end of one series of his comments on Wordsworth, 'Imagination has nothing to do with Memory'.[20] Wordsworth can write neither in immediate response to natural objects nor in total absence from them. Like Proust and many others in whom the sensibility is highly developed, he relies on the intervening stage when the first response is revived by a later memory. Blake will not compromise in this way. He refuses to rely on sensibility and memory to provide a place where reality and imagination can meet. Inspiration must be direct and total.

Yet this cleavage should not blind us to the fact that both poets are ultimately talking the same language. If they disagree about the method, both see the meeting of imagination and the natural world as the object of their deepest concern. Blake's impatience with those who look only at the natural world does not preclude a vivid concern for men who suffer the

physical ills of that world; and it was Wordsworth, not Blake,
who created the phrase, 'the Vision and the Faculty divine'.[21]
Blake and Wordsworth are complementary, not opposing
figures. The positive assertions of each assist one to understand
the other—each shows the dark side of the other's sphere.

And the basic weaknesses of Blake's mythology are related to
his unwillingness to compromise concerning inspiration. Thus
he proclaims the unqualified power of vision without indicating
the exact status of the visionary revelation. Is his total mythology primarily a matter of the mind, intended to work on the
minds of his readers and to help them restore the Eternal Man
within themselves? Often it seems so:

> If the Spectator could Enter into these Images in his Imagination
> approaching them on the Fiery Chariot of his Contemplative
> Thought if he could Enter into Noahs Rainbow or into his bosom
> or could make a Friend & Companion of one of these Images of
> wonder which always intreats him to leave mortal things as he
> must know then would he arise from his Grave then would he meet
> the Lord in the Air & then he would be happy.[22]

But at other times he is evidently so possessed by his interpretations that he imagines them to be of a more basic validity,
eventually to be confirmed in the physical world, where a Last
Judgment in the flesh will be followed by restoration of the
universe to its pristine paradisal state. That he should do so is
less surprising when we remember that Shelley, also, cherished
hopes of a paradise literally restored; but his failure to come to a
definite conclusion on the subject is a source of occasional
bewilderment.

The other apparent confusion in Blake's thinking can, however, be cleared up. Did he really approve of the flesh or not?
Throughout this study apparent contradictions in his references
to the body will have been noticed. Sometimes, as he sings the
praises of 'desire' he seems to be extolling sexual fulfilment; at
other times he seems to deplore it as a sure way to 'vegetation'.
The commentators take over the confusion and do not help:
sometimes they speak of physical love in his work as if it were
the highest form of human experience; at others, they stress
that he sees the physical bonds formed between men and
women as a source of peril.

Here it is useful to turn back to Wordsworth. To read him after Blake is to see the element missing from the conspectus of the latter's work. Wordsworth refers back constantly to the affections that bind together the creation: the babe on the mother's arm; the devotion of a dog for its master; the love of man for man. Affection is the 'gravitation and the filial bond'[23] of his universe—something to fall back on, a resource permanently available to men even if a rational and commercial civilization estranges them from it by isolating them from each other.

For Blake, such a feeling could not be basic. Despite his passionate concern for human justice, his sympathies with the suffering and the oppressed, he placed only a limited value on the physical bonds that bind men to each other and to the whole creation. Wordsworth's image of the 'homely nurse' whose task it is to make up to man for his loss of pristine vision[24] would have left him cold. For him the earth and its affections are potentially an imprisoning power: men should recognize their common humanity, but if they are to be truly bound together it will be by a common human Vision, not by physical ties.

It is surprising that a man who could write so movingly as Blake of human beings and animals should show a certain distrust of affectionate sensibility, but his writings betray the fact over and over again. One reason that he disliked men such as Hayley was the predominance of this trait in their characters. To him it smacked of feebleness and effeminacy.

Blake was, perhaps, to this very limited extent, an early victim of the Industrial Revolution, cut off from that immediate contact with the earth which results in a sense of familiarity and unity with all living things. There is acute observation of birds, animals and insects in his writings, yet his personality had been moulded in separation from the earth: that immediate and unconscious sense of it which is the birthright of every country child was lacking in him. At the same time, he did not have the fear of the earth which characterizes the overcivilized. The earth was there to be accepted, and it was always there. It was vision that was needed: only vision could lead to a right use of the earth. Over-devotion to the earth would lead to 'vegetation': when Blake wanted to find a place for the affections he set them in Beulah—the necessary place of rest which was also a potential prison.

Blake's attitude to nature cannot, moreover, have been overwhelmingly affected by his being brought up in a city. The London of Blake's youth was still surrounded by farms and villages; he was less cut off from nature than the city children of today. It is only some physical and immediate link that is severed: his compassion and humanity are hardly touched.

The Industrial Revolution also helped to mould him in a different way. The new technology had brought with it an interest of energy in every form: and if Blake was distrustful of overindulged affections and vegetation of the flesh, that was partly because he, too, shared this passionate concern with energy.

This fact, largely missed by the commentators, is vital. It helps to clarify Blake's attitude in a large number of places. When he surveys sexual relationships, for example, it is the *energy* of desire that is accepted and found significant, while physical attraction in less active forms is ignored or distrusted. It is the energy of Satan that attracts Blake; the energy of the serpent that renders it subtle in his symbolism; the energy of the tiger that makes it crucially ambiguous for good or evil.

Blake was not unaware of other elements in the human condition. But his enthusiasm for energy meant that he felt some things more directly than others. The concept is a touchstone in understanding him: it helps us to grasp the idiosyncratic element in his use of words such as 'desire' and 'power'.

There are also repercussions in his view of art. His greater stylistic felicities, verbal or pictorial, are achieved in the depiction of active rather than passive states. And his criticism of other artists is correspondingly biased. His violent attacks on Sir Joshua Reynolds are due to his lack of sympathy with the contemporary art of sensibility. Instead, he proclaims his faith in the 'bounding line', invoking the names of Dürer, Raphael and Michelangelo.[25]

The distinction reaches to the very roots of his personality. Those who read studies of Blake in which he is presented as an innocent visionary must be surprised, to say the least, when they turn to the poems published from his notebooks, and discover the vigour and virulence with which his enemies are attacked. The more scabrous poems in *An Island in the Moon* are equally unexpected.

Such a marked division of personality leads one to look again at the unusual twin portrait from the Tatham manuscript, the frontispiece to the present volume. In the foreground appears the face of a pugnacious elderly man, very present in the body; behind it another, radiant face, resembling the early portrait attributed to Mrs Blake.[26] The portrait is usually seen as a representation of Blake in youth and old age: further interpretation may, however, be suggested. It is likely that even in his old age, his friends were aware of two Blakes: the firm, snub-nosed man, downright in enthusiasms and antipathies; and, deep within, sometimes breaking through the features of pugnacity, the radiant lineaments of the visionary.

Blake found it hard to link his two faces. The Blake who energetically expelled a soldier from his cottage garden, or who wrote scurrilous epigrams about his patron, could not easily come to terms with the Blake who loved the eye of innocence: the world made too rigid a separation between the two. Hayley and many of his contemporaries bridged the gap by means of a cultivated benevolence and sensibility. Blake found this merely emasculating. Equally, he was too positive a man to adopt the conventions which allow men of the world to communicate socially without penetrating beneath the surface layers—too positive, even, to develop the massive controlling irony of a Swift as a permanent mask for his vision.

His lack of contact with the earth did not cause, but it exacerbated his condition. The verses to Dr Johnson or Klopstock[27] betray, by the faintly self-conscious tone of their references to excrement, a very slight uneasiness with the earth. Blake's coarseness, though never objectionable and often enjoyable, is a coarseness of the town rather than the country. Even his references to death carry an element of paradox: he can come to terms with the grave only because he sees it as a gateway to the release of visionary energies.

Had Blake possessed the full contact with the earth which would have made his energies and his inward vision an organic

unity instead of a loose association, he would conceivably have
been a greater artist. He might have produced a body of work
which reconciled the forms of the imagination with the diverse
rhythms of life, ranging from the dramatic beat of energy to the
subtle pulsation of living organisms. As it is, he always produces the rhythms of energy in his verse and painting; the
rhythms of organic life are sometimes lacking. While one
responds to the hammer-beat of Los and the flames of Orc,
one misses the even more varied and sustaining rhythms of
Dionysus.

It is the same with Blake's vision of nature. One would
rather have an artist who sees the sun as an innumerable company of the Heavenly host crying, 'Holy, Holy, Holy is the
Lord God Almighty' than an analyst who sees it as a round disk
of fire somewhat like a guinea: but these are not the only ways of
looking at the sun. Blake's way makes a distinction between
the energy in nature and those parts which are apparently
without energy. (One is reminded of his story that when the
'spiritual Sun' appeared to him, he insisted that he was not the
Greek Apollo—whom he contemptuously identified with the
sky.)[28] In the vision of some other poets, however, one finds a
view of the sun which unites it more fully with the rest of
creation. In the later part of *The Ancient Mariner*, or in Dylan
Thomas's *Poem on his Birthday*, the sun is seen with a wholeness
of vision that brings together its innocent glory, its energy and
its relation to the innermost demands of the human imagination.

To compare Blake with these poets, however, is to exhibit the
degree of his visionary commitment. Coleridge and Thomas
both recognized that their view of the sun was connected to a
childhood unity of imagination which their contemporary
civilization could not accept. Coleridge writes *The Ancient
Mariner* in ballad rhythms which suggest an earlier state of
civilization; Thomas feels it necessary to defend the connection
between the imagination of his boyhood and that of the grown
man. Blake refuses to be defensive: he will be at once a mature
man and a visionary, and will refuse to acknowledge any
contradiction between the two roles.

Blake's endeavour to remain true to both sides of his nature makes him, more than any other figure of the Romantic period, an exemplar of the division within post-Renaissance man. A man so richly endowed in body and imagination was bound to be deeply aware of the contemporary etiolation of the human personality, eroded physically by the prohibitions of the moral law and mentally by the development of analytic techniques. The progress of humanity towards mastery of nature was cutting men off from graces both of body and mind.

In the fourth book of *The Excursion* Wordsworth comments more soberly on the same phenomenon in respect of religion. After the valiant efforts of the Reformers to remove idolatry it now appears to the Wanderer that some other gift, present to devotees of earlier religions when they worshipped the great forms of nature, has been removed. Man, reformed, is in danger of descending to littleness of soul.[29]

A century later, the mechanics of the process were examined by James Joyce in *Stephen Hero*:

> The modern spirit is vivisective. Vivisection itself is the most modern process one can conceive. The ancient spirit accepted phenomena with a bad grace. The ancient method investigated law with the lantern of justice, morality with the lantern of revelation, art with the lantern of tradition. But all these lanterns have magical properties: they transform and disfigure. The modern method examines its territory by the light of day.[30]

The situation has been similarly conceived by many artists. But Blake, by the nature of his interests, brings to it a peculiarly individual response which both shows the division at its sharpest and sets him apart from other critics of modern civilization.

Certainly his philosophy has little or nothing to do with the intellectual presuppositions of a technological society. It stands or falls by his assertion that 'all men partake of vision, but it is lost by not being cultivated.'[31] The cultivation of vision is precisely the occupation which is discouraged in perfecting the techniques of analysis and regard to material fact which are required for the advancement of technology.

At the same time, his twin preoccupations with vision and energy cut him off from both the traditions which have risen up in opposition to the predominance of technology. His belief in the human imagination marks him off from the broad benevolence of writers like Fielding and Cobbett, whose strongest feelings are for the ties of earth. Even Dickens, who sees more clearly the demands of the imagination, bases himself squarely upon a nostalgia for breadth of character and richness of physical living.

At the other extreme, Blake's delight in energy marks him off from the central tradition of the perennial philosophy. One cannot regard as an ascetic a man who so delighted in the energies of the human body. One cannot firmly align with the Platonists an artist who delighted not in the passive contemplation of ideal Forms but in the bounding lines of that energetic action which creates its own forms.

Yet he was looking for the same things. He wanted to see men living in the breadth and richness of their own humanity as much as did Fielding; he wanted to see them living under the light of eternity as much as did any seventeenth-century mystical poet. It was the tug of both desires that ultimately prohibited wholehearted allegiance to either tradition as it existed in this time.

The twofold allegiance to vision and energy which he did maintain is particularly evident in his most characteristic work. When one is nearest to the 'essential' Blake, these two qualities are at their fullest stretch. In his early work, for example, his conception of energy came near to compassing all the forces of nature. We have already shown how he apprehends, even if he does not fully seize, the importance of the earth. A man who could write the *Songs of Innocence and of Experience*, whose ultimate vision was of a Man walking in a Garden, was not dissociated from the primal sympathies to which Wordsworth clung. Yet some final barrier, reared within his personality, prohibited him from trusting the earth wholeheartedly.

As he grows older, energy weakens, coming more under the sway of vision. But even in the most visionary designs of his later years, it is at work just below the surface, lending to the work a character which could derive from no one but him.

His enthusiasm for energy is also a key to his achievement in the visual arts. In his painting and engraving he is concerned not with the isolation of platonic Forms but with rendering the bounding lines of activity. One understands his treatment of the human face the better as one recognizes that it is the work of a man who has looked hard and long at human beings for signs of the lineaments of their inward energies.

In his poetry, the counterpointing of vision and energy is central. From the *Songs of Innocence and of Experience* to the late prophetic books, his style constantly comes to life when both are active. It flags, slightly, when energy disappears, for then vision is left dangerously exposed. The idea of energy existing in isolation from vision, on the other hand, is the theme that most excites him. It is not for nothing that *The Tyger* is the poem which we most readily associate with him.

The double preoccupation pervades his whole view of human life. The idea of life having its own healing rhythms, which forms the basis of most human comfort, does not greatly attract him. He puts his faith in the thin, dancing line of energy which unites the whole of human experience, grave or gay:

Man was made for Joy & Woe
And when this we rightly know
Thro the World we safely go
Joy & Woe are woven fine
A Clothing for the Soul divine
Under every grief & pine
Runs a joy with silken twine[32]

The condition where imagination and energy intertwine is, in fact, that of his Eternal Man, who has little to do with the decay of the flesh. Shortly before his death he wrote,

I have been very near the Gates of Death and have returned very weak & an Old Man feeble and tottering, but not in Spirit and Life not in The Real Man The Imagination which Liveth for Ever. In that I am stronger & stronger as this Foolish Body decays.[33]

Gilchrist tells the story of a lady, considered extremely beautiful as a child, who remembered being taken to an evening party and there presented to Blake.

He looked at her very kindly for a long while. without speaking; and then, stroking her head and long ringlets, said: 'May God make this world to you, my child, as beautiful as it has been to me!' She thought it strange, at the time . . . that such a poor old man, dressed in shabby clothes, could imagine that the world

had ever been so beautiful to him as it must be to her, nursed in
all the elegancies and luxuries of wealth . . .[34]

The persisting sense of beauty is one guarantee of the integrity
and worth of Blake's long struggle. And if he did not succeed
in bringing vision and human experience together in the extended, epic form that he hoped for, there were many limited
revelations, Joycean 'epiphanies', which brought a temporary
sense of full reality. By the time that he wrote his *Jerusalem* his
inspiration found its most ready expression in the production of
single plates, or short runs of plates, which he then presented,
in loose order, within a larger general framework.

The process was carried a stage further with the production of
the 'Visionary heads'. Blake would sit late at night until the
likeness of some famous historical figure appeared in front of
him, which he would then reproduce swiftly on paper. On such
occasions he would appear like a portrait painter with a subject
sitting to him.[35] The culmination of these drawings is 'The
Ghost of a Flea'—probably the nearest that Blake ever came to
portraying evil, yet witty rather than solemn, a perfect assimi-
lation of the lineaments of man and flea.[36] In a similar way, the
design for 'The Ancient of Days' (Fig. 24) is said to have
hovered over his head at the top of his staircase in No. 13,
Hercules Buildings.[37]

This is one of several ways in which order supervenes to
crown the strivings of Blake's art. At the other extreme from
such direct visionary experiences one must set the impact of
many of Blake's most successful designs upon the reader, who is
aware of a fuller realism than could be deduced from the artist's
apparent intentions. Blake's immediate appeal to the unsophisticated eye is legendary.

In modern times, the appeal to the unsophisticated is assisted
by the very fact that we have been stressing. The technological
revolution has brought about a new consciousness of energy, to
which traditional art has been slow to respond. The art-forms
peculiar to the twentieth-century, on the other hand, such as
jazz music or fiction with a strong narrative content, appeal
directly to our feeling for movement. The greatest feats of
modern physical construction have been achieved not in 'static'
buildings but in the architecture of motion. Motion is a central

reality in our age: as soon as our most typical men stop moving they are lost.

It is natural that such modern readers should feel an immediate attraction to Blake; it is equally natural that that attraction should not last very long. His attitude to energy is too equivocal. He stands back from the road of modern motion to invoke the virtues of a humanity which moves in art and generosity rather than in mechanical construction and self-interest.

With the fixed 'reality' of modern civilization, Blake has little to do. It is of the nature of his art that its 'reality'—that is, the mode by which it is to be apprehended, varies continuously. Sometimes a direct response will be evoked; sometimes the artist's achievement can only be reached by the sort of investigation which has appeared in these pages. At other times, an intuitive leap of sympathy is required, to bring one into tune with Blake's mood at the time of composition—and here his various artistic works will be found to illuminate one another: one may not understand a poem until one sees some design which was conceived in the same visionary mode. Or again, the point of illumination may be more direct. In *Milton*, for example, Leutha is described as shining upon the assembly with 'moth-like elegance'.[38] The reader who sought a subtle symbolic point would be mistaken; Blake's communication here relies only upon the reader having seen a moth with its wings folded in the lines of an elegant cloak. All these types of reading, the direct response, the intuitive reach of sympathy, the observant eye and the patient effort to follow Blake's thinking through its long path of development are required if his works are to yield their fullest content. Each approach accomplishes something: the final task is to bring them together and to know at each point which is most appropriate.

In the end, however, all are interrelated, from the directly sensuous to the sharply intellectual. Blake's positive achievements are not fully understood without an appreciation of his accompanying negative sense. One of the reasons that we still respond so strongly to his work after more than a century is that his inner conflicts are still alive in every heir to the Anglo-Saxon tradition of moral seriousness and analytic thought.

Somewhere in the interstices of our record of technological progress we find ourselves sharing his sense of loss and diminishment, his longing for generosity and splendour.

Blake's sense of loss was peculiarly sharp, not merely because he was sensitive to the new spirit in his society, but because he had seen that spirit made manifest in an intense and concentrated form at a particular period of time. Here again one sees a link with Wordsworth.

Both poets had lived through the French Revolution; both had been possessed for a time by the new vision of life which it seemed to be unfolding. It had seemed that all human beings were about to reach forward and possess a new society, an association of individuals united by a common vision in liberty and joy.

When the early hope was swallowed up in disillusionment, both poets passed into a period of withdrawal. The divergency of their personal experience, however, shaped their courses differently. For Wordsworth, the Revolution had been accompanied by his love-affair with Annette Vallon. His withdrawal was thus a total withdrawal from passion, which was ultimately to bring in its wake the loss of imaginative power. He would find his final point of rest in the 'hiding-places of man's power',[39] the primal sympathies of nature which survive all changes and chances.

For Blake, on the other hand, the time of the Revolution was associated with the death of his brother Robert. Disillusioned by the events in France, he withdrew to the memory of his brother's released spirit ascending heavenward 'clapping its hands for joy' and found in that a permanent testimony to the presence of the Eternal Man in all men. The Revolution had not succeeded in liberating it for more than a moment, but it lay dormant in every individual. Wordsworth's primal sympathies led him inevitably to a respect for convention; Blake's sense of the eternal in the human imagination led to enthusiasm for liberty, immortality and, above all, for the bounding lines of energy. If liberty could not be achieved politically it could be brought about in the cultivation of art. Art, indeed, is the true home of liberty, for there the forms of energy exist in their own identity, neither breaking out into destruction nor freezing into

solid forms of restraint and tyranny. In the images of art, therefore, men see, permanently represented, the forms of their truest
freedom.

Here, then, is a final key to the subterranean element in
Blake's work. As with Wordsworth, his buried integrity was
that of a disappointed social revolutionary. Perhaps only some-
one who has lived through the experience of a public event
which momentarily transforms men out of their everyday selves,
and in so doing reveals their true identities, can fully enter into
the preoccupations and enthusiasms of artists like these.

Such events on a large scale are rare; the nearest equivalent
in the twentieth century has been the communist revolution.
As it happens, however, the development in Blake's attitude
was paralleled closely by the experience of a disappointed
revolutionary in Russia. Dr. Zhivago, according to his creator,
moved back in the same way from disillusionment concerning
political action to a faith in the lasting forms of life as they are
revealed in art. Pasternak's account of his later years, therefore,
provides, as well, a fitting tribute to Blake's final achievement:

> . . . he mourned that distant summer . . . when the revolution
> had been a god come down to earth from heaven, the god of that
> summer when everyone had gone mad in his own way, and when
> everyone's life existed in its own right and not as an illustration
> to a thesis in support of higher policy.
>
> As he scribbled his odds and ends, he made a note reaffirming
> his belief that art always serves beauty, and beauty is the joy of
> possessing form, and form is the key to organic life since no living
> thing can exist without it, so that every work of art, including
> tragedy, witnesses to the joy of existence.[40]

Appendix One
The Development of Blake's Mythology

The reader may find it useful to have for reference a brief account of Blake's mythical personages. To 'schematize' his mythologizing is of course somewhat misleading, since his mythical characters are never simple equivalents for things or qualities. His myth-making is always controlled by patterns of ideas and it is only within the dynamic structure of these patterns that individual characters assume significance.

The patterns themselves often have a symmetrical structure. Blake is fond of the dialectic form, for example; he also finds a fitness in creating groups of four. It is equally typical of him that the patterns are by no means sacrosanct: a character who appeared to be comfortably 'placed' in one story may, in the next work, emerge with different status. Under the pressure of a new idea his significance may indeed actually shift.

It is possible that other books were written which elaborated the myths further and that knowledge of them might help to explain those that remain. From the existing books, however, we can largely infer the nature of the general patterns. A full consideration would require detailed examination of the books, from *Tiriel* to *Jerusalem*, which are mythical in character. Here we are more concerned with the names and ideas which have appeared in the 'social' works. A development on the following lines may be suggested:

1. An early period of mythologizing (based partly on allegorizing the story of Adam, Eve and the serpent) which results in the poems *Tiriel* and *Thel* and which produces as main characters *Mnetha, Har* and *Heva; Tiriel* and *Myratana* and their sons; *Thel* and *Luvah.* From the compressed symbolism involved Blake develops his more complicated later patterns; the only characters which survive from these early formulations are Har and Heva (figures of a paradisal innocence which has

etiolated through failure to pass through the fires of experience)
and Luvah, prince of Love representing a lost human Sun-
figure in whom love and light were creatively incarnate.

2. *A period of political and social concern* resulted in the emergence
of new figures to express Blake's enthusiasm for liberty and his
indignation at social wrongs. These feelings are first expressed
in the *Songs of Experience*, where specific wrongs are attacked and
the decline of humanity from its original state of liberated vision
and desire is ascribed to a figure known as 'Starry Jealousy'.
In *Visions of the Daughters of Albion* 'Starry Jealousy' is named as
Urizen, creator of the universe of Law and abstract thought.
Most of Blake's other mythical creations at this time presuppose
the eighteenth-century universe and show the various forces at
work in it. *Oothoon* expresses the spirit which yearns for love,
Leutha the spirit of free love and fulfilled desire. *Bromion* expresses the spirit of law which dominates the eighteenth-
century intellectual world, *Theotormon* the negative spirit of
doubt and refusal which results from that dominance. In subsequent works two more such figures are introduced, representing
the primary emotional forces which are left in a world dominated by law. *Rintrah* at his best represents honest indignation,
Palamabron pity and benevolence. Rintrah is usually spoken of
with approval, Palamabron more guardedly respected, for pity,
not involving the automatic honesty which is likely to accompany the exercise of energy in wrath, may well become a hypocritical mask for self-assertion or emotional impotence.

Rintrah dominates *The Marriage of Heaven and Hell*; Rintrah
and Palamabron both appear in *Europe*; Theotormon reappears
briefly in *The Song of Los* where he represents the failure of
traditional Christianity to acknowledge the energies of sexual
love. In the later *Milton*, where Palamabron is a main partici-
pant, the hypocritical element in benevolence is stressed very
strongly. Rintrah, Palamabron, Bromion and Theotormon do
not appear together in any one book until *Milton* where they are
mentioned at one point as the 'mighty ones' who remain to
Los. (It may be observed, incidentally, that names ending in
-ah usually express *energy* in some form, whereas those ending
in -on or -en usually indicate a failure of vision. This is particu-

larly noticeable in the present group.) I am inclined to think nevertheless that Blake always conceived of them as a group, forming one of his favoured patterns of four.

3. A new 'biblical' myth. Towards the end of *The Marriage of Heaven and Hell* Blake promises his reader 'The Bible of Hell', of which the first instalment is offered in the concluding 'Song of Liberty'. The Exodus story is retold as a conflict between tyranny and liberty, between the Moses of the tablets of law and the Moses of the burning bush, between the 'Starry king' and the 'new-born fire'. (In *The Book of Ahania*, which repeats the confrontation, the fire-spirit is called Fuzon.) In Blake's re-fashioning of the Bible, the God of Genesis, equally, is separated into the God of Restraining Law and the God of creating energy, named respectively as Urizen and *Los*. From this time forward, Los becomes steadily more important.

4. The first attempt at an extended myth. This involves two main themes:
(i) *The Myth of Atlantis,* conceived of as a lost city where sublime and pathos were both allowed a place; where the light-giving palaces of light on the mountains were matched by innocence in the pastoral plains. In some primeval catastrophe, the whole was swamped by forces generated by the blind worship of law and quantitative measurement: the Sea of Time and Space rushed in, the lands of innocence and pathos were covered, and of the former mountains of vision only the tips remained, rocks of reason in an Atlantic of opaque vision.
(ii) *Blake's scheme of energies,* first adumbrated in a Proverb of Hell in *The Marriage of Heaven and Hell*:

The head Sublime, the heart Pathos, the genitals Beauty, the hands & feet Proportion.

The first ordering of Blake's figures of human energy follows this bodily pattern and is related also to the four elements and to the chief elements in his view of man, as follows:

Urizen	head	light	lost vision
Luvah	heart	heat	lost love
Ariston	genitals	stream of life	sexual beauty driven into secrecy
Urthona	hands and feet	earth	the creative impulse.

This pattern dominates *America,* where the myth of the lost Atlantis is particularly relevant to the confrontation between the 'starry king' of English tyranny and the 'new-born fire' of American revolution. This confrontation is seen as perpetuating the situation which precipitated the original cataclysm. From hints which are dropped in the prophetic books the story would be something like the following. Ariston, beautiful and full of sexual energy, revolted against his father, the ageing king, and stole a bride whom he took into the forest; there he built a secret palace for her. In the struggle which followed he was slain in the forest (like Absalom or Adonis) and his grieving father led his followers away teaching them obedience to the Law. In the wilderness they degenerated into Druids of reason who were willing to sacrifice human beings to the Law. This myth is repeated again and again in human affairs—particularly in time of revolution; it is also mirrored cosmically in the heavens where the original universe, dominated by the light of an Eternal Humanity, has polarized (in Swedenborgian fashion) into energy and light: 'Mars' became the centre, giving birth to the sun of our universe which is as destructive as it is creative, while the former starry fires of sublimity have degenerated into blank patterns of light in the heavens, organized by the mathematicians according to abstract laws.

5. The inclusion of creative forces. These themes, which were adequate to stand mythically behind a short poem like *America,* proved intractable material for an extended myth. They formed a pattern of decline which was altogether too negative for a long creative work. To introduce a more positive element Blake brought in two new characters: *Tharmas* (with his feminine counterpart or 'emanation' *Enion*) and Los (with his emanation *Enitharmon*—who contains within her name the names of the previous two). These represent respectively the quest for a unified vision and the function of creative energy in a visionless world. Enion and Tharmas are like Isis and Typhon, or Psyche and Cupid: the female always pursues the male, but is seeking him in his lost form (Osiris; the winged Cupid). Los and Enitharmon dwell in Time and Space respectively, representing the creative elements in each.

Although their lack of vision blinds them into jealousy they create continuously. It is they who are pictured as presiding over the history of Europe from the Greeks to the present day. In a world that has seen the slow decline of vision in favour of abstract thought and which has allowed the moral law to forbid the expression of human desire, they are, for all their limitations, the chief positive forces at work.

6. The artist as hero. In the later prophetic books where Blake is preoccupied with the heroic function of the artist as the only possible saviour of a world that has declined in this way, Los becomes increasingly important. In Jerusalem he is the artist who, not possessing vision, yet guards it by the very fact of continuing to create; in *Milton* he embodies the artistic energy which only awaits the descent of vision to become artistic genius. In this work however the wheel has come full circle: the hero is not Los but a character who is John Milton reincarnate as William Blake. The initiative which rested with the infra-human forces in previous poems is finally restored to the artist in his historical setting.

7. The permanent myth. The other great organizing principle in Blake's mythologizing, that of the four 'levels of vision', exists independently of all these developments. I have assumed throughout this study that the idea of the four levels was already present when he began his serious writing. It should be recognized, however, that the terms 'single', 'twofold', 'threefold' and 'fourfold' do not appear in his extant writings until after 1800. I believe that the pattern involved was working in his mind long before and derived from his early reading of Boehme, but this is a question which must be argued elsewhere. The more general pattern involved in the 'four levels' takes a dialectic form (see below, p. 230).

This pattern, which derives from his early reading of Boehme and Swedenborg, is constant throughout his writing. The 'levels of vision' idea sets the state of 'Light' above that of 'Heat' but otherwise retains the basic organization of this pattern. It also stresses further Blake's conviction that although in each of these four states the basic vision of man is fundamentally changed, each *includes* the levels below it.

ETERNAL HUMANITY

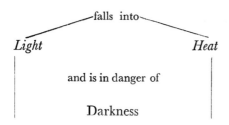

Light   Heat

and is in danger of

Darkness

Appendix Two
The Gates of Paradise

The development of Blake's thinking in the early part of his career can be followed in some detail by looking at the successive organizations which he imposed on the series of designs which were eventually published in 1793 as *For Children: The Gates of Paradise* and re-issued about 1818 with the changed title *For the Sexes: The Gates of Paradise*. As they stand the designs form a somewhat puzzling series and the explanations offered by critics have usually been perfunctory. Their obscurity, however, is partly due to the compression of thought and organization which lies behind them. Many of Blake's most important ideas played a part in evolving the final pattern by which he selected and arranged them.

One point which has not been properly taken into account is that most of the plates had already appeared as drawings in the notebook known as the Rossetti Manuscript and that these early pencil sketches often had different inscriptions beneath them. The existence of these earlier versions suggests that the evolution of the series was not a simple one.

The first designs exist in great profusion, one to a page. At some point, Blake went through them and numbered some of them in a different order, no doubt intending this order to be used in a projected publication. The fact that he renumbered them already suggests that he was beginning to form them into some sort of pattern, even if not a highly articulated one. Moreover, the earliest numbers in the series correspond roughly to those adopted in *The Gates of Paradise*.

In the original series, no number 1 can be distinguished in the facsimile edition. Number 2 is a drawing not used for the *Gates*, accompanied by the quotation

Whose changeless brow ne'er smiles nor frowns.[1]

Some other plates which appear in the numbered series have similar inscriptions—thus

8 Ah luckless babe born under cruel star
   And in dead parent baleful ashes bred
   That little weenest now what sorrows are
   Left thee for portion of thy livelihood!
                                Spenser.

21 I have said to corruption thou art
    my father to the worm thou art
    my mother & my sister.
                        Job.

24 The drift of hollow states hard to be spelled.
                                        Milton.

36 Yet can I not persuade me thou art dead.
40 Are glad when they can find the grave.
50 Begone & trouble me no more.[2]

There are more quotations, many of them to drawings not numbered in the series. In general they follow the pattern which one finds in the 'graveyard' poets of the eighteenth century: a pessimism concerning life in this world, accompanied by the reflection that such pessimism makes death more welcome as harbinger of a happier state of things in the next world. The exact nature of Blake's reflections cannot be deduced from such a fragmentary set of quotations, which in themselves merely reflect the familiar pessimism, with perhaps the additional idea that this world is governed by a fatal and remorseless destiny.

To interpret the series we must revert to Blake's own ideas. Damon is probably right to see in the drawing of a deathbed resurrection a reminiscence of Blake's own experience by the deathbed of his brother Robert:[3] that experience had been crucial, establishing in his mind the contrast between this world and eternity, and making him see eternity not as a 'future' state but a 'present' one, constantly revealing itself amid the lawbound events of this world. The range of authors represented in the quotations also shows the extent of Blake's reading at this time. The Bible, Shakespeare, Spenser, Donne, Milton and Dryden are all represented, often by quotations from their minor works. Blake, possessed by the force of his new ideas, had evidently ransacked their writings for passages which dealt with metaphysical issues—particularly the problems of birth, life and death.

If these general ideas give a common theme to the drawings in the notebook, however, a glance at the engravings reproduced in *The Gates of Paradise* (Figs. 4–10, 12–23)[4] suggests that further structuring was introduced when Blake picked out these particular drawings and gave them their captions. The themes of birth and death dominate the beginning and end of the series respectively. In the earliest set, the Frontispiece and first engraving have the captions 'What is Man?' (showing a baby in the form of a caterpillar chrysalis on a leaf) and 'I found him beneath a Tree' (showing a mother pulling up a baby like a mandrake from the soil). Similarly, the last four engravings form a series on the subject of death. The death-bed resurrection scene ('Fear and Hope are—Vision') is followed by 'The Traveller hasteth in the evening', 'Death's Door' (an old man entering the grave, his hair blown by a wind from this world), and a figure of earth, wrapped in grave-clothes and still bearing its traveller's staff, with a worm at its back and side (here the quotation from Job is reduced to 'I have said to the Worm: Thou art my mother & my sister'). Startling as this last drawing is at first sight—particularly when we remember that the series is entitled 'For Children'—Blake intended it to be taken literally. A proper vision of the relationship between this world and eternity would, he felt, induce an attitude to the earth which would take the horror even from the grave and the devouring worm—those favourite emblems of eighteenth-century moralizing.

Further patterns can be observed in the other engravings, where two clear sets, of four plates each, can be seen. The first set is inscribed with the names of the four elements:

Water   Earth   Air   Fire

Additional captions, engraved later, emphasize that they are intended to exist as a group by forming a quatrain:

Thou Waterest him with Tears
He struggles into Life
On Cloudy Doubts & Reasoning Cares
That end in endless Strife.

The second series of captions, on the other hand, consists of four exclamations:

Alas!   My Son! My Son!   I Want! I Want!   Help! Help!

The first plate later received the additional words, 'What are these? the female Martyr, / Is She also the Divine Image?'

The relation between these two sets of four is important for our understanding of the series as a whole. The first four are images of Despair, the second are reproaches to mankind. The intervening design is therefore crucial, since it may well provide the link between them. This design, which seems to be related to the chrysalis baby of the frontispiece, since it shows a winged baby bursting from a shell, is the one that originally bore the quotation from Spenser beginning, 'Ah luckless babe . . . '. The quotation now attached to it is 'At length for hatching ripe he breaks the shell', which also appears against it in the Rossetti Manuscript with Dryden's name added.

The 'breaking of the shell' could be simply the birth of a child into this world. Such an interpretation would be consonant with the subsequent drawings, which show a boy catching small human creatures, as boys sometimes run after butterflies; a youth aiming a dart at his father—and then, successively, crying for the moon; sinking in the ocean; clipping the wings of the young in his 'aged ignorance'; and finally imprisoning the father and the sons (a reference to the binding of the senses). At the same time, it is difficult to see how the first sequence of four would fit this simple pattern. It could of course refer to the elements which constitute the child in the womb, but the quatrain suggests further significances. The child and man of the later sequence could be taken to represent a pattern of darkening vision, but what are we to make of the grown man who appears, despairing, in each of the earlier ones?

The idea of 'bursting the shell' has often been used to express not birth into this world, but birth into immortality. We know that Blake was acquainted with the more philosophical poems of Donne at this time: he would hardly have missed the line in 'Of the Progress of the Soul' that describes immortality:

Thinke thy shell broke, thinke thy Soule hatch'd but now.[5]

Similarly, Young's *Night Thoughts* must long have been
familiar to him: and when he came to make his illustrations for
the work in later years he used the emblem of the child and the
shell to illustrate two extracts: the line ending

... helpless Immortal! Insect *infinite*!

and then the lines,

Embryos we must be, till we burst the Shell,
Yon ambient, azure shell, the spring to Life,
The life of Gods; O Transport! and of Man.[6]

The illustration to the latter passage shows the soul breaking
from its blue shell into immortality, while a nearby chrysalis on
a leaf reiterates the point.

Does the illustration, then, portray the awakening of the
human soul into immortality? As before, the interpretation
does not fit satisfactorily. Why should immortality be introduced at the beginning of a series depicting a human lifetime,
instead of at the end?

The image is to be related, not to any chronological event in
a human life but to the mythological emblem in orphic religion,
by which Creation begins when Love bursts from its shell in the
midst of Chaos and the warring elements are reconciled. Blake's
use of the emblem is ambiguous and satirical however, corresponding to the ambiguity of human desire. The breaking egg
may release either a winged Eros or a serpent of destruction and
the child that Blake depicts has the potential lineaments of
both. This ambiguity invites a closer look at the transition from
the first group of designs to the second. While the first three
designs of the earlier group show a man in various attitudes of
doubt and despair the fourth shows him rising with sword and
shield in fire—the accoutrements, in Blake, of the 'spectre'.
Moreover, when the design first appeared in a notebook it was
accompanied by the lines from Milton,

Forthwith upright he rears from off the pool
His mighty stature.[7]

The Satanic theme seems to be continued in figures 13 and
14, which could recall the encounter with sin and death at the
gates of Hell. If the one interpretation is tentative, the other is

fairly clear, for the design represents with surprising faithfulness
the scene which prompts the cry of Sin to Death when he rises
to attack his father Satan:

> What fury, O son,
> Possesses thee to bend that mortal dart
> Against thy father's head?[8]

Again, figure 15 is reminiscent of Satan's flight through the
aether to seek out Paradise. With this apparent run of sense, it
is fair to suppose that the 'breaking of the shell' reflects Satan's
eruption from the bounds of Hell. The interpretation is reinforced by Blake's serpent-lore, where the coiled serpent breaks
out of the shell of reason to become the fiery serpent of destruction.

The internal structure of the series reflects some of the basic
ideas in the early prophetic books. The first group of four
designs, bearing the names of the elements, are images of man's
sense of alienation and doubt when he contemplates the universe. Cut off from the earth, lacking vision, he exists in a
limbo between the two.

When these designs first appeared in the notebook, they
appeared in a slightly different order, with the following
quotations:

(Water) O that the Everlasting had not fixd
His canon against Self slaughter
Shakespeare

(Earth) Rest, rest perturbd spirit
Shakespeare

(Air) Thou hast set thy heart as the heart of God
Ezekiel

(Fire) Forthwith upright he rears from off the pool
His mighty stature.
Milton[9]

The second quotation, which is addressed by Hamlet to the
ghost of his father as he 'works in the earth', is evidently taken
by Blake as emblematic of the restlessness of man, weaned from
the earth which yielded his mortal clay. The third reflects his
other restlessness—his desire to sit above the earth in judgment

and control, by the power of the mind within him. But in so setting himself apart from the universe, man does not achieve liberty: on the contrary, he finds himself imprisoned by the limitations of his five senses. To quote from *There is no Natural Religion*, 'If it were not for the Poetic or Prophetic character the Philosophic & Experimental would soon be at the ratio of all things, & stand still unable to do other than repeat the same dull round over again'.[10] That is the state of man here. And so, if the soul is not content to remain in this perpetual cycle, its only remedy is to break out by exploiting its own energies. Yet to do so is to set up its own self as a value—and this is to enter the state of Satan. The Selfhood becomes paramount, man is possessed by his own fallen energies. Indeed, when one looks again at the baby of figure 12, one sees that its expression suggests the lustiness of human desire. The small boy chasing faery creatures has the same lineaments of incipient 'lust' (Blake did not, however, disapprove of chasing butterflies, provided that they were allowed to fly free again, as he shows in his introduction to *Europe*).[11] The second series of four, then, consists of images of Desire. Here Blake's irony is allowed full play, for although the world of Desire is higher than the darkened world of Reason, it is equally liable to misuse. In each of the images this possibility of corruption is shown: the 'female martyr' who is a victim of the possessive love which destroys her; the instinct to kill which results from atrophy of the life-instinct; the inordinate desire, the crying for the moon, which betrays the possessiveness of man, unable to see himself in the context of eternity. Although in each image the human being is shown as possessive and lustful, his face betraying the fact, the same Desire, if he only knew it, is the key to his eternal nature. Possessiveness could turn into self-giving; the energy of the son against his father could be used creatively for mankind. Even the crying for the moon is the beginning of wisdom—for, as Blake puts it in *There is no Natural Religion*,

> If the many become the same as the few when possess'd, More! More! is the cry of a mistaken soul, less than All cannot satisfy Man.
> If any could desire what he is incapable of possessing, despair must be his eternal lot.

> The desire of Man being Infinite the possession is Infinite &
> himself Infinite[12]

These aphorisms reverberate through the rest of the designs.
If the general outline follows the natural pattern of eighteenth-
century thought, counterpoising time and eternity, the internal
structure of the series is dominated by Blake's own opposition
between Reason and Energy, and his conception of the ambiguity of Energy as being the potential link between man and
eternity as well as the means of greatest evil. Born into a state
where Vision has faded, man finds himself in a world of cold
reason, surrounded by 'Cloudy Doubts & Reasoning Cares'.
He can either remain there or break out; if he does break out,
he finds himself in the state of Satan: the Desire to which he
gives himself turns into a rage for possession and destruction.
The boy chasing butterflies prefigures the grown man who will
'martyr' the female; the hardening of the same desire will
eventually lead to the murder of life. The aspirations of endless
will become self-imprisoning; the soul which tries to climb a
ladder into infinity will find itself sinking in the sea of time and
space. Eventually, vision and desire both dead, he will begin to
hinder the young, clipping their wings of vision and enclosing
them within the dictates of his moral law. The happiest course
for man is to live in the expectation that when he dies he will be
liberated into eternity, his flesh being simultaneously restored
to the earth which is the ground of his desire.

One source remains to be examined—the passage from
Dryden containing the line 'At length for hatching ripe he
breaks the shell' which is the inscription to the crucial design.
The context is not one of Dryden's well-known works, but his
translation into contemporary verse of *The Knight's Tale*. Its
relevance to *The Gates of Paradise* is everywhere apparent:

> The Cause and Spring of Motion, from above
> Hung down on Earth the Golden Chain of Love:
> Great was th'Effect, and high was his Intent,
> When Peace among the jarring Seeds he sent.
> Fire, Flood, and Earth, and Air by this were bound,
> And Love, the common Link, the new Creation crown'd.
> The Chain still holds; for though the Forms decay
> Eternal Matter never wears away:

The same First Mover certain Bounds has plac'd,
How long those perishable Forms shall last;
Nor can they last beyond the Time assign'd
By that All-seeing, and All-making Mind:
Shorten their Hours they may; for Will is free;
But never pass th'appointed Destiny.
So Men oppress'd, when weary of their Breath,
Throw off the Burden, and subborn their Death.
Then since those Forms begin, and have their End,
On some unalter'd Cause they sure depend:
Parts of the Whole are we; but God the Whole;
Who gives us Life, and animating Soul.
For Nature cannot from a Part derive
That Being, which the Whole can only give:
He perfect, stable; but imperfect We,
Subject to Change, and diff'rent in Degree.
Plants, Beasts, and Man; and as our Organs are,
We more or less of his Perfection share.
But by a long Descent, th'Etherial Fire
Corrupts; and Forms, the mortal Part, expire:
As he withdraws his Vertue, so they pass,
And the same Matter makes another Mass:
This Law th'Omniscient Pow'r was pleas'd to give,
That every Kind should by Succession live;
That Individuals die, his Will ordains;
The propagated Species still remains.
The Monarch Oak, the Patriarch of the Trees,
Shoots rising up, and spreads by slow Degrees:
Three Centuries he grows, and three he stays,
Supreme in State; and in three more decays:
So wears the paving Pebble in the Street,
And Towns and Tow'rs their fatal Periods meet.
So Rivers, rapid once, now naked lie,
Forsaken of their Springs; and leave their Channels dry.
So Man, at first a Drop, dilates with Heat,
Then form'd, the little Heart begins to beat;
Secret he feeds, unknowing in the Cell;
At length, for Hatching ripe, he breaks the Shell,
And struggles into Breath, and cries for Aid;
Then, helpless, in his Mothers Lap is laid.
He creeps, he walks, and issuing into Man,
Grudges their Life, from whence his own began.
Retchless of Laws, affects to rule alone,
Anxious to reign, and restless on the Throne:

First vegetive, then feels and reasons last;
Rich of Three Souls, and lives all three to waste.
Some thus; but thousands more in Flow'r of Age:
For few arrive to run the latter Stage.
Sunk in the first, in Battel some are slain,
And others whelm'd beneath the stormy Main . . .[13]

The passage, which is taken from the speech made by Theseus to reconcile the court to the death of Palamon, consists very largely of an exposition of the philosophy of Boethius, including a defence of 'Great Necessity'. As usual, we need to be on our guard. Blake was the last person in the world to accept wholeheartedly the doctrine of Necessity. He would react firmly against the supposition that forms decay yet matter remains. His own belief was precisely the opposite.

Blake's series of plates is, in fact, not a straight illustration of Dryden's ideas, but the result of a meditation upon them. Dryden's insistence on the traditional belief that the four elements are harmonized by the intervention of Love[14] is replaced by a vision of the four elements warring in Chaos (as in *Paradise Lost*)[15]—which Blake uses to symbolize the fruits of that analytical consciousness by which the creation is seen only in its component parts. Reliance on his five senses allows man to stand above nature in separate lordship: but it also leads to an overwhelming feeling of futility and imprisonment. In desperation he resorts instead to unlimited exploitation of his own energies:

He creeps, he walks, and issuing into Man,
Grudges their Life from whence his own began. . . .

Dryden's threefold classification, which follows the Aristotelean division of souls into vegetative, feeling and reasoning, is reinterpreted by Blake into an order of his own. The vegetative state reflects the decline of Vision, the feeling state the decline of Desire. Finally, reduced to the reasoning state, alone, without vision or desire, tyrannical and unperceptive, man imposes his own will on others.

The Gates of Paradise, at first sight an inconsequential collection of designs, is a tightly knit sequence, reflecting an intricate pattern of thought in Blake's mind. His reading of Dryden and his reflections on it set the seal on previous speculations concerning Energy and Reason, and brought the conflict into new focus. On the other hand, it is also characteristic of his intellectual state at this time that his excitement is only partially transferred into art. The finished product, though fine in places, has a preponderantly negative quality, demanding a familiarity with Blake's vision before it can be made to yield its full meaning.

The paradigm remained for Blake a fruitful one, which he carried forward into his later thinking. Many years later, in producing a new edition, he renamed it 'For the Sexes: The Gates of Paradise' and wrote a long verse commentary which, while mentioning individual plates, brings them into a further pattern.[16] Two passages deserve especial attention. Having described the creation of himself as a Natural Man when his 'Eternal Man set in Repose', he comes to the point where he rises up in the fire and finds himself as

> Two Horn'd Reasoning Cloven Fiction
> In Doubt which is Self contradiction
> A dark Hermaphrodite We stood
> Rational Truth Root of Evil & Good
> Round me flew the Flaming Sword
> Round her snowy Whirlwinds roard
> Freezing her Veil the Mundane Shell

At this point, Energy and Nature stand mutually opposed as man and woman. And in these terms, the 'breaking out' consists of the male ravishing the female. What follows is obscure.

> I rent the Veil where the Dead dwell

> When weary Man enters his Cave
> He meets his Saviour in the Grave
> Some find a Female Garment there
> And some a Male, woven with care
> Lest the Sexual Garments sweet
> Should grow a devouring Winding sheet.

The point of this seems to be that Man, although deprived of his Eternal vision, is at least able to produce children in whom his early vision is renewed, and thus prevent total stagnation. Yet the child, like the sexual activity which produces it, can become perverted towards death instead of life.

Only at the end of the poem is the proper state of sexual activity hinted at:

15 The Door of Death I open found
    And the Worm Weaving in the Ground
16 Thou'rt my Mother from the Womb
    Wife, Sister, Daughter, to the Tomb
    Weaving to Dreams the Sexual strife
    And weeping over the Web of Life

As in *The Book of Thel*, a close relationship is supposed between sexual love and death: one of the most common subjects of seventeenth-century wit is given a serious point. When the imagination is brought into play in love-making, a state of threefold vision is created; in the grave, worms create new life out of corruption. Neither Vision nor physical energy is ever destroyed: both spring up again in new manifestations of living form. Whereas the rational man fears death, the imaginative man accepts it, knowing that vision and desire are eternal. Sexual experience is invoked by Blake not as a 'worldly' activity but as the 'shadow of desire', the experience which can offer to man an intimation of immortality—and incidentally give him the vicarious immortality involved in transmitting his living form to human descendants. It draws fallen man towards a reconciliation with the earth, which otherwise horrifies him.

This reconciliation is sealed by the imagination. The final and most comprehensive answer to the speech of Dryden's Theseus is to be found in *The Marriage of Heaven and Hell*, where the whole universe, including the earth, is made the heritage of energy and vision. Against Theseus' stoic assertion that if 'forms' decay matter remains, the Voice of the Devil affirms that though matter decay, the 'forms' of energy, as seized by the imagination, remain.

Some years later Blake made the same point more explicitly, using the very imagery of Dryden. The central point of Theseus' argument rests in his image of the oak:

The Monarch Oak, the Patriarch of the Trees,
Shoots rising up, and spreads by slow Degrees:
Three Centuries he grows, and three he stays,
Supreme in State; and in three more decays . . .[17]

Theseus goes on to say that 'the propagated Species still remains', but this is not enough for Blake, who writes in his
'Vision of the Last Judgment',

> . . . the Oak dies as well as the Lettuce but Its Eternal
> Image & Individuality never dies. but renews by its seed. just
> so the Imaginative Image returns by the seed of Contemplative
> Thought. . . .[18]

Notes

Place of publication is London unless otherwise stated; date of publication is given at first entry

Chapter One

1 *Jerusalem*, 38(34). 29. NB 480; NC 665; E 178.

2 Coleridge, *Biographia Literaria*, ch. ii, 1907, I, 20–1. See also the discussion in my *Coleridge the Visionary*, 1959, pp. 226–8.

3 See, e.g., Mona Wilson, *Life of William Blake*, 1948, pp. 65–7; 71. D. Figgis, *Paintings of William Blake*, 1925, ch. vii.

4 *Soviet Weekly*, contemporary report.

5 J. Bronowski, *A Man without a Mask*, 1943, pp. 85–6.

6 H. M. Margoliouth, *William Blake*, 1951, pp. 124–5. Margoliouth's evidence is mainly Blake's letters to Hayley of 1 April 1800 and 6 June 1800.

7 H. M. Margoliouth, *William Blake's 'Vala'*, Oxford, 1956, p. xix.

8 John Wain, letter to the *Spectator*, 10 January 1958, p. 47.

9 D. W. Harding, in *Penguin Guide to English Literature*, V, 'From Blake to Byron', 1957, pp. 67–84.

10 N. Frye, *Fearful Symmetry*, Princeton, 1947, pp. 431–2.

11 Notes on Spurzheim's *Observations on . . . Insanity* (1817). NB 817; NC 772; E 652.

12 See L. A. G. Strong, 'Reminiscences of W. B. Yeats', *The Listener*, 22 April 1954, pp. 689–90.

13 'The Everlasting Gospel', d. 75–6. NB 136; NC 752; E 511.

14 'A vision of the Last Judgment' (from a notebook). NB 639; NC 605–6; E 545.

15 H. M. Margoliouth, 'Blake's Drawings for Young's *Night Thoughts*' in *The Divine Vision* (ed. V. de Sola Pinto), 1957, p. 198; cf. illustration facing p. 197.

16 NB 579; NC 771; E 266.

17 C. P. Snow, *The Two Cultures and the Scientific Revolution*, Cambridge, 1959, pp. 5–6.

18 NB 74; NC 216; E 26.

19 NB 686; NC 58; E 452.

20 Aldous Huxley, *Point Counter Point*, 1928, ch. ix, p. 144.

Chapter Two

1 *Marriage of Heaven and Hell*, pl. 5. NB 182; NC 149–50; E 34–5.

2 In his *Dedication of Aeneis*, 1697. *Essays* (ed. W. P. Ker), Oxford, 1900, II, 165.

3 Walter Bagehot, *Literary Studies*, 1879, I, 211–12.

4 Cambridge, 1947, and London, 1961, respectively.

5 *Paradise Lost*, iv, 453–76; x, 504–47; xi, 829–38.
6 C. S. Lewis, *A Preface to 'Paradise Lost'*, 1942, p. 94.
7 Shelley, *Defence of Poetry. Works* (ed. R. Ingpen and W. E. Peck), 1930, vii, 129.
8 Pope, *Satire V*, 102.
9 E. J. Morley, *Henry Crabb Robinson on Books and their Writers*, 1938, I, 330.
10 N. Frye, essay in *The Divine Vision* (ed. V. de Sola Pinto), 1957, p. 101n.
11 Milton, *Prose Works*, 1931, IV, 86.
12 *Paradise Lost*, ix, 1011–1 (Darbishire text).
13 See below, pp. 88–9.
14 Letter to Butts, 22 November 1802. NB 861–2; NC 818–19; E 693–4.
15 Mona Wilson, *Life of William Blake*, p. 22.
16 Quoted, J. G. Davies, *The Theology of William Blake*, 1948, p. 34.
17 Desirée Hirst, *Hidden Riches*, 1964, p. 65, quoting Paracelsus, *Archidoxes* (tr. J. H.) 1660, p. 7.
18 *Ibid.*, quoting Paracelsus, *Interpretatio alia Totius Astronomiae, Opera Omnia*, Tom. II, Geneva, 1659, p. 670a (tr. John Hargrave).
19 Hirst, *op. cit.*, pp. 66–7, quoting the same ed., p. 472 (tr. Dr C. H. Josten).
20 NB 737; NC 90; E 592. Quoted Hirst, *op. cit.*, pp. 206–7.

Chapter Three

1 William Blake, *The Book of Urizen*. Reproduced in Facsimile with a note by Dorothy Plowman, London, 1929, p. 17. Mrs Plowman also mentions Uranus as a possible source for the name.
2 N. Frye, *Fearful Symmetry*, p. 239; S. F. Damon, *William Blake, his Philosophy and Symbols*, 1924, p. 329.
3 The last two identifications are my own.
4 N. Frye, *op. cit.*, p. 238. H. G. Hewlett (*Contemporary Review*, 1876, XXVIII, 779) cites names such as *Oithona*, *Tonthormod*, *Brumo* and *Lutha* from Ossian.
5 Donne, Elegy XIX, l. 27.
6 NB 66; NC 211; E 19.
7 Johnson, 'The Vanity of Human Wishes', II, 37–44. *Poems* (ed. D. Nichol Smith and E. L. McAdam), Oxford, 1941, p. 32.
8 Swedenborg, *Last Judgment*, 45. This belief was embodied in the resolutions adopted by the conference of Swedenborgians in 1789 as no. XXXVIII. (See J. G. Davies, *The Theology of William Blake*, 1948, p. 34.)
9 S. F. Damon, *op. cit.*, p. 316; Harold Bloom, *Blake's Apocalypse*, 1963, p. 76.
10 *Thel*, pl. 5, 11. 9–10. NB 164; NC 130; E 5.
11 E. J. Morley, *Henry Crabb Robinson on Books and their Writers*, I, 328.
12 How dydd I knowe that every darte
    That cutte the airie waye,
  Might not fynd passage to my heart
    And close my eyes for aie?
  (Chatterton, 'The Dethe of Sir Charles Bawdin'; mentioned by H. Bloom, *op. cit.*, p. 83.)

13 NB 148–9; NC 98; E 2–3.
14 Desirée Hirst, *Hidden Riches*, pp. 222–3, quoting Swedenborg's *Apocalypse Revealed*, Manchester, 1791, I, no. 484.
15 See, e.g., Plutarch, *De Iside et Osiride Liber*: *Graece et Anglice*, ed. S. Squire, Cambridge, 1744 (II), pp. 41–3.
16 *The Prelude*, 1850, v, 50–140.
17 David Erdman, *Blake, Prophet against Empire*, Princeton, 1954, p. 165n., citing Martin Nurmi.
18 In 'The Everlasting Gospel'. NB 133–43; NC 748–56; E 510–16.

Chapter Four

1 S. F. Damon, *William Blake, his Philosophy and Symbols*, p. 277.
2 Hazard Adams, *Blake and Yeats: the Contrary Vision*, Cornell, 1955, p. 239.
3 J. Bronowski, *A Man without a Mask*, p. 116.
4 S. Gardner, *Infinity on the Anvil*, Oxford, 1954, p. 124.
5 S. F. Damon, *op. cit.*, p. 277. See Blake's picture, 'Epitome of James Hervey's Meditations among the Tombs'. Reprod., M. Butlin, *Catalogue of Works of William Blake in the Tate Gallery*, 1957, pl. 39.
6 D. W. Harding, in *The Pelican Guide to English Literature*, V, 1957, p. 69.
7 *Ibid.*, p. 70.
8 See A. S. Roe, *Blake's Illustrations to the Divine Comedy*, Princeton, 1953.
9 David Erdman, *Blake: Prophet against Empire*, pp. 110–12.
10 'In all the heavens there exists no other idea of God than that of man.' For this (from *Divine Love and Wisdom*, 11) and many other similar quotations from Swedenborg, see J. G. Davies, *The Theology of William Blake*, pp. 35–7.
11 E. M. W. Tillyard, *Poetry Direct and Oblique*, 1945, pp. 11–15.
12 E 717.
13 See Geoffrey Grigson, *The Harp of Aeolus*, 1948, ch. v.
14 See below, pp. 233–8 and Fig. 17
15 See his essay in *The Divine Vision* (ed. V. de Sola Pinto), pp. 79–81.
16 G. M. Harper, 'The Source of Blake's "Ah! Sunflower" '. *Modern Language Review*, 1953, XLVIII, 139–42.
17 F. R. Leavis, *Revaluation*, 1936, pp. 140–2. Text from E 18.
18 'Of the Progresse of the Soule', III, 77–80. *Poems*, ed. H. J. C. Grierson, Oxford, 1912, I, 253.
19 NB 608–9; NC 578; E 533.
20 *Antony and Cleopatra*, IV, xv, 66. Cf. the discussion of the imagery in G. Wilson Knight's *The Imperial Theme* (1931) and Caroline Spurgeon's *Shakespeare's Imagery* (1935).
21 See above, p. 44.
22 Coleridge, *Poems* (ed. E. H. Coleridge), I, 285–92. See my *Coleridge the Visionary*, p. 180.
23 *The Faerie Queene*, I, iii, 5–6.
24 *The Divine Vision* (ed. V. de Sola Pinto), pp. 31–2; William Empson, letter to the *Spectator*, 13 December 1957, p. 833.
25 See above, pp. 47–8.
26 ('Upon the promising Fruitfulness of a Tree.') John Bunyan, *Book for Boys and Girls*, 1686, p. 33.

27 *The Divine Vision* (ed. V. de Sola Pinto), pp. 86–7.
28 Edward Young, *The Complaint: or Night Thoughts on Life, Death, and Immortality* (1742), I, 353–7. Cf. *Twelfth Night*, II, iv, 111–13.
29 See the original illustration in the British Museum Print Room, Album 14, I, 24.
30 NB 87; NC 163; E 458.
31 NB 116; NC 429; E 479.
32 NB 110–13; NC 424–7; E 475–7.
33 Kathleen Raine, 'A Traditional Language of Symbols', in *The Listener*, 9 October 1958, pp. 559–60.
34 *Ibid.* The apocalyptic reference is hard to pin down, however. The prophet Joel mentions withering trees as a sign of woes (e.g., Joel i, 12–19). In Revelation, 8, 7, a third part of the trees is burnt at the opening of the Seventh Seal.
35 *Ibid.*, p. 560. The story of Uzzah is in II Sam. vi, 6–8. Blake paints it in his illustrations to Dante. He also refers to it allegorically in his Annotations to Lavater: 'Man is the ark of God . . . if thou seekest by human policy to guide this ark, remember Uzzah, II Saml. VIch . . .' (NB 727; NC 82; E 585). The biblical account makes no mention of the withering of an arm, however: Blake may be thinking of King Jeroboam, whose hand was dried up when he stretched it forth against the man of God (I Kings xiii, 4). A painting of his on the subject is now in the Fletcher Moss Museum at Didsbury, Manchester.

Chapter Five

1 Mona Wilson, *Life of Blake*, pp. 41–2, quoting Gilchrist and Tatham.
2 David Erdman, *Blake, Prophet against Empire*, Part Three.
3 S. F. Damon, *William Blake, his Philosophy and Symbols*, p. 82.
4 David Erdman, *op. cit.*, p. 151 and n.
5 *Ibid.*, p. 154.
6 *Paradise Lost*, x, 504–9.
7 Blake probably formed this name by running together 'Orcus' (Hell), the Greek ὄρχεις (the genitals), and 'Orc' meaning a whale (Erdman, *op. cit.*, p. 24n.). He thus suggested three important images of the energy for which Orc stands. Bernard Blackstone has recently suggested that Orc as 'fiery boy' traces his ancestry to Gray's 'Descent of Odin' (II, 63–70)

> In the caverns of the west,
> By *Odin's* fierce embrace comprest,
> A wond'rous boy shall *Rinda* bear,
> Who ne'er shall comb his raven hair,
> Nor wash his visage in the stream,
> Nor see the sun's departing beam,
> Till he on *Hoder's* corse shall smile
> Flaming on the funeral pile.

(*The Lost Travellers*, 1962, p. 75.) The memory is probably there. When Blake illustrated the lines in his *Illustrations to Gray's Poems* (Oxford, 1922), he pictured the 'wond'rous boy' not as Orc but as a stooping visionary like his Newton, perhaps with satirical irony.

8 Reproduced, *William Blake's Illuminated Books: A Census* (ed. G. Keynes and Wolf), Grolier Club, New York, 1953, pl. 6.

9 See N.E.D. s.v. 'Nostoc'. Coleridge was also aware of this tradition. See his *Notebooks*, ed. Kathleen Coburn, 1957, vol. I, 1703, for his note, accompanied by a valuable discussion of sources by the editor.

10 Ovid, *Metamorphoses* ii, 235–56.

11 This tradition was of topical interest in Blake's time, since James Bruce, explorer of the Nile, had returned from Abyssinia with the lost Ethiopic Book of Enoch which, as he described, has a lengthy version of the story. James Bruce, *Travels to Discover the Source of the Nile*, Edinburgh, 1790, I, 497–500.

12 The water-colour known as 'The Ascension of the Dead' in the British Museum Print Room supports this interpretation.

13 Erdman, *op. cit.*, p. 24n.

14 *Ibid.*, pp. 55–6.

15 *Ibid.*, p. 58.

16 *The Faerie Queene*, I, xii.

17 *Paradise Lost*, vii, 226–31. This version is in the Print Room of the British Museum. See S. F. Damon, *William Blake: his Philosophy and Symbols*, pp. 347–8. Damon points out that the quotation is not in Blake's hand; but since each design carries a quotation he feels sure that the suggestion was his.

18 *The Notebook of William Blake* (ed. G. Keynes), 1935, p. 161.

19 *Milton*, 41.12–14.

20 Hela was the goddess of death in Scandinavian mythology.

21 Desirée Hirst (*Hidden Riches*, pp. 130–2) has noticed that several phrases in the Preludium seem to relate to the writings of Robert Fludd and Richard Clarke. The image of the inverted tree here recalls the illustration of the sephirotic tree, its roots against the sun, its branches stretching out below, that appears in Fludd's *Meteorologica Cosmica*. 'The overflowing stars rain down prolific pains' recalls Fludd's description of the 'Antipathetical jar', 'when the severe Attributes of God, do rain down into the starry world, influences of a contrary nature . . .' (*Mosaicall Philosophy*, 1659, pp. 192–3). 'Thou dost stamp them with a signet' recalls the descriptions of God's 'sephirotic seal', as in the works of Clarke. Her further point that the roped head in *Jerusalem*, plate 62, may derive from the frontispiece to Fludd's *Works* sounds less convincing, since the rope there surrounds the whole universe of symbols. One notices, however, that the figure of the bound head appears also in the illustration to the Preludium. It seems likely, therefore, that Blake derived from the rope of the design an emblem of the binding force of Reason, which he afterwards deployed in various illustrations. His whole handling of Fludd suggests that this philosopher, whose interests ranged from mechanics to mysticism, gave him many ideas about the relationship between the rational and imaginative universes.

22 Andrew Tooke, *The Pantheon* . . . 1738, pp. 12–13; Isa. vii, 14–15.

23 See above, pp. 98–101.

24 Gen. xxviii, 10–18. Jacob's vision is the subject of one of Blake's best pictures: see D. Figgis, *Paintings of William Blake*, 1925, pl. 80.

25 *Twelfth Night*, I, i, 5–7; Song of Solomon iv, 16.

26 Rev. i, 4; 11.

27 See also below, p. 135.

28 See, for example, his *Three Principles of the Divine Essence*, ch. xvii (J. Boehme, *Works*, ed. W. Law, 1764–81, I (ii), 146–65).

29 NB 54; NC 125; E 9.

30 See above, pp. 107–8.

Chapter Six

1 Letter of 12 September 1800. NB 841; NC 799; E 680.

2 Letter to Mrs Flaxman, 14 September 1800. NB 842; NC 800; E 681.

3 NB 621; NC 592; E 561.

4 NB 657; NC 545; E 498.

5 *Milton*, 9.4–6. NB 384; NC 489; E 102.

6 'I write when commanded by the spirits, and the moment I have written I see the words fly about the room in all directions. It is then published and the Spirits can read.' This statement to Crabb Robinson can be matched by a letter to Butts, in which he says that he has written 'from immediate Dictation twelve or sometimes twenty or thirty lines at a time without Premeditation & even against my Will. the Time it has taken in writing was thus renderd Non Existent. & an immense Poem Exists which seems to be the Labour of a long Life all producd without Labour or Study.' E. J. Morley, *Crabb Robinson on Books and Writers*, I, 333; Blake's letter of 25 April 1803. NB 866–7; NC 823; E 697.

7 NB 785; NC 457; E 635.

8 *Paradise Lost*, ii, 305; 559; 561.

9 'Hell's Concave'. *Paradise Lost*, i, 542.

10 *Paradise Lost*, i, 752–761.

11 NB 81; NC 221; E 32.

12 Cf. my *Coleridge the Visionary*, pp. 199, 251.

13 Rev. xi, 3–8.

14 John xi, 11.

15 With his phrase 'the double drum' Blake is probably recalling Dryden's 'Song for St Cecilia's Day'; 'The double double double beat/Of the thundring DRUM.' *Poems* (ed. J. Kinsley), vol. II, p. 538.

16 See my *Coleridge the Visionary*, pp. 154–6.

17 See S. F. Damon, *William Blake: his Philosophy and Symbols*, p. 312.

18 *Paradise Lost*, x, 282–323.

19 *Paradise Lost*, iv, 223–35.

20 The Wicker Man is the 'colossus of osiers', described by Caesar and Strabo, in which the Druids burned animals and men. There seems to be no particular connection between it and Scandinavia, but Druidism was supposed to have been practised all over the northern countries. A seventeenth-century illustration is reproduced as Fig. 51. For a full account see A. L. Owen, *The Famous Druids*, 1962, pp. 20–1; 158–9 and 228–30.

21 *Paradise Lost*, i, 392–521.

22 The first two books of *Paradise Lost* contain the following words which appear in the extract: 'ruin' (i, 46; 91; 593); 'pit' (i, 91; 381; 657); 'pitchy' (i, 340); 'nitre' (ii, 937); 'burning' (i, 210; 296); 'ore' (i, 673; 703); plains (i, 104). 'Marble' is Blake's own, but may owe something to Milton's 'marle' (i, 296).

23 NB 625; NC 596; E 565.
24 NB 806; NC 474; E 648.
25 NB 638; NC 605; E 545. See p. 243 below.
26 NB 647; NC 613; E 551.
27 NB 652; NC 617; E 555.

Chapter Seven

1 NB 122; NC 434; E 487.
2 Reproduced in *Vala or the Four Zoas* (ed. G. E. Bentley, Jr.), Oxford, 1963, *passim*, and Geoffrey Keynes, *Pencil Drawings by William Blake*, 1927, pl. 80, respectively.
3 *Vala or the Four Zoas*, IX, 709. NB 367; NC 376; E 388.
4 *Jerusalem*, pl. 26. NC 649; E 169.
5 Reproduced in M. Butlin, *Catalogue of Works of William Blake in the Tate Gallery*, pl. 2.
6 NB 589; NC 560; E 518.
7 Letter to Hayley of 28 October 1804. NB 899–900; NC 851–2; E 702–3.
8 Mona Wilson's account (*Life of William Blake*, pp. 151–6) may be supplemented by David Erdman's (*Blake, Prophet against Empire*, pp. 375–386).
9 Letter to Butts, 16 August 1803. NB 873; NC 828; E 699–700.
10 D. Figgis, *The Paintings of William Blake*, pl. 71.
11 *Ibid.*, pl. 75.
12 *Ibid.*, pl. 70.
13 *Ibid.*, pl. 1. See above, pp. 119–20 and n. 17.
14 *Ibid.*, pl. 73.
15 In the Fitzwilliam Museum, Cambridge.
16 *Ibid.*, pl. 13.
17 *Ibid.*, pl. 12.
18 NB 599–600; NC 570; E 526.
19 NB 596; NC 567; E 523–4.
20 This is the endpaper to Geoffrey Keynes's *William Blake's Engravings*, 1950.
21 John Milton, *Poems in English* with illustrations by William Blake (ed. G. Keynes), 1926, vol I, facing p. 180.
22 *Ibid.*, facing I, 104.
23 *Ibid.*, facing I, 130.
24 *Ibid.*, facing I, 136.
25 *Ibid.*, facing I, 250.
26 *Ibid.*, facing I, 352.
27 No. 60 in *The Blake Collection of W. Graham Robertson* (ed. Kerrison Preston, 1952).
28 John Milton, *Poems in English* (ed. Keynes), I, 10; 48.
29 *Ibid.*, facing I, 268.
30 *Ibid.*, facing I, 344.
31 *Ibid.*, facing II, 76 and 166.
32 *Ibid.*, facing II, 30.
33 *Ibid.*, facing II, 32.

Chapter Eight

1 NB 118–21; NC 431–4; E 481–4.
2 Thomas Traherne, *Centuries of Meditations and Thanksgivings*, III, 3 (ed. H. M. Margoliouth), Oxford, 1958, vol. I, 111. Quoted *variatim*, B. Blackstone, *English Blake*, Cambridge, 1949, p. 36.
3 Edwin Muir, *An Autobiography*, 1954, p. 33.
4 *Jerusalem*, 27. NB 463–4; NC 649; E 170.
5 NB 99; NC 184; E 465.
6 See Arthur Bryant, *The Age of Elegance*, 1950, pp. 273–6 and chs. viii–x *passim*.
7 The main outbreaks took place in 1831, 1848, 1853, and 1865.
8 See above, p. 75.
9 *Joseph Andrews* (ed. de Castro), 1929, III, i, p. 199.
10 See, e.g., G. D. H. Cole, *Life of William Cobbett*, 1924, p. 10.
11 William Law, 'The Spirit of Prayer', *Works*, 1762, VII, 3.
12 *Ibid.*, 16–17.
13 *Ibid.*, 49–76.
14 Isa. 51, 9; Joshua ii, 1–3; 6, 17–25.
15 Northrop Frye's discussion of 'Rahab' seems to lay itself open to this objection (*Fearful Symmetry*, pp. 139–40 etc.). But it is often a matter of innuendo rather than statement.
16 Blake, Letter to Butts, 22 November 1802. NB 860; NC 817; E 692. Wordsworth, 'The Thorn'.
17 NB 821–3; NC 782–4; E 654–6.
18 It is implicit in the whole structure of *A la Recherche du Temps Perdu*. Individual passages relating to the point can be found in *Remembrance of Things Past* (tr. Scott Moncrieff) 1941, IV, 46–7 and 227; VIII, 194. Cf. also IV, 288; VI, 124; IX 23, 26, 81–4 and 272; and XII, 359–60.
19 NB 822; NC 783; E 655.
20 *Ibid.*
21 *The Excursion*, i, 79. (*Poems*, ed. de Selincourt, V, 10.)
22 NB 644–5; NC 611; E 550.
23 Wordsworth, *The Prelude* (1850), ii, 243.
24 Wordsworth, *Ode on the Intimations of Immortality*, st. vi.
25 NB 617; NC 585; E 540.
26 Reproduced as illustration to M. Wilson's *Life of Blake* (1948 ed.).
27 NB 682, 103; NC 54, 186–7; E 448–9, 491–2.
28 See above, pp. 187 and 51.
29 *The Excursion*, iv.
30 James Joyce, *Stephen Hero*, 1944, p. 165.
31 '(Blake) thinks all men partake of it, but it is lost by not being cultivated.' E. J. Morley, *Henry Crabb Robinson on Books and their Writers*, I, 330.
32 From 'Auguries of Innocence'. NB 119; NC 432; E 482.
33 Letter to George Cumberland, 12 April 1827. NB 926; NC 878; E 707.
34 A. Gilchrist, *Life of William Blake*, 1907, ch. xxxiv, pp. 328–9.
35 *Ibid.*, ch. xxviii, pp. 271–5. M. Wilson, *Life of William Blake*, pp. 269–75.
36 Reprod., G. Keynes, *Pencil Drawings of William Blake*, I, 1927, pl. 49.
37 A. Gilchrist, *op. cit.*, ch. xiv, p. 127.

38 *Milton*, 11. 32–3. NB 387; NC 492; E 104.
39 *The Prelude* (1850), xii, 279.
40 Boris Pasternak, *Dr Zhivago*, 1958, pp. 406–7.

Appendix Two

1 *The Notebook of William Blake, called the Rossetti Manuscript* (ed. G. Keynes), 1935, p. 160 (MS. p. 85). From Donne, 'The Progress of the Soul', st. iv.
2 *Ibid.*, MS. pp. 19, 45, 27, 73, 17, 101. The first four are from Spenser (*Faerie Queene*, II, ii, 2.1); Job xvii, 14; Milton, sonnet 'To Sir Henry Vane the Younger', l. 6; and his 'On the Death of a fair Infant dying of a Cough', l. 29, respectively. The last two have not been identified, and may be Blake's own.
3 S. F. Damon, *William Blake: his Philosophy and Symbols*, p. 86, n. 3.
4 NB 568–577; NC 760–771; E 256–266. The plates are reproduced also in G. W. Digby's *Symbol and Image in William Blake*, Oxford, 1957, pl. 1–19; these show the various inscriptions as engraved by Blake.
5 Donne, 'Of the Progress of the Soul: The Second Anniversary', 1. 184. *Poems* (ed. H. J. C. Grierson), Oxford, 1912, vol. I, p. 256.
6 E. Young, *The Complaint; or, Night-Thoughts on Life, Death, and Immortality* (1742), I, 80; 32–4.
7 *Paradise Lost*, i, 221–2.
8 *Paradise Lost*, ii, 728–30.
9 From *Hamlet* I, ii, 131; *Hamlet*, I, v, 183; Ezek. xxviii, 6; *Paradise Lost*, i, 221. (*The Notebook of William Blake, op. cit.*, MS. pp. 92, 95, 94, 91).
10 NB 147; NC 97; E 1.
11 NB 212; NC 237–8; E 59.
12 NB 148; NC 97; E 2.
13 Dryden, *Fables*, 'Palamon and Arcite', iii, 1024–81. Dryden, *Poems*, ed. James Kinsley, Oxford, 1958, IV, 1526–7.
14 See, e.g., A. O. Lovejoy, *The Great Chain of Being*, Cambridge, Mass., 1936. E. M. W. Tillyard, *The Elizabethan World Picture*, 1943, ch. 8. Sir John Davies's poem, *Orchestra* (1596), is particularly relevant.
15 *Paradise Lost*, ii, 894–910.
16 NB 577–8; NC 770–1; E 265–6.
17 See above, p. 239.
18 *Vision of the Last Judgment* (MS. pp. 68–9). NB 638; NC 605; E 545.

The Illustrations: a Commentary

The figures which follow illustrate points which have been discussed in the text. They also provide an opportunity to compare Blake's handling of his visual sources with his use of earlier literature. Blake was an ardent student of the work of his artistic predecessors and is reputed to have possessed an unusually large collection of engravings. His possible debts to other artists have been the subject of several studies, notably George Wingfield Digby's *Symbol and Image in William Blake* (Oxford, 1957), Professor Anthony Blunt's *The Art of William Blake* (London, 1959) and J. Hagstrum's *William Blake, Poet and Painter* (Chicago, 1964). The concern of each of these writers has been to relate Blake's work to particular traditions; my aim in the handful of examples presented here is to suggest that Blake often took themes from his predecessors and subsumed them into his own vision just as he had taken literary phrases which could be made to fit his own poetic vision.

Lucas Cranach's 'The Fall', my first example (Fig. 2) is of course only one of many treatments of the theme; it bears very closely on Blake's in certain respects, however. Blake particularly admired the work of Albrecht Dürer; and it may be from Dürer's representations of St Jerome, in which the face of Jerome's lion resembles the face of his master, that he first conceived the idea of making the animals in his designs represent the passions of the human beings. The theme is present, vestigially, in Cranach's woodcut; in Blake's illustration to *Paradise Lost* (Fig. 3) it has become an important controlling factor. Blake's Adam and Eve also bear a striking visual resemblance to Cranach's (the hair of the two Adams may be compared—Dürer's treatment of the hair of Adam and Eve in some designs resembles Blake's still more closely) but an important difference must be noted. Blake's faces carry the lineaments of particular states of human vision; Cranach's seem more like particular individuals.

This tendency of Blake's to see in other artistic works themes which could be interpreted through his own vision also characterizes his interest in the Portland Vase (Figs. 26 and 27). Sir Geoffrey Keynes has shown that Blake almost certainly engraved these plates of the Portland Vase for Erasmus Darwin's *Botanic Garden* (1791) (see his *Blake Studies*, 1949, pp. 67–75); the question of its possible significance in Blake's work of the time has, however, been little explored. In the context of the present study it can be argued that he would have seen the two designs as representations of man in the states of fallen vision and resurrection to Vision, respectively. The theory is supported by the existence of similar plates in *America*. The enclosed male and anxious woman of *America* (Fig. 28) may be compared with the hostile male and drooping woman of the vase (Fig. 26); the awakening male and the prophetess with serpent in her lap of *America* (Fig. 29) may be compared with the risen man (now sexual), the winged cherub and the prophetess with serpent in her lap of the vase (Fig. 27). The comparison of the first pair is inconclusive, that of the second is very convincing.

Just as Blake found in a figure from Michelangelo's 'Crucifixion of St Peter' a model for his representation of the eternal visionary Druid, the Gothic artist of all ages, so in the figure of Minos in 'The Last Judgment' (Fig. 36) he discovered a model for his figure of man enwreathed by a serpent to emblematize the imprisoning 'selfhood' formed by visionless energies (Figs. 34–5; 37–41). The Royal Academy Library, which Blake used, has both a drawing (Fig. 36) and an engraved detail of Minos, either of which might have been known to him.

Blake's enthusiasm for Dürer makes it also not unlikely that he found in the latter's 'Apollo and Diana' (Fig. 42) a model for his ideal man of vision, carrying the sceptre of innocence and the sun of experience. (It is even conceivable that the backward 'APOLO' of Dürer's drawing suggested the name of Los, Blake's fallen guardian of the eternal Sol.)

Blake's interest in earlier engravings would lead him naturally to examine some of the more elaborately executed title-pages which were common in the seventeenth century. Ralegh's *History of the World* (1614), for example, with its angels trumpeting fame, good and bad (Fig. 46), seems to have furnished the illustrations of Blake's *Europe* with the serpentine trumpets of the fallen angels of reason, the plague-seeds which they blow into the harvest, and the plague-spotted victim of Newton's analysis (Figs. 47 and 49). The title-page of Hobbes's *Leviathan* (Fig. 50) may equally have coalesced in Blake's mind with that of the Wicker Image (from Sammes's *Britannia Antiqua Illustrata*, Fig. 51) to create that composite concept of all men brought under one Law which he called 'The Wicker Man of Scandinavia' (*Milton* 37.11). Such attempts to reduce men to a single image corresponded in his eyes to the cruel sacrifices of the Druids. Drayton's *Polyolbion* (1612) (Fig. 52) could equally have suggested the complementary theme (that of embodying natural landscape within the outline of a human body in order to suggest fertility, happiness and a vision that humanizes all things) which he uses in 'A Sunshine Holiday' (Fig. 53).

Blake rarely imitates directly, but he often uses the themes of other men when they have been transmuted through his own vision. We are always driven back to the organization of that vision for a full interpretation of what he is doing, therefore. In certain respects his visual art was better adapted than his literary for the communication of that vision. A complicated design can bring together the various elements in a dialectic, for example, without being obliged to force them into a sequence: they can coexist and stand in varying relationships to one another.

Fig. 3 is a good example of the effects that can be achieved by this method. Adam and Eve are shown in Eden, in 'organized innocence'. The bower in which they are sitting is composed of the plants and flowers of innocence and threefold vision; in the distance stands the tree of experience, the serpent woven round its trunk, surrounded by beasts representing the human passions. The vessel which Eve is carrying probably emblematizes threefold vision, as in Blake's painting of the Wise and Foolish Virgins. The angel, whose crown and flame-enfolded wings are emblems of the supreme, fourfold vision, is indicating the foliage of innocence with one hand and the distant tree of experience with the other. Adam listens to his admonitions with some incredulity, unable to believe that the desire and vision which are organized in Paradise could ever come to exist in separation from one another.

The plates of the sequence entitled *The Gates of Paradise* illustrate the effects of this separation in detail. As shown in Appendix Two, they present the images of reason and energy in their human limitations and suggest the dynamic pattern that links them. They are products of Blake's wit rather than of his vision: it is his human insight which is most in evidence. But the organization of his vision is necessary to explain them.

The contraries of reason and energy are represented vividly in Figs. 24 and 25. Urizen's compasses in the one express his limiting actions; his own limitations are in their turn suggested by the wan sun-disk behind him. Milton, in the other, is possessed by the energy of the fiery sun-ball at his back, an energy which is half-terrifying to him by reason of its uncontrollability.

The visual imagery of *America* shows the world that is produced by this opposition. The failure of the male, lost in reasonings and abstractions, and the consequent anxiety of the female induce an insurgent rebelliousness in their child which is expressed in his facial lineaments (Fig. 28); Fig. 29 shows the reawakening of the male and his response to a prophetess, whose serpent (repeated at the foot of the page) is an emblem of energy organized.

Subsequent plates show the pattern in other forms: innocent female desire is associated with the waves of the sea; visionless, manacled male desire with flames of fire (Fig. 30). In the lowest state (Fig. 31) the female, imprisoned in a wave, hovers over a man who is completely enclosed. In the ideal state (Figs. 32 and 33) the male runs freely through the flames of energy while the mother and child float above waves of gratified desire.

The oppositions of reason and energy are also used to interpret the story of the Creation and Fall. Since Urizen is a god of fading vision the man that he creates is bound in by his own energies (the serpentine windings around his legs (Fig. 34)). Consequently his energies rise up as spectre wings: the man becomes a figure of violence and destruction with sword and shield, while the woman, imprisoned by the same energies, lies under the domination of the serpent (Fig. 35). The energies that might have been expressed in the crown and wings of four-fold vision have turned into an imprisoning 'selfhood' which cuts man off from vision. The Fall of the Eternals (Fig. 37) is an emphatic illustration of the point.

Blake's illustrations to *Paradise Lost* develop the theme. Adam and Eve making love in the bower of Experience are watched by a Satan who enacts the danger represented by their selfhoods by his own enwreathing serpent; the precarious-ness of their state is suggested by the moon and star of threefold vision that illuminate the scene (Fig. 38). At the Fall (Fig. 39) Eve's act of submission to the serpent-selfhood is accompanied by jagged lightning and a spectre-like jagging of the veins of the tree of Experience. Adam and Eve emerge subsequently into a world (Fig. 40) where the guardian cherubs above the gate and the dangerous serpent beneath their feet mirror the separation between reason and energy, respectively. Jesus on the Cross (Fig. 41) displays in his love and forgiveness a victory over the selfhood which is represented in the nailed eye of the serpent and fallen bodies of the Tyrant and the Whore. It becomes possible for Earth to rise again and seek her Creator.

This, however, is a prophetic vision rather than an apocalyp-tic awakening. Such an awakening would be embodied by Blake rather in the images of Albion putting down the spectrous sun of false vision (Fig. 43) and of his rising again in the form of Satan in his original glory or of the Great Sun, a being of humanized vision (Fig. 44 and 45).

Reason is angelic in its original form: the figure of Newton with his compasses (Fig. 48) is a repetition of that of Urizen in Fig. 24. But Newton's limitations are shown by the fact that he carries out his investigations at the bottom of the sea of time and space, where only a dim light can filter through: when the angels of reason practice visionless analysis they blow plague-seeds into the harvest and Newton looks up in the prison of his single vision to see with horror the plague-spotted victim of his doctrines going off to spread his contagious disease (Figs. 47 and 49). Reason and Moral Law form an idolatrous single mould of man into which individual men are herded as into the Wicker Image which the Druids used for human sacrifice (Fig. 51).

258

In the proper state of humanity the opposite would be the case: all nature would be humanized and men would see their own best qualities reflected in the lesser forms of nature. The fullness of this vision is reserved at present for the young visionary, the youthful poet of Milton's 'L'Allegro' in whose fourfold vision the sun is replaced by a sphere containing the active forms of humanity. 'Here they are no longer talking of what is Good & Evil or of what is Right or Wrong & puzzling themselves in Satans Labyrinth. But are Conversing with Eternal Realities as they Exist in the Human Imagination.' (*A Vision of the Last Judgment.*)

Visionary or vegetative? The contradictions of human nature (from *The Gates of Paradise*) **4** Title page **5** 'What is Man?' **6** 'I found him beneath a tree'

4

6

The Sons of Reason (from *The Gates of Paradise*) **7** 'Water' **8** 'Earth'
9 'Air' **10** 'Fire'

Images of disorganized desire (from *The Gates of Paradise*) **12** 'At length for hatching ripe he breaks the shell' **13** 'Alas' **14** 'My Son! My Son!' **15** 'I want! I want!'

12

13

14

15

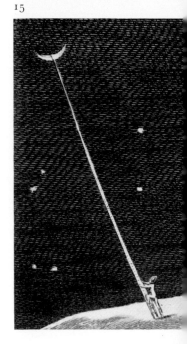

Images of imprisoned desire and of the keys of the prison (from *The Gates of Paradise*) **16** 'Help! Help!' **17** 'Aged Ignorance' **18** 'Does thy God O Priest take such vengeance as this?' **19** 'Fear & Hope are—Vision'

16

17

18

19

Images of hope (from *The Gates of Paradise*) **20** 'The Traveller hasteth in the evening' **21** 'Death's Door' **22** 'I have said to the Worm: Thou art my mother and sister' **23** Conclusion

20

21

22

23

(Blake's engravings from the Portland Vase) **26** The images of failed desire **27** The images of awakened desire

26

The first Compartment.

27

The second Compartment.

31

32

The Serpent and the Selfhood **34** The Serpent-self created in subordina-
tion **35** The Selfhood dominant

34

35

The Serpent and the Selfhood **36** Fallen man, serpent-encircled (Michelangelo) **37** The Eternals dominated by their selfhoods

36

37

The Serpent-selfhood in Eden **38** Organized Innocence in danger
39 The Selfhood bids for supremacy **40** The Serpent-selfhood as enemy
41 The Serpent-selfhood overcome

38

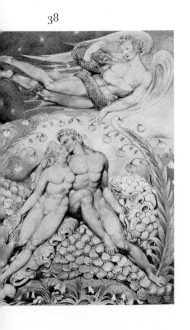

39

40

41

The Sun **42** *Apollo and Diana* by Albrecht Dürer **43** Albion with the
spectrous sun of false vision and the moon and stars of surviving imagination
44 Human genius glorified ('Satan in his original glory') **45** The sun
humanized ('When the Great Sun begins his state . . .')

42

43

44

45

The plagues of reason   **46** Angels of Good and Ill Fame (Ralegh's *History of the World*)   **47** Angels of fallen reason (Blake's *Europe*)

46

47

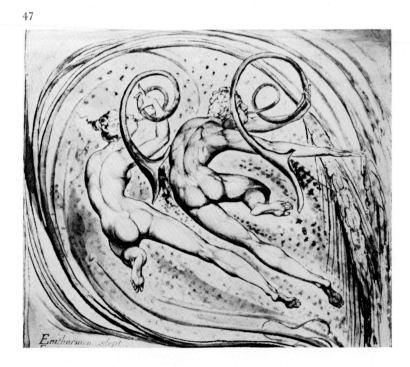

48

49

All men under one law   **50** Humanity under the Law (Hobbes's *Leviathan*)
51 Humanity sacrificed to Law (from Sammes's *Britannia Antiqua*)

All things humanized   **52** Humanized emblems of England (Drayton's *Polyolbion*, detail)   **53** Nature humanized ('On a Sunshine holiday . . .')

50

51

52

53

Index

Unless otherwise indicated italicized items are literary or visual works by Blake. Indexing of common Blakean topics is often selective. Bold type indicates a central discussion